D1253830

SCHOPENHAUER

The Arguments of
the Philosophers

EDITOR: TED HONDERICH

Reader in Philosophy, University College, London

The group of books of which this is one will include an
essentially analytic and critical account of each of the
considerable number of the great and the influential
philosophers. The group of books taken
together will comprise a contemporary
assessment and history of the entire course
of philosophical thought.

Already published in this series

Plato	J. C. B. Gosling
Meinong	Reinhardt Grossman
Santayana	Timothy L. S. Sprigge
Wittgenstein	R. J. Fogelin
Hume	B. Stroud
Descartes	Margaret Dauler Wilson
Berkeley	George Pitcher
Kant	Ralph Walker
The Presocratic Philosophers (2 vols)	Jonathan Barnes
Russell	Mark Sainsbury
Karl Popper	A. O'Hear

SCHOPENHAUER
The Arguments of the Philosophers

D.W. Hamlyn

Professor of Philosophy
Birkbeck College, London

Routledge & Kegan Paul

London, Boston and Henley

First published in 1980
by Routledge & Kegan Paul Ltd
39 Store Street,
London WC1E 7DD,
Broadway House,
Newtown Road,
Henley-on-Thames,
Oxon RG9 1EN and
9 Park Street,
Boston, Mass. 02108, USA
Set in Journal 11/12 point
by Columns of Reading
and printed in Great Britain by
Thomson Litho

British Library Cataloguing in Publication Data
Hamlyn, David Walter
1. Schopenhauer, Arthur. − (Arguments of the
philosophers).
I. Series
193   B3148   80-40874

ISBN 0 7100 0522 9

Contents

CONTENTS

Preface

Many people have come to know of Schopenhauer through collections of his essays, for the most part selections from his *Parerga and Paralipomena*, that have appeared in various translations and in many forms. That, as I shall indicate, is not the best way to arrive at an understanding of his philosophy. For that it is essential to go to his main work *Die Welt als Wille und Vorstellung*. That book has appeared in many German editions. For a very long time the only English translation of the work was that by R. B. Haldane and J. Kemp (1883). There is now available, however, a newer and in many ways more accurate translation by E. F. J. Payne, based on the German edition of Schopenhauer's works edited by Arthur Hübscher. Both this translation and Hübscher's edition of the German text of Schopenhauer's main work are available in paperback form, and are the most readily accessible versions for anyone who wishes to purchase the work (although Payne's translation is published in the USA). Payne's translation is a fine one and I have made extensive use of it, although there are perhaps points at which it lacks a certain philosophical sophistication.

Nevertheless, the Haldane and Kemp translation has many virtues, even if it is not based on a recent or the most accurate edition of the text. Moreover, it is likely to be the version to be found in many libraries. In my references to passages from Schopenhauer's main work I have therefore given references to both translations. The first reference in each case is to the volume, section and page of the Payne translation, the second is to the volume and page of the Haldane and Kemp translation. The references are prefaced by *WR* and *WI* respectively, to correspond to the two titles *The World as Will and Representation* and *The World as Will and Idea*.

In the case of the other works by Schopenhauer there is less of a problem. *The Fourfold Root of the Principle of Sufficient Reason* was for long available in English only in the translation by Madame K. Hillebrand, together with *The Will in Nature*, in Bohn's Philosophical Library, published by G. Bell and Sons. That version remains the only source in English for *The Will in Nature* and reference must be made to it. *The Fourfold Root* is now available in a translation by E. F. J. Payne, and although published in paperback in the USA is readily obtainable. It is unlikely that many readers will have access to the Hillebrand translation. I have therefore given references to the Payne translation (section and page reference in each case, prefaced by *FR*). For the two essays *On the Freedom of the Will* and *On the Basis of Morality* I have made reference to the translations by K. Kolenda and E. F. J. Payne respectively, both published in paperback by Bobbs-Merrill in the USA in the Library of Living Arts, and readily obtainable. I have referred to them as *FW*, followed by page reference, and *BM*, followed by section number and page reference. The complete *Parerga and Paralipomena* are published in a translation by E. F. J. Payne by Clarendon Press and my references are to that edition (*PP*, followed by volume number and page reference). Further details of all these works are given in the bibliography. I have not made reference to any other collection of essays.

There are very few good books in English on Schopenhauer. The one by Patrick Gardiner published by Penguin is almost the only exception to that rule and I have consulted it extensively.

Despite my heavy reliance on the translations given above, I have consulted the German text also and the translations of passages quoted are in all cases my own. Despite this an acknowledgment of debt to E. F. J. Payne's translations is inevitable and certainly called for. I therefore acknowledge a great debt to his fine work with gratitude.

I have lectured to students at Birkbeck College on matters connected with the book and I am grateful for their comments, and also those of some of my colleagues. I am particularly grateful to Ruby Meager, with whom I have discussed several issues concerning Schopenhauer, often over lunch and with obvious risk to her digestion.

I am grateful, finally, to Miss Hilary Crewes for secretarial assistance of various kinds.

1

Introduction

It is sometimes said of Schopenhauer that he was not a very systematic thinker. There is a sense in which this judgment is undeniable. Many of the discussions of individual issues in his works tend to wander, and it is not always easy to see how different arguments fit together. Moreover, the impression of lack of system has been encouraged both by the way in which Schopenhauer presented his views to the public and by the way in which the public, or at any rate the Anglo-Saxon public, has received them. On Schopenhauer's own side there is the fact that he tended to revise his main works and to add to them in successive editions. There is his phenomenal learning that leads him to make frequent references to many aspects of western and eastern thought, both philosophical and non-philosophical. There is his polemical style and his special antipathy to his German contemporaries, especially Hegel, and those whom he called the 'professors of philosophy'; it was a style both of thought and writing which, whatever its cause, offended many in his own time, and has continued to do so since. There is the fact that essays on specific subjects play what is perhaps a much larger part in his philosophical output than is the case with many other major philosophers. This last point has affected also the way in which the public has received Schopenhauer's views. The essays contain thoughts on a great number of subjects, and some of the thoughts are very striking indeed. They have, however, created the impression that Schopenhauer was just a man of ideas, of aphorisms, and of thoughts on sundry aspects of life, some of which are in a curious way anticipatory of later ideas.

If that were all that there is to it, Schopenhauer would have no place in this series. It is not, however, all that there is to it. The main structure of Schopenhauer's major work *Das Welt als Wille und Vorstellung* is really quite clear, and contains a continuous argument which takes in the bulk of his philosophy. In the preface to the first edition of the work he describes himself as offering a single thought, and elsewhere he says that what he has to say is simply the unfolding of such a single thought. Schopenhauer lived from 1788 until 1860. He first published the main work in 1819, but a revised second edition appeared in 1844, and a third edition in 1859. The effect of these revisions was not only a general enlargement of the original work but also the additional inclusion of fifty essays by way of supplements to each of the four books of the original work. Most of these essays are related to individual chapters of the original work (now the first volume) and this fact is indicated. Comprising as they do the second volume of the final version, they provide essential comment upon and elucidation of the material of the first volume, as well as a great deal of additional material.

Schopenhauer gave the reader advice on how to read the book. In the preface to the first edition he instructed readers to read the whole book twice; in the preface to the second edition he relaxed his standards somewhat, but he advised readers to read the second volume by itself after reading the first. (It is not in fact clear that the advice is in every case right.) It cannot be denied, however, that this type of revision, rather than a complete re-writing of the original work, makes an appreciation of the whole system difficult. The structure of the argument nevertheless remains the same, and the supplementary essays follow the structure of the original. The works that Schopenhauer wrote between the first and second editions of the main work – *On the Will in Nature* (1836), *On the Freedom of the Will* (1839), *On the Basis of Morality* (1840) (the latter two published together in 1841 as *The Two Fundamental Problems of Ethics*), and the collection of essays *Parerga and Paralipomena* (1851) – are really all subsidiary to the main work, even if they have some importance in themselves. Hence, for an appreciation of Schopenhauer's argument it is necessary to give pride of place to the main work.

There is one other book, apart from an early essay on *Vision and Colours* (1816) written in support of Goethe's theory of colours, which I have not mentioned. It is one which is, on Schopenhauer's own admission, of great importance for an understanding of his philosophy. This is his doctoral dissertation *The Fourfold Root of the Principle of Sufficient Reason*, written in 1813, and revised and enlarged in 1847. Schopenhauer insisted that it should be read as an introduction to his main work, and the advice deserves to be treated seriously. Hence I too shall begin with a survey of what is said in that book. Much of what Schopenhauer says in the first of the four books of the main work covers similar ground, but the real argument is to be found in *The Fourfold Root*. There is much more to Schopenhauer's philosophy than what is to be found there, but it is an invaluable introduction to it. The book also makes clear another fundamental point about Schopenhauer – his relation to Kant. Schopenhauer had very definite views about other philosophers, but in most cases he was willing to give credit where he thought that credit was due, even when he was inclined to be critical. The exceptions to that rule were his German contemporaries, Fichte, Schelling and Hegel. In the last in particular he could find nothing that was good. It is not always easy to see why. It may be in part due to his own abortive academic career, although this cannot be the whole explanation. During a brief appointment at the University of Berlin he chose to lecture at the same hour as Hegel, with disastrous results as far as concerns an audience. For the rest of his life he lived on a private income, but the feeling against those who pursued philosophy for money persisted. For whatever reason he was a solitary figure who received little recognition during his life-time until near the end of it. He was, however, always ready to acknowledge his debt to the 'great Kant', even if he was also critical of him. One has the impression that for him Plato and Kant were the great giants of philosophy, but it was Kant who had the greater influence upon him. The main work contains in the first volume an appendix which consists of a critical, indeed very critical, appreciation of Kant; it is an appreciation all the same.

In effect Schopenhauer took over the main framework of Kant's *Critique of Pure Reason*, and in particular its transcendental idealism and the distinction between phenomena and things-in-themselves (except that for Schopenhauer, as it turns out, there is only one of the latter).[1] He disliked, however, most of Kant's architectonic, not just because it was architectonic but because he thought it wrong. He believed that Kant was right and greatly to be admired for what he had said in the 'Aesthetic' of the *Critique*; it was thereafter that he had gone wrong. There is nothing like a theory of categories in Schopenhauer. Nevertheless, *The Fourfold Root* and the first book of the main work remain remarkably Kantian in spirit. One of his chief complaints about his contemporaries was their neglect of Kant; for that same reason Hegelianism was in his eyes a corruption of philosophy, nothing but meretricious sophistry pretending to be philosophy. Kant was not, however, merely a source of influence. Schopenhauer's entire approach to philosophy was very much the same, although his

3

style of writing was very different. Schopenhauer's style is marvellous; nobody who knows anything of the two philosophers could think when reading Schopenhauer that he was reading Kant. There are, however, differences of doctrine between the two philosophers, some of which go to the very roots. I shall mention two now, though others will appear in what I have to say later.

First, Schopenhauer believed that there was nothing wrong with the idea that a metaphysics, even if *a priori* in itself, could have, as he put it, an 'empirical source'. Indeed, it was round this point in relation to ethics that there revolve some of the issues lying behind his heated complaint against the Royal Danish Academy of Sciences, who in 1840 refused him the prize for his essay *On the Basis of Morality*, despite the fact that he was the only entrant for it. Also, while he accepted Kant's doctrine that phenomena are transcendentally ideal although empirically real (that is to say that the ordinary distinction between appearance and reality is a genuine one but is to be drawn at the level of, and within, experiences only) he thought that he could give an empirical account of the origins of such experiences in terms of the effect of objects of perception on the brain and its effects on perception itself. Thus Schopenhauer saw a much closer relation between Kant's transcendental idealism and Berkeley's subjective idealism than Kant himself saw and other philosophers since have been prepared to see. More than this, Schopenhauer saw Locke's causal or representative theory of perception, against which Berkeley himself reacted, as something of the source of his own idealism. We shall see later that his attempt to graft on to his version of Kant's transcendental idealism certain aspects of an empirical theory of perception, with a praiseworthy distinction between sensation and perception, scarcely adds to the coherence of the overall account.

Second, although this takes us in the opposite direction, Schopenhauer thought that Kant had made an illegitimate distinction between representations and their objects. It is necessary at this point to make some comment on the word 'representation'. It may have been noted that I have not so far given an English translation of the title of Schopenhauer's main work. The translation that was for long the only translation in English of the main work (that by R. B. Haldane and J. Kemp) gave the title as *The World as Will and Idea* and translated 'Vorstellung' as 'idea' throughout. That translation is fine as long as it is realized that the word 'idea' is being used in something like the Lockean sense, as anything that comes before the mind as a state of consciousness. The term 'Vorstellung' covers perceptions, concepts, images and any object of consciousness of that kind, not just ideas in the more ordinary sense. To speak of the world as idea is thus, in the Schopenhauerian context, simply an expression of idealism. The more recent translation of the main work by E. F. J. Payne uses the title *The World as Will and Representation*. If that avoids the misleadingness of the earlier translation it unfortunately imports some of its own, since the term 'representation' suggests that there is something to be a representation of. Schopenhauer does sometimes associate 'Vorstellungen' with mental pictures or pictures in the head or brain. On the other hand, the Schopenhauerian criticism of Kant that I mentioned earlier is to the effect that Kant makes a mistake in making a distinction between representations and their objects — what they are of. Moreover, the fact that the term covers any object of consciousness, including concepts, makes it wrong to translate it as 'representation or mental picture', as Payne often does. It might have been better to use a more neutral term such as 'presentation', although it is doubtful whether even that would remove all misleadingness. (I shall try not to make too much of a meal of this point in what follows.) However all this may be, the point of Schopenhauer's criticism of Kant is to reinforce the idealism, over which Schopenhauer in effect finds an ambiguity or indefiniteness in Kant's expression of his views, even if he thinks that the true idealism is in fact implied by Kant's doctrine. For Schopenhauer himself there exist simply representations and thing-in-itself. There are no other objects.

Since the thing-in-itself comes eventually to be identified with the will, it seems to follow that there exist only will and representations; that is what the world is. There is, however, something of a difficulty in this, since representations are representations to a knowing consciousness or subject, and even if it turns out, as it does, that we ourselves are will as thing-in-itself, knowledge and the subject who has it have to enter the picture somehow. Schopenhauer uses in this connection the image of the will as a strong, blind man carrying the intellect as a lame but sighted man on his back. The image is suggestive, but it remains a problem how it is to be given a literal interpretation in Schopenhauer's scheme of things. The same problem, although without the reference to the will, exists for Kant. On his view too each of us, *qua* noumenal self, is a thing-in-itself (something behind and beyond phenomena), but phenomena or representations are such, not for that noumenal self, but for the 'I' that is presupposed in what Kant called the transcendental unity of apperception — the 'I think' that accompanies all our representations. For transcendental idealism there is no question of there being a representation of such an 'I'; the 'I think' is rather a necessary condition of the possibility of repre-

5

sentations constituting experience. The noumenal self, as thing-in-itself, cannot be conceived as having any part in this, even if it is in some sense its ground. Hence the link between that noumenal self and the 'I think' remains obscure.

For Kant, since nothing positive could be said about things-in-themselves, the problem could be left to that extent as a mystery. Schopenhauer, however, thinks that something positive *can* be said about the thing-in-itself and that there is a good argument for this conclusion; the thing-in-itself is will. In that case, however, the mystery of the connection between it and the knowing subject ought not to be left as such. It is so left, as will appear, and that perhaps is one of the most unsatisfactory aspects of his philosophy. Strictly speaking, if he were asked what at bottom exists, he ought to say 'The thing-in-itself'. In that case, however, in what sense do representations exist? If their existence is an existence for a subject, what is that, and how does the knowledge that they entail come into the picture? The world is after all will *and* representation. These are questions which will exercise us as we go on.

As far as concerns Schopenhauer's argument, knowledge or a knowing consciousness or subject for which there are representations is the starting-point of his inquiry. It is perhaps as well to comment briefly on Schopenhauer's conception of knowledge at the very outset, as well as on the general idea of a starting-point in this connection. Schopenhauer shows little interest in the question which so much occupies modern epistemologists – what knowledge is. The notion (which is barely distinguished from that of consciousness) is taken as a datum, and Schopenhauer shows no interest in what some have called its analysis or in the conditions that make its objectivity possible. Moreover, knowledge or consciousness is for him very much something that involves a relation between an individual knower and an object. Schopenhauer belongs to the tradition, initiated perhaps by Descartes, which takes the individual knower (not a community of knowers) as the starting-point for his philosophical inquiry. (I shall return to this point in my final chapter.) At the same time, as I shall indicate in more detail later, he works on the assumption that what is true in this respect for me must be true for all men, and he shows no inclination to any form of solipsism or interest in a problem of 'other minds'. Each of us is a knower and has consciousness of a range of objects in the form of representations. It is what this implies that is his concern.

To turn to the general idea of a starting-point – every metaphysics which seeks to present an argument leading to conclusions about what fundamentally exists must start somewhere, and the necessity of the conclusions will be relative to that starting-point. Thus, for example, Aristotle's doctrine of the categories, as a doctrine about the most general kinds of thing that ultimately exist, is derived from an initial position about language in relation to the world. The doctrine can be construed as an unfolding of the implications of that initial position. In a similar way, the ontology that is set out in P. F. Strawson's *Individuals*, to take a more modern example, is derived from an initial position about speaker-hearer identification of things, and the ontology that results is arrived at by a kind of unfolding of what is implied in that initial position. In Kantian terms it is an 'exposition' of a concept or scheme of concepts, and it is the inverse of a transcendental argument which takes the conclusion and argues for something as necessary to its possibility. In such arguments what I have described as the initial position constitutes a sort of 'given'. For both Kant and Schopenhauer it is in effect the transcendental idealism that is that 'given' -- the 'fact' that there are representations for a knowing consciousness. If there is a difference, it is that Kant starts from the representations themselves and argues that they pre-suppose a knowing consciousness — in opposition to a Humean position according to which there need be no such implication; Schopenhauer, on the other hand, starts from the knowing consciousness and argues for what this entails about representations as its contents.[2] There is, finally, the other difference, referred to earlier, that Schopenhauer thinks that it is possible to produce empirical support for the idealism itself, while for Kant it remains a 'given' in every sense.

In *The Fourfold Root* Schopenhauer starts from the idea of a knowing consciousness for which there are representations, and argues for the thesis that any such representations must be subject to a condition which constitutes one form or other of the principle of sufficient reason. Every representation is conditioned in this way and is thus necessary relative to something (some further representation) which is its condition, ground or reason. Schopenhauer thinks that there are four, and only four, such forms of the principle of sufficient reason, and therefore four, and only four, kinds of way in which representations are conditioned for us. There are for the same reason four, and only four, kinds of object for a knowing consciousness. The world as representation is so structured and so governed by principles in four different ways. None of these conditions or forms of the principle of sufficient reason takes us beyond representations; the principles are all internal to the realm of representations alone. The first step in outlining and assessing Schopenhauer's argument will involve a

7

consideration of this particular argument.

The first book of the main work takes up the issues at that point in a more general way and sets them in a general context. It is here that we are confronted with the argument for transcendental idealism in its greatest detail, although it has to be said that it appears that it was only when Schopenhauer came to write the supplementary essays in the second volume that he felt any great need for such an argument at all. Schopenhauer also sets out the relations between perception, understanding and reason, as he understands those notions, and has something to say about the forms of knowledge which they make possible. It is in this context also that he offers his theory of the nature of metaphysics itself.

The second book of the main work presents the crucial argument for taking the sort of step that Kant thought impossible — to the identification of the thing-in-itself with the will. That argument, while certainly invalid, is of considerable interest, and relies upon certain considerations that have implications beyond the merely Schopenhauerian context. Once he has arrived at the notion of the will, Schopenhauer can and does give consideration to the ways in which the will may be thought to have expression in nature in general. This has implications not only for an understanding of teleology, instinct and the like, but for natural law in general. The essay *On the Will in Nature* also has much to say about such matters.

The third book of the main work takes us back to representation in the light of the foregoing. Schopenhauer has in the previous book introduced the notion of grades of objectification of the will, which he associates with that of Platonic Ideas, considered in effect as that to which objects of a given kind are tending. Ideas form a distinct class of representations. Knowledge of them demands a kind of divorce from the will, and thus involves a form of pure contemplation, without any of the striving that is to be found in ordinary perception because of the influence of the will. This is for Schopenhauer the source of aesthetic awareness and forms the basis for his consideration of the various arts. His invocation of the Platonic Ideas presents, however, many difficulties, and this part of his theory may be to many an unsatisfactory part of his system.

The final book goes back to the will and presents his views on ethics. These are based on the 'fact' of our real identity as will, indeed as one single will. This is the basis of the sympathy or compassion which Schopenhauer thinks the only basis of morality. It is in this book that, basing himself on the conception of human nature that he takes his metaphysics to provide, Schopenhauer offers what little he has to say about political philosophy, as well as ethics. In this respect, as well as in his observations about free will the book has links with *The Two Fundamental Problems of Ethics*. In this book too are to be found Schopenhauer's observations on death, suicide, sex, and finally salvation in the will's denial of itself.

The general structure of Schopenhauer's argument is therefore clear, in the same way as the very different structure of Kant's argument is clear. As with Kant's argument again, the lack of system is in the details, not in the general structure. Through these details, however, there runs a central consideration which almost justifies Schopenhauer's claim to be unfolding a single thought. Once he has taken the crucial step to the identification of the thing-in-itself with the will, most of what is claimed in the final book of the main work, with all its richness and expansiveness, follows directly, or can be seen as doing so, in a most impressive way. Schopenhauer was not afraid to take the argument to its rigorous conclusion as he saw it. It is difficult not to be impressed by this. To be so impressed is not simply to find a fascination in the many ideas that he throws out or to be taken in by his truly marvellous style. It is to find as a matter for admiration the way in which the ideas are fitted together and derived from a definite structure of thought, and so presented to us. Some flavour of this is to be got from many individual passages in his work, but from none so much perhaps as the words that conclude the fourth book of the first volume of *The World as Will and Representation* (*WR* I 71, p. 411; *WI* I, p. 532). Schopenhauer is replying to the objection that what the denial of the will produces is nothingness. He says, 'We freely acknowledge it: what remains behind after the complete abolition of the will is, for all those who are still full of the will, indeed nothing. But also conversely, to those in whom the will has turned and denied itself, this so very real world of ours with all its suns and galaxies is — nothing.' Despite all his apparently bad-mannered vituperation against his fellow philosophers, Schopenhauer seems genuinely to accept that, whether or not he attained that state himself.

2

The Fourfold Root

The Fourfold Root of the Principle of Sufficient Reason was
Schopenhauer's doctoral thesis and was first published in 1813. He
published a second edition, revising and enlarging the original text,
in 1847, the year in which he was 59. In the preface to that second
edition he refers in biting terms to the difference in style that may
be apparent between the mild and unassuming tone of the young
man and the firm but occasionally harsh voice of the 'old man'. He
also makes in passing one of his characteristic attacks on Hegel,
the 'clumsy charlatan', and speaks sadly and bitterly about the
state of German philosophy. In the interval between the two editions he had published most of his other works, including two
editions of his main work; and in the preface to the first edition of
The World as Will and Representation he had urged readers to read
The Fourfold Root first as an essential introduction to the main
work. Indeed, he had said that he would have printed it along with
and as an introduction to the text of the main work, if it had not
been written 'several years' before. It had in fact been published
five years previously, and it is legitimate to wonder whether five
years is enough to warrant departing from a policy which otherwise seemed desirable. The truth is no doubt that to have printed
The Fourfold Root at the beginning of the main work would have
upset the scale and structure of that work, since *The Fourfold
Root* is quite a substantial book in its own right. The only other
thing to be said on that score is that the publication of the second
edition of the main work with its large scale selection of supplementary essays upset its balance in any case. However that may be,
The Fourfold Root remained a separate work, and it is the 1847
edition that is available in translation and is the version generally
referred to.

It is indeed a separate work in its own right. It contains, how-ever, little more than a few suggestive reflections of Schopenhauer's full-scale metaphysical views, let alone his ethics and aesthetics. While, therefore, it has been for long a work much admired by many philosophers (including myself), it might be argued that one does not get from it the full flavour of Schopenhauer's philosophi-cal views. That is no doubt true. At the same time, it would be unwise not to take seriously Schopenhauer's own estimation of the work. For anyone concerned with Schopenhauer's *argument* for his metaphysical position it is indeed the essential first stage in that argument. Schopenhauer never went back on what he argued in it. It is, as the title suggests, a systematic exposition of the role played by the principle of sufficient reason in four forms and in relation to four possible objects for a 'knowing consciousness'. As that reference to knowledge makes clear the work is essentially Schopenhauer's epistemology, if anything deserves that title. More than that, it provides, given Schopenhauer's idealism the essential framework for the 'world as representation'.

I said above that the work contains a systematic exposition of the role played by the principle of sufficient reason. I did not say that it contained an argument for the principle itself, nor did I speak of roles in the plural. Each of these points requires comment. Schopenhauer did not think that it was possible to provide an argument for the principle, which in its most general form can be stated, as he says, in the terms in which it was put by Christian Wolff — 'Nothing is without a reason why it should be rather than not be' (*FR* 5, p. 6). Nor did he ever attempt to set out such a proof and *The Fourfold Root* should not be interpreted as doing so. Schopenhauer thinks that the principle is in fact presupposed in any argument or proof; hence to ask for a proof of the principle itself involves a circle, in that the principle is presupposed in the very demand (*FR* 14, pp. 32-3). It might be suggested that this very fact gives rise to the possibility of a proof of sorts — a proof that is dialectical in the sense implied in what Aristotle says with regard to the principle of contradiction. Aristotle suggests that in the case of the principle of contradiction anyone who denies it can be shown to presuppose it; the sceptic is, so to speak, refuted out of his own mouth. In the case of the principle of sufficient reason, however, the sceptic would have to do more than speak; he would have to argue. An unargued scepticism about the principle of suffi-cient reason might be gratuitous, but it would not be incoherent in the way that a denial of the principle of contradiction might be held to be. (I shall discuss later Schopenhauer's own attitude to the principle of contradiction.)

11

Aristotle's treatment of the principle of contradiction involves in effect a version of what Kant was to call, although in a special application to possible experience, a transcendental argument — an argument to the effect that something must be so because the very possibility of something else presupposes it. Could Schopenhauer have allowed a transcendental argument for the principle of sufficient reason? He certainly thought that the principle was presupposed in all possible relations that a knowing consciousness could have to an object. It is for the same reason presupposed in any argument for the truth of something, including *a fortiori* its own truth. To say that is to say that the principle constitutes a transcendental truth — and that Schopenhauer certainly wanted to assert. It is not, however, to say that we have here an argument for the absolute necessity of its truth; that Schopenhauer would certainly have wanted to deny, along with all absolute necessities (cf. *FR* 49, pp. 225-7; I shall return to this issue later in this chapter, and also in relation to Kant in the next chapter). We may recognize or be got to recognize the truth of the principle *a priori*, but that does not mean that there is any proof of it, not even a transcendental proof. What Schopenhauer provides in *The Fourfold Root*, therefore, is not an argument for the principle but an exposition of its role which may point towards a recognition of its truth — as truth it is, in his view.

Similar considerations apply to the other point that I mentioned, when I spoke of the role, rather than the roles, of the principle. To speak of roles might suggest that there is involved here a heterogeneity of principles; but there is, according to Schopenhauer, only one principle, which asserts that everything results from a given reason. There may be different applications for such a principle, and the applications may take different forms according to the characteristics of that to which it is applied. The principle itself, however, has a single root (which I shall set out in due course), even if its applications can take four forms. To that extent, speaking of the 'fourfold root' may be misleading. There are not four roots; there is only one root, but there are four forms that the principle can take in its application to different kinds of object of consciousness. Hence too the principle has only one role, although one needs to state that role in differing ways according to the circumstances.

Schopenhauer puts the point at the very beginning of the work in terms of two other transcendental principles, to which he recurs at intervals later in the work. These are the laws of homogeneity and specification. They require us to seek for, on the one hand, a single concept or genus under which the phenomena in question can be subsumed, and, on the other hand, the proper number of kinds or species in terms of which the phenomena are to be classified. Such laws, for which Schopenhauer invokes the authority of Plato and Aristotle, are clearly at best methodological or heuristic principles; they will find an application to the extent that the subject-matter admits of it and to that extent alone. What Schopenhauer is suggesting in the present context is that, wherever something constitutes the ground for something else (and there will always be some ground), we can find a single principle which sums this up, whatever be the nature of that ground. Conversely there will be a definite number of possible kinds of ground. Schopenhauer thinks that there are in fact four such kinds of ground, but this fact has its own source in the nature of the relation of a knowing consciousness to its object. This is the root of the principle and it is fourfold in that sense.

Why four, however? Fundamentally the answer to this question is that there are as many kinds of reason or ground as there are kinds of object for a knowing consciousness; and Schopenhauer thinks that an examination or exposition of what is involved in this reveals that there are only four kinds of object for our cognitive faculty — a faculty that manifests itself in the forms of sensibility, understanding and reason. Schopenhauer here embraces a kind of faculty psychology or scheme of faculties which he has inherited from Kant, although he constantly protests, as we shall see later, that Kant did not have a correct view of the relation between understanding and reason. At all events, an examination of the human mind in this way is supposed to reveal only four kinds of object for a subject, and it is inferred from this that there can be only four kinds of reason, ground or condition for such objects. Once again, there can be no proof of this, although it is a truth that one may be got to see. Schopenhauer adds in the closing section of the work (FR 52, p. 234) that if there were a fifth kind of object for a subject there would have to be a fifth kind of ground and, therefore, a fifth form of the principle of sufficient reason; but he clearly thinks that we have no idea of what this would be like. The four forms of the principle that emerge from an examination of the relation of a knowing consciousness to an object are supposed to be all that we can make sense of in relation to human-beings as knowing subjects, and in that way constitute a kind of limit to what we can find intelligible.

It follows from all this that we shall appreciate the answer to the question 'Why four?', if we do so at all, only by following Schopenhauer through his examination of what is involved in the relation of a knowing consciousness to an object. The same applies to the question 'Which four?'. It would be idle, however, to claim that when we read through *The Fourfold Root* we get the impression of being involved in a voyage of discovery. The treatment is too systematic for that, and we are presented with Schopenhauer's findings, not the process of discovery itself. Moreover, it is clear that he was helped to his conclusions by things said by his predecessors. He devotes the second chapter of the work, in fact, to a summary of things said by other philosophers on the subject in general. The most obvious influence is Christian Wolff, who distinguished three kinds of *ratio* (reason) or *principium* (principle) — those of *fiendi* (becoming), *essendi* (being) and *cognoscendi* (knowing) — although there are of course much earlier precedents for such distinctions. Schopenhauer also notes that Wolff mentions under the heading of *causa* an 'impulsive cause, or reason determining the will', which corresponds in some way to his own fourth kind of reason or ground — that of *agendi* (acting). How this fits in with the others we shall see in due course.

The structure of Schopenhauer's discussion comprises (a) the statement of the single root of the principle of sufficient reason and (b) the exposition of the four forms that this takes in the light of what is said about the root. The first takes up part of the very short third chapter; the discussions of the four forms take up a chapter each, and the first receives by far the fullest treatment. There is finally a short conclusion, some part of which has already been mentioned. The statement of the root itself is important and I shall quote it in full (*FR* 16, pp. 41-2):

> *Our knowing consciousness, manifesting itself as outer and inner sensibility (receptivity), understanding and reason, divides into subject and object, and contains nothing else. To be object for the subject, and to be our representation, are the same thing. All our representations are objects of the subject, and all objects of the subject are our representations. Now it is found that all our representations stand to one another in a law-like connection, one that is in form determinable A PRIORI. By virtue of which nothing existing by itself and independent, and also nothing single and detached, can become an object for us.*

The first part of this implicitly states Schopenhauer's idealism, although it may not do so quite explicitly. All forms of knowledge or cognition, he says, involve a relation between a subject and an object, but the only thing that counts as such an object for a subject is a representation. Hence, we cannot have knowledge of anything that is not fundamentally a matter of representation. In his main work Schopenhauer tends to state his idealism by means of the formula 'No object without a subject'. He does not quite say that here; he simply confines his attention to objects for a subject and asserts that they are all representations (there might, as far as that goes, be other objects — not for a subject). The second part of the passage, on the other hand, asserts that all representations stand, and must stand, to each other in some connection, so that their occurrence is both regular and conditioned. No representation can occur by itself but must be subject to some condition by other representations which constitute its ground. This will turn out to be of fundamental importance.

So much for the root. Why, however, is it that? It is difficult to answer that question without reference to the discussion of the four forms of the general principle that follows. What he has produced in the statement of the root is in effect a framework within which, and within which alone, the conditioned nature of phenomena is to be seen. All such forms of being subject to conditions apply to representations alone, and all representations are subject to such conditions. This is so because, in effect, that is what cognition is like. Thus the nature of human cognition provides the key to the ways in which the principle of sufficient reason gets an application to phenomena. Our understanding of the four forms of the principle must involve in each case relating the form to that root. It will be of importance to see by the same means how the form of the principle in each case can be thought to be *a priori*.

It remains to set out and discuss the ways in which this is worked out in detail. Schopenhauer says in chapter 8 (*FR* 46, pp. 221-2) that the systematic arrangement which the classes of reasons should follow ought to be (1) the principle of reason of being (first in respect of time and then in respect of space), (2) the principle of reason of becoming or law of causality, (3) the principle of reason of acting or law of motivation, and (4) the principle of reason of knowing. The reason for this ordering is, he says, that the first three are concerned with immediate representations, while the last is concerned with representations from representations (one might almost say representations *of* representations). He gives no reasons for the ordering of the other three, but presumably the point is that it is natural to attend to the structural aspects of the arrangement of representations before attending to what might be called their dynamic features. In his actual exposition, however, Schopenhauer does not follow that order, but that of becoming, knowing, being and acting. He does that, he says, for the sake of clarity, dealing with what is familiar and better known first. However that may be, I shall simply follow his order of exposition.

15

The principle of sufficient reason
of becoming — causality

Perhaps the most obvious instance of the general principle that
'nothing is without a reason why it should be rather than not be' is
the principle of universal causality, and it is thus understandable
that Schopenhauer deals with it first. His treatment of it constitutes, as I said earlier, by far the longest chapter (chapter 4) of
The Fourfold Root. A good deal of it, however, is given up to
matters that at first sight might not seem to belong there. There is
a fairly extensive criticism of Kant on causality, and that is understandable (although I shall, by and large, reserve consideration of
that until the next chapter). What may be less obviously predictable is that there is to be found here Schopenhauer's theory of
sense-perception. It is in fact an essential part of his argument for
the *a priori* character of the principle. It must be confessed, however, that his treatment of it, involving, as it does, an extensive use
of the principle of causality, is far from happy, despite a laudable
insistence on a strict distinction between sensation and perception.

Schopenhauer's actual explanation of the notion of a cause is
relatively simple, whether or not it is right. He insists that causality has to do, not simply with events as they succeed each other in
time, but with *changes*, i.e., as he puts it, the appearance and dis-
appearance of states in time. It is in this sense that causality has to
do with becoming — with the coming about of a new state in time.
The cause of the coming to be of a state is another state (considered, of course, as representation) which is a sufficient reason for
the state that comes to be, and without which it would not come
to be. Strictly speaking, Schopenhauer says, the cause is the *entire
state* that pre-exists the state that comes to be. A state is and must
be, however, the state of an object or objects; hence a change presupposes a relatively persistent object. Moreover, even if objects
themselves can in the end cease to exist, there is presupposed a
persistent matter, and Schopenhauer thinks that the permanence
of matter is known *a priori* and with certainty. Unfortunately, as
seems to be the case, the only ground that Schopenhauer has for
thinking that this claim has more than an empirical certainty is
that there is no room for the conception of the arising or passing
away of matter, since these notions apply only to states of things,
not to that which is the ultimate bearer of those states. Hence the
weight of the argument for the permanence of matter is put upon
the causal principle itself and his interpretation of it as applying to
states which presuppose the existence of something of which they
are the states.

Nevertheless, Schopenhauer's claim that causality has to do with changes has something to recommend it, at any rate as far as concerns the place of causality in the material world. It is less clear how it applies elsewhere. Schopenhauer goes on to distinguish three kinds of cause. The one that we have been concerned with so far is really that which applies, as he puts it (FR 20, p. 70), to the 'inorganic kingdom', where, he says, Newton's Third Law, that action and reaction are equal and opposite, applies. When we are concerned with organic life, i.e. with plants and 'the unconscious part of animal life', causes appear as stimuli, and action and reaction need not be equal. Where there is consciousness, causes appear as motives; here knowledge is presupposed for the motives to function. We shall return to this third kind of cause in the fourth section of this chapter, in connection with the fourth kind of sufficient reason, but it may be remarked here that it is not at all obvious how Schopenhauer's general formula concerning the connection of causality with the coming to be of the states of bodies applies in this case.

The claim on behalf of the principle of causality in this sense, however, needs to be related to the root if it's validity, on Schopenhauer's view, is to be evident. That is to say that, given the way in which the root was expressed, the principle needs to be set out in terms of how representations are as objects for a subject. Indeed Schopenhauer starts his chapter in this way by setting out the class of objects for which this form of the principle of sufficient reason has application. It is the class of intuitive, complete and empirical representations, i.e. those of perception (FR 17 p. 45), the forms of which are those of space and time (FR 18 p. 46). The perceivability of space and time is in fact matter. Indeed it is the fact that space and time are presupposed here that makes possible what Schopenhauer comes to say about causality and changes in the states of bodies. For, as he says (FR 18 p. 46), permanence in an object is recognized only through a contrast with changes occurring in other objects which exist simultaneously but are spatially differentiated from it; and changes, as we have already seen, presuppose a permanent something in which the changes occur. Hence the principle of causality gets an application only to representations which have a spatio-temporal form. So far this is a straight Kantianism, as is also his insistence that it implies a transcendental idealism, despite the reference to an empirical reality. That is to say that everything that appears to be said about an empirical reality has to be interpreted in terms of representations for a subject, while what is so said has no application to anything that may lie beyond representations as a thing-in-itself. Hence, what

17

has been said about objects and their states is still, strictly speaking, to be construed in terms of representations.

In a sense, however, Schopenhauer's idealism is more fundamental than that. With Kant he argues that it is not merely sensibility that gives the subject representations which constitute empirical objects, but sensibility together with the understanding (although, as we shall see, he gives a rather different account of what the understanding is from that which Kant gives). It is the understanding which involves use of the principle of sufficient reason. If it is true that empirical representations cannot stand alone, but must occur for the subject in an ordered connection according to the principle of sufficient reason in the form being considered at present, this is a truth which results from the workings of the understanding. So far so good; so, with the qualification made above, Kant. However, Schopenhauer also claims (*FR* 19, p. 48) that *immediate* knowledge is available to the subject only through the inner sense, the outer being again object of the inner, so that the inner sense perceives the perceptions of the outer sense; and he adds that for this reason, as far as concerns the *immediate presence* of representations in consciousness, the subject remains under the form of time alone.[1]

There is, second and, I think, connected with the former point, the fact that Schopenhauer wants to make a firm distinction between sensation and perception (and elsewhere he takes Kant to task for failing to make the distinction). In a way Kant's transcendental idealism depends on *not* making such a distinction, but on taking representations as something produced in us in the way that sensations are. That way of thinking Kant had inherited from his empiricist forebears, such as Berkeley. Although Kant thought that perception of the empirical world of phenomena was more than a matter of sensibility, more than a matter of the reception of representations, since it also involved the understanding, the understanding was not supposed to go beyond representations, but rather to bring them under principles of judgment. Schopenhauer did not agree with the idea that the understanding had anything to do with judgment, but he agreed with the rest. He still wished to distinguish between sensation and perception.

It is possible to make a distinction between sensation and perception in a way that does not necessarily go against that point of view. That is to say that it is possible, while making the distinction, to refuse to allow that perception involves any inference or any other kind of cognitive move from sensations. That, for example, was how Thomas Reid made the distinction, since, in his view, while perception involved sensation, the latter had merely a

18

kind of causal role in contributing to perception, and did not constitute any kind of epistemological 'given' on which perception
was based, as it were inferentially. Schopenhauer refers approvingly
to Reid on the distinction between sensation and perception in his
main work (*WR* II 2, pp. 20-1; *WI* II, p. 186), but only because he
thinks that Reid thereby shows in a negative way 'the intellectuality of perception'.[2] Hence there is no indication that Schopenhauer really appreciated the importance of the way in which Reid
made the distinction. What he himself wants to say, and claims to
be the first to say 'in consequence of the Kantian doctrine', is that
the understanding makes possible the move from the sensations
given in sensibility to a perception of the world constituted by
representations of outer sense. That is why such representations
are not, strictly speaking, immediate; they are mediated by the
understanding. The fact that such representations are not possible
at all without that mediation is supposed to show that the principle
by which the understanding works — the principle of causality — is
presupposed in perception, and cannot for that reason be derived
from perception. It must therefore be *a priori*.

How does it work? Sensation, Schopenhauer says (*FR* 21, p.
76), is a poor, wretched thing; it is something that occurs 'within
the organism' and is confined to 'the region underneath the skin'.
While a sensation can be pleasant or unpleasant, and to that
extent has a connection with the will, it is essentially subjective
and we become conscious of it only under the form of time; there
is nothing objective about it. It is the understanding that grasps
that the sensation is the effect of something, applies the law of
causality *a priori*, and summoning space to its assistance (as something 'lying predisposed in the intellect, i.e. the brain' (*FR* 21, p.
77)), places the cause outside the organism. Schopenhauer goes
into some detail concerning the tasks that the understanding or
intellect has to perform, including (a) the setting right the impression of the object which is produced upside down on the retina,
(b) the making of a single perception out of a double sensation
produced in the two eyes, (c) the addition of the third dimension
by constructing bodies out of the 'mere surfaces previously obtained' (*FR* 21, p. 93), and (d) the recognition of the distance of
objects. This is all in addition to the task of fitting sight together
with the other senses, or at least touch.

It would be profitless to go into the details of all this. Schopenhauer relies heavily on contemporary optics, but apart from limitations of that kind it remains inutterably obscure what basis the
understanding has for carrying out the tasks in question. Even if it
were granted that we know *a priori* that all changes are due to

some cause, it could not be maintained that we know *a priori which* causes they are due to. Hence, if it were true that we are given sensations, we still could not know *a priori* what they are caused by. Schopenhauer says (*FR* 21, p. 85) that the retina of the eye possesses the faculty of immediately feeling from what direction the light that impinges on it comes. Apart from the doubtfulness of the claim in itself, it is impossible to see what it could mean on Schopenhauer's terms of reference, since sensations as such do not conform to the form of space. Even if the intellect could be said to supply that form, it could not supply the details required in any given instance. On top of all this is the fact that it seems very difficult, to say the least, to apply in this context what Schopenhauer says about causes effecting changes of state in objects. If sensations are caused by objects and are taken by the understanding as being so, what is the state that is so changed, and what is it a state of? It might be suggested that it is a state of the body, but Schopenhauer makes clear (*FR* 22, p. 121) that the representation that the sensation consists in is not a representation of the body, since that would make it a perception, not a sensation. A sensation is not a representation *of* anything; hence if the sensation brought about were a new state of the body, it could not be one which we were aware of as such. That makes it even more difficult to see how it could be the basis for the work of the intellect or understanding.

It is impossible to avoid the conclusion that this is a rather unfortunate section of Schopenhauer's book. While it is right to make a distinction between sensation and perception, and while Schopenhauer is largely right in the way in which he makes it, the distinction cannot then be used in the way in which he uses it. While a distinction between sensation and perception could be added to, without making it part of, a Kantian transcendental idealism, so allowing for a distinction between different states of consciousness, it cannot be made part of the workings of that transcendental idealism as Schopenhauer tries to make it. In effect, on his view, the understanding produces intuitive perceptions, and thus representations (of the world, as we should ordinarily say), by means of its own laws, basing itself on other representations, i,e. sensations. It is noteworthy that there is no reference in all this to the notion of judgment; indeed Schopenhauer overtly repudiates such a reference, as well as that to any processes of reflection, these being, in his view, the province of reason, not of the understanding. For Kant the function of the understanding was to bring intuitions under concepts according to certain laws or principles. For Schopenhauer its function is in effect to produce new intuitions out of those involved in sensation alone. The principle of sufficient reason on which it relies, however, can only provide the form of a connection between such intuitions or representations; it cannot provide the details of that connection, nor can it, strictly speaking, provide new representations. It has to do both these things on Schopenhauer's account.

It might be thought that the whole account could be omitted and replaced by some more satisfactory account of perception. One might even appeal, as Schopenhauer does some of the time, to the part played by the brain and nervous system in bringing about some of the results which he thinks the understanding brings about, e.g. the making of a single perception out of the double excitations produced in the two eyes. This would surely imply, however, that such mechanisms are either innate or the result of maturation, not of learning. Whatever be the facts on this matter, Schopenhauer is fairly definite (*FR* 21, p. 104) that the understanding's application of the principle of sufficient reason is the result of experience. In any case, Schopenhauer's account in section 21 of *The Fourfold Root*, where all this occurs, is meant to provide a basis for the claim for the *a priori* character of the principle of sufficient reason in this form. If Schopenhauer were right the truth of the principle that every representation of sensation has a cause in outer objects, even if not the fully general principle that every representation has a cause in other representations, would be presupposed in the workings of the understanding in producing those representations which constitute perceptions of the world. All perception would thus presuppose the truth of the principle, at least in its restricted form, in the sense that nothing could validly be called 'perception' if it were not true. In that case there would be a genuine sense in which at least the restricted form of the principle of sufficient reason of becoming would be *a priori*. Since Schopenhauer cannot be right in the account offered, one is left, if one wants a basis for the claim for the *a priori* character of the principle of causality, only with something of the kind that Kant offered in the 'Second Analogy' of the *Critique*. This Schopenhauer rejects, even if the sum total of what Kant says in the three 'Analogies' has some relation to what Schopenhauer says concerning what causality actually is, especially its connection with the permanence of matter and bodies. Hence, while Schopenhauer offers some interesting considerations about the nature of causality and the connection between that notion and those of objects and matter, his account of the *a priori* character of the principle of sufficient reason in this form is, I believe, no less than disastrous.[3]

The principle of sufficient reason of knowing —
reason and truth

Despite what I have said about the disastrous nature of Schopenhauer's account in the previous section, what he intended to suggest as true was at least that the occurrence of any representation is conditional upon the occurrence of some other representation or representations as its ground or reason. The only necessity to be attached to representations is thus a relative one only, i.e. they must occur *if* others are to occur. If in saying that such a connection between representations was the work of the understanding Schopenhauer had meant to say that it had something to do with concepts, he could have been taken to say that any necessary connections between representations is due to the way in which they are subsumed under concepts. Necessity would in that case be a product of our way of thinking about things, not something that belongs intrinsically to whatever concepts are applied to. Such a view might have some appeal to philosophers who want to deny that there is any necessity about events themselves, and to insist that, if we want to attribute any necessity to the actual course of events, such a necessity must be taken to arise simply from our way of thinking about those events, in subsuming them under concepts and indeed under systems of connected concepts.

However that may be, it cannot be what Schopenhauer thinks; for he does not think that concepts are the work of the understanding. In this he thinks of himself as putting right misconceptions that others, including Kant, have had about the understanding. It is indeed true that as he uses the term 'understanding' that use corresponds more to our ordinary use of the term, by contrast with the Kantian use which is to some extent technical. For Kant the understanding is discursive and involves bringing intuitions under concepts in judgment. For Schopenhauer, as we shall see in more detail later, the objects of understanding are things; its one function is that of providing immediate knowledge of the connection between cause and effect in relation to those things. It is reason which is discursive. Lack of understanding amounts to stupidity, while deficiency in reason is foolishness; in general, reason is concerned with truth, understanding with reality (*WR* I 6, p. 24; *WI* I, p. 30). He also thinks that the persistence of illusions despite what our reason tells us also shows the difference between understanding, which is always involved in perception, whether veridical or illusory, and reason (*ibid.* and *FR* 21, pp. 103-4). One might think that such understanding would nevertheless presuppose concepts, even if it is not their source. That does not, however, appear to be Schopenhauer's view. Animals, in his view, have understanding, since they perceive objects, but he does not allow that they have concepts (*WR* II 5, pp. 59ff; *WI* II, pp. 228ff; cf. *FR* 26, pp. 145ff.). There is thus, on his view, a gap between understanding and concepts, and this perhaps reflects our ordinary ways of speaking and thinking much less.

However that may be, with concepts we move to the second class of objects for a subject and thus to a second form of the principle of sufficient reason. They are the representations provided by the faculty of reason, and the second form of the principle of sufficient reason is thus one in which such representations have their ground in others. Concepts are, for Schopenhauer, abstract representations derived from the representations of perception; they might, he says, be termed representations from representations. The more abstract they become, however, the less they include of what was there in perception. We should have no grasp on them at all were they not fixed for our consciousness by an arbitrary sign; hence there is a connection between concepts and words, a fact which is enough, in Schopenhauer's view, to show that animals cannot have concepts. An image or phantasm is not of itself a concept, but a representative of a concept. Schopenhauer sometimes suggests (e.g. *WR* II 7, p. 72; *WI* II, p. 245) that all really original thinking is done in pictures or images, because these enable the thinker to relate concepts and abstract thought to perception.

There is much in this that is highly dubious, particularly the doctrine of abstraction that it presupposes. Schopenhauer sometimes suggests (e.g. *WR* I 8, p. 39; *WI* I, p. 50) that reason has one function — the formation of concepts — just as the understanding has the one function of providing immediate knowledge of the connection between cause and effect. How reason is supposed to abstract from perceptions remains, as with all doctrines of abstraction, unclear. If the abstraction is a cognitive act it must work on what is already known in the perceptual instances; but if something is indeed known in them they must surely presuppose already some concept of the object perceived. How then is that concept obtained? On the other hand, if the abstraction is not a cognitive act of that kind, but the concept comes into being, so to speak mechanically, it remains quite obscure what principles govern the selection of instances in such a way that they give rise to the concept.[4] What Schopenhauer has to say about the role of images may, however, have some importance; it constitutes an emphasis on intuitive as opposed to ratiocinative thought, and an assertion of the importance of the former for the latter.

Abstract thinking, Schopenhauer seems to suggest (*FR* 28, p. 153), is either a matter of proceeding from one concept to another or a matter of subsuming representations of perception under a concept or concepts. It is the latter that he characterizes as the activity of the power of judgment, and to that extent he agrees with Kant. Schopenhauer, however, thinks that the power of judgment mediates not between intuition and understanding, as Kant thought, but between understanding and reason — as one might expect, given what I have already said about his conception of those faculties. Yet when Schopenhauer comes to characterize judgment formally, with the aim of setting out the principle of sufficient reason of knowing (*FR* 29, p. 156), he speaks as if a judgment is merely the combining or separating of concepts, at any rate if the relationship is clearly conceived and expressed. This has a certain consequence as regards what he has to say about truth, as will appear. Apart from that, what Schopenhauer has to say provides no adequate account of what a judgment is; it does not, in particular, distinguish the combination or separation of concepts that is supposed to occur in judgment from that which may occur in other contexts, e.g. the association of ideas. He does say that the combination or separation of concepts in judgments takes place under various restrictions and modifications, and that these are given by logic in the theory of judgments; but he gives no further indication in *The Fourfold Root* of what he has in mind, nor does he offer any further details of what a judgment is. What, in particular, are judgments about? Their content is, he says, taken from the intuitions from which the concepts in question are derived by abstraction. This, however, says nothing in itself about what it is for a judgment to be about something or what it is to judge something about a subject.

What Schopenhauer seems to have in mind, and this is brought out further in what he says about the principle of sufficient reason in this context, is that a judgment involves a passage from one concept to another, and that the connection presupposed in this, as with the connection between empirical representations earlier, requires a ground or reason. He puts this by saying (*FR* 29, p. 156) that if a judgment is to express knowledge it must have a sufficient reason, and 'by reason of this quality it then receives the predicate *true*.' Hence the principle of sufficient reason in question is that of knowing. There are, however, certain possible objections to be made to this.

First, the 'if' in 'if a judgment is to express knowledge' suggests that the necessity of the ground is one relative to the possibility of

24

knowledge, i.e. it suggests that Schopenhauer is saying that a necessary condition of the possibility of knowledge is that any judgment that expresses it must have a sufficient reason. The parallel to this in the first version of the principle of sufficient reason would be that if a connection of representations is to constitute possible experience or empirical reality it must be subject to a sufficient reason in the form of a cause. I do not think, however, that that is what Schopenhauer there says. To suppose that he did say that would be to think of him as arguing by means of a 'transcendental argument' aimed at showing the necessary conditions for the possibility of something. It is of course true that the ground that he offers for the *a priori* character of the principle of causality is that perception of the world would not be possible without its truth; and he does later classify the principle of causality as a transcendental truth such that its ground is the possibility of experience (even if this reference to *experience* rules out a similar characterization of other forms of the principle of sufficient reason). To argue in this way is not, however, his overall aim; rather he is trying to show or, rather, get us to accept that the relation of a knowing consciousness to an object of any kind implies the existence of a ground or reason for that object in the form of other objects of that kind.

Thus, in the case of concepts, the situation ought to be that the relationship of a knowing consciousness to a concept as object involves the grounding of that concept in other concepts. In other words, we cannot think *that* without thinking *this other* which is the ground for the thinking of *that*. Knowledge would then come in only through the knowing consciousness which is presupposed in the 'root'. If the situation is to be construed otherwise, it will have to be because a concept must itself involve knowledge, and similarly for judgment. That would in fact be a plausible view of what having a concept is. That is to say that it is plausible to view the having of the concept of X as knowing what it is for something to be X; and because judgment presupposes concepts it would equally presuppose knowledge. How far what Schopenhauer says about the having of concepts can be construed in that way is arguable (a concept is after all an object of a knowing consciousness and concepts are derived from the objects which are their instances), but it is not the way in which he explains the sufficient reason of knowing. What he seems to offer is simply one of the necessary conditions of knowledge, i.e. that any judgment that constitutes knowledge must have a ground. Although that sounds highly plausible in itself, it does not directly relate to the 'root' and the place of concepts as objects of a knowing consciousness.

A second point is that Schopenhauer appears to make truth or its ascription a consequence of knowledge. Surely, however, a judgment can constitute knowledge only if it is already true; furthermore there may be grounds for calling something true without this amounting to knowledge. Schopenhauer, however, goes on immediately to define truth as the reference of a judgment to something different from itself; and while that sounds promising enough he adds that that something is the reason or ground for the judgment (rather than, e.g. the fact that the judgment states — a fact which in the case of empirical judgments at least would reflect empirical reality). The truth of a judgment is therefore the reference of that judgment to the reason for it — to what may be called, perhaps, its verification. On the face of it there seems to be a certain similarity between this account of truth and that put forward in recent times by Michael Dummett, an account that has come to be called 'anti-realism'.[5] There seems to be no reference in what Schopenhauer has to say to what are called verification-transcendent truth-conditions. Truth is for him irrevocably associated with knowledge of grounds. One might even find in this suggestions of a coherence theory of truth, a theory which has had some connection historically with idealism because of idealism's rejection of a reality independent of ideas or representations. It is not clear, however, why Schopenhauer would have to favour such a theory; there is no reason why, even on his view, the truth of a judgment should not be a matter of its reference to the representations that it is about. On the other hand, it was the inadequacy of Schopenhauer's account of judgment in that very respect (i.e. in explaining what it is for a judgment to be about something) that I commented on earlier. Hence, while there is in Schopenhauer's theory a definite connection between truth and knowledge, the resemblances between what he says and modern anti-realism, whatever may be said about that theory, may be superficial only.

Despite the defects of Schopenhauer's account of judgments and their truth, the uses to which he puts that account in the following sections of *The Fourfold Root* are at a much higher level of value. He there distinguishes between different kinds of truth by reference to the ways in which a true judgment may be related to its ground. It is important to be clear about what he is doing in this, since he uses terminology which has been more commonly used for other purposes; moreover, his distinctions are not, and for good reason, exclusive. The first kind of truth distinguished is logical or formal truth. A judgment that has this kind of truth is one the truth of which follows from that of another. It is thus not logical truth in the modern sense of a truth which is so for purely logical reasons, however that is to be defined; it is not analytic truth. As Schopenhauer goes on to say (*FR* 30, p. 157), a judgment that has logical truth can also have material truth if the judgment from which it follows logically has such material truth or depends upon a material truth somewhere in the chain of judgments that entail it. This is quite consistent with his general definition of truth as the reference of a judgment to its ground. The question is simply one about the nature of that reference.

The second kind of truth is the material truth already referred to, and a judgment has this when its ground is experience; if it is so grounded *directly* on experience then it is said to have empirical truth. In order to contrast this with logical truth one might be inclined to take what Schopenhauer says as meaning that the grounds for speaking of the judgment in question as true do not amount to entailment, and that the support that it receives from other judgments is less than that, as would be the case with, say, the relation of an experiential judgment to a generalization based on it. Once again, however, this does not seem to be what Schopenhauer has in mind. For he speaks of the ground of judgments of this kind as experience itself (*FR* 31, p. 159), and he refers back to the faculty or power of judgment as being the mediator between intuition and abstract thought, and so between understanding and reason. A judgment has material truth, he says, when its concepts are connected, separated or limited by each other as is required by the intuitive representations through which it is established. Hence its verification grounds, and, as he sees it, truth grounds are experience itself.

The third kind of truth is transcendental truth. A judgment has this when its ground is not just experience but the conditions of the possibility of experience, i.e. when the judgment is determined 'either by the forms of space and time intuitively perceived by us *a priori* or by the law of causality known to us *a priori*.' Apart from the restriction to the law of causality in the second case, this is orthodox Kantianism. Examples will be truths of mathematics and such truths as 'Nothing happens without a cause' and 'Matter can neither come into existence nor pass away', i.e. the sort of judgments that Kant called synthetic *a priori*. Schopenhauer implies that these judgments have not only transcendental truth but also material truth, despite the fact that they are synthetic *a priori*. This is because there is a sense in which our having experience is a condition of their truth, so that if we are to spell out the grounds for that truth some reference will have to be made to experience. It is the reference to the possibility of such experience that makes truths of this kind transcendental for both Kant and

Schopenhauer. It could well be said, however, that reference to the possibility of experience is not quite the same as reference to experience itself, so that there is at least an awkwardness about the claim that transcendental truth involves material truth also.

There is, finally, metalogical truth — truth the ground of which is constituted by the formal conditions of all thought. That is to say that a judgment has metalogical truth when its ground is in effect the conditions of the possibility of any thought whatever and not merely that involved in experience. Schopenhauer thinks that there are only four such judgments — the laws of identity, contradiction, and excluded middle, and the principle of sufficient reason itself. He makes clear in the section concerned with these (*FR* 33, pp. 161-3), as he has done elsewhere, that the distinctions between kinds of truth are not meant to be exclusive. The principle of sufficient reason revealed here as a metalogical truth was treated earlier as a transcendental truth, when it had the form of the principle of causality. Schopenhauer goes on in the final and most extended section of this chapter (*FR* 34, pp. 163-89) to make remarks about the power or faculty of reason in general. What he has to say is in many ways in line with Kant's criticisms of pure reason, despite his objection to what he considers Kant's muddled understanding of the term 'reason' itself. The important point, however, is that in his view reason has 'absolutely no *material*, but only a *formal*, content' (p. 171). That should in fact be evident from the classification of kinds of truth that I have surveyed. Schopenhauer's conception of reason involves a concern simply with the relations that the mind takes to exist between various judgments and their ground. These all constitute applications of the principle of sufficient reason, and that, in his view, is what reason consists in.

It is worthy of note that Schopenhauer has no place for truths which are their own ground, so to speak. In discussing logical truth he allows of the possibility of truths the ground of which is ultimately one of the laws of thought, but he rejects firmly the idea the such judgments can be said to have *intrinsic truth*. Although he does not explicitly say so, analytic truths would be a case in point. For him, however, the notion of an intrinsic truth is really a contradiction; 'every truth is the reference of a judgment to something *outside* it' (*FR* 30, p. 159). Analytic truths, so-called, depend on the laws of thought, but these in turn, as metalogical truths, depend on the formal conditions of all thought. If they are truths it is because an attempt to think without conformity to them would be in some sense self-stultifying.[6]

It may be wondered why I said earlier that what Schopenhauer has to say about the classification of kinds of truth is of a higher level of value than what he has to say about judgment and truth in general. Have I not expressed or implied considerable doubts about the details? One is here up against the kind of consideration that is often invoked in connection with Kant also — the promising character of the general programme and scheme as compared with the details of the execution of that programme. There is a great deal of obscurity in the notion of *reference*, when Schopenhauer says that truth consists in the reference of a judgment to its ground. It remains true that there are interesting distinctions to be made between the various kinds of relation that a truth may have to 'what makes it true'. It is indeed arguable, to say the least, that no truth can have any kind of intrinsic status apart from its truth; on the other hand, we may have abundant reason for interest in the various ways that it can stand to what makes it true. That would mean that there is truth *simpliciter*, not contingent truth, necessary truth or anything like that (it is indeed an essential part of what Schopenhauer wants to say, as we shall see later, that all necessity and contingency is relative). It would mean also that there may be a variety of considerations that tell in favour of something's being true; and nothing is true without there being something that makes it true. Such a view would be at least consistent with what Schopenhauer says about the application of the principle of sufficient reason in this context. Indeed to put the matter as I have done might be less misleading than his apparent wish to produce a classification of truths or kinds of truth, when (as the non-exclusiveness of the distinctions itself indicates) he is really interested in the relation of truths to their ground. The trouble arises from the suggestion that truth just *is* the reference of a judgment to its ground. That is not what truth is, but the style of reference to a ground in each case remains a matter of importance.

There are two further points to be made. First, what I have just said indicates why Schopenhauer would have been right to bring these considerations under the heading of the principle of sufficient reason of knowing, even if he had not had other reasons for invoking that idea. I raised a doubt earlier about his use of the phrase 'if a judgment is to express knowledge'. It remains true that in so far as the sufficient reason provides a ground for speaking of truth it provides one for speaking of possible knowledge. Second, it is easy to see in this case why the form of this version of the principle of sufficient reason is determinable *a priori*. If Schopenhauer were right in what he says, the idea of the reference of a judgment to its truth ground would not be something that we get or could get empirically; the idea is one that ties up with the very notion of a judgment or of that in relation to knowledge.

The principle of sufficient reason of being — space, time and mathematics

Schopenhauer's treatment of the matters included under this heading is extremely brief. It is Kantian in a fairly orthodox way,[7] and it may be that that is the reason for the brevity. It cannot be denied, however, that Schopenhauer gives us the bare bones without the flesh. In this chapter we return from concepts to intuitions. The objects for a knowing consciousness with which we are now concerned are 'the formal part of complete representations, i.e. the intuitions given *a priori* of the forms of outer and inner sense, i.e. of space and time' (*FR* 35, p. 193). All this is in conformity with the Kantian thesis that space and time are pure *a priori* intuitions. What distinguishes this class of representations, Schopenhauer says, from that discussed under the first heading, where spatial and temporal characteristics were said to be sensuously perceived, is that there matter was involved; it was indeed said that matter was simply the perceptibility of space and time. The principle of sufficient reason of being concerns the determination of the parts of space and time by each other, in terms of position and succession. Such a determination is quite different from that involved in causality, and although insight into the ground of being may become a ground of knowledge the determination of the parts of space and time by each other is different from either the determination provided by the ground of becoming or the determination provided by the ground of knowing. It is this kind of reciprocal determination (and reciprocal it is, as Schopenhauer emphasises) that constitutes the basis for mathematical truth — geometry presupposing the relations between parts of space or spatial positions, arithmetic presupposing the relations of succession between parts of time (and in a much simpler way than is the case with space, because time has only one dimension).

One might think Schopenhauer's invocation of the *principium essendi* in this connection a rather restricted and perhaps artificial application of that notion. It is not what previous philosophers had in mind in speaking of a principle of being. Wolff, as Schopenhauer himself indicates (*FR* 10, p. 25), defined the *principium essendi* as *ratio possibilitatis alterius* (the reason for the possibility of another thing) and explained it in terms of, for example, the reason for a stone's being able to receive heat lying in the essence or mode of composition of the stone. Thus Wolff connected, as many previous philosophers had done, being with essence. The purpose of the *principium essendi* on that account is to explain why a thing is as it is. Schopenhauer hotly rejects that suggestion in connection with the kind of example that Wolff invokes, on the grounds that the stone's composition could be considered only as part of the state which produced the subsequent state of the stone in conformity with the law of causality. So Schopenhauer rejects any kind of essentialism in explaining why things are as they are — as indeed he should do given his general view about the relativity of all necessity, as opposed to the kind of absolute necessity that seems to be involved in any talk of essences. It might be thought, however, that what he says about space and time involves a kind of essentialism in regard to them, and that this too is involved in the thesis that mathematical truth depends on the essence of space and time. However, space and time are not for Schopenhauer in any sense things. They are forms of intuition, forms of perception, and to maintain that is simply to say that, even apart from the representations of ordinary perception, we may have an awareness of the forms that perception must take; their structure must conform to certain principles. If one asks why that is so, why perceptions must take those forms, the only possible answer for Schopenhauer is that that is what a knowing consciousness is like. If there is any appeal to essences in all this it is only to the essence of a knowing consciousness as we understand it. Schopenhauer says explicitly (*FR* 37, p. 197) that no proof of what he has to say about space is possible. The truths in question are transcendental, being grounded in 'the intuition of space given *a priori*'. That is to say that their ground is the conditions of the possibility of experience, and the *a priori* intuition of space (and similarly for time) is such a precondition.

There is nothing in all this that conflicts with Schopenhauer's general position, therefore, nor with Kant's. The idea that mathematics depends on intuitions of space and time has generally come under scathing criticism in connection with Kant. There is certainly nothing to be said for the thesis that arithmetic presupposes for its validity the intuition of time. Like Kant, Schopenhauer appeals to the succession that is evident in counting. Even if it were agreed that arithmetic has counting as its foundation, the kind of succession that is involved in one number succeeding another is not the succession involved in counting — bringing into the set that item, then that other, and so on. It is arguable in any case whether counting is in fact an essential feature of our estimate of the number of things. It is conceivable that children should be taught to recognise the number of things in a collection without counting

31

them, and might then learn the principles of arithmetic by application to sets of things of varying size recognized in that way, without counting coming into the picture. What is clear is that the feature of our experience which gives application to arithmetic and in terms of which it thus receives an interpretation is plurality, however an estimate of its degree is arrived at.

In the case of geometry it is often said that Kant's views on this were refuted by the discovery of alternative geometries to the Euclidean one. Schopenhauer also is limited in his view of geometry to Euclidean geometry, and what he says about geometrical proof is restricted to what Euclid says. It does not seem to me, however, to be the case that the discovery of alternative geometries need be taken as completely upsetting what Kant and Schopenhauer have to say on this matter. A geometry is in a sense the unfolding or 'exposition' in metrical terms of a certain conception of space. Which conception best fits our experience and under what conditions is an empirical question. The central Kantian point, however, is that space itself is not a concept, not simply a way of thinking about the world. Which is in fact the most adequate way of thinking about the world in spatial terms depends on how the world actually is for us in spatial terms. Hence spatiality at least is a feature of how things are perceived to be and how, given our sensibility, they must be perceived to be. In so far, therefore, as space is something objective and not simply an aspect of our way of thinking about the world, and in so far as in Kantian terms concepts (ways of thinking) are opposed to intuitions, it is not really wrong, when speaking in Kantian terms, to associate space with intuition. Alternative geometries then become alternative ways of spelling out in metrical terms the conception that best corresponds to that intuition. Hence there is a genuine sense in which geometry does presuppose an intuition of space in a way that arithmetic does not presuppose an intuition of time. (There is also of course a sense in which geometry, being metrical, presupposes arithmetic, as Schopenhauer points out (*WR* I 12, p. 54; *WI* I, pp. 69-70). That does not affect the general point.)

What I have said about the way in which geometry involves not only intuition but also a concept which is supposed to fit that intuition receives a partial echo in what Schopenhauer says about the individual items which mathematics has to deal with, i.e. spatial figures and numbers. These are what he calls, following Kant, *normal intuitions*, and they are such that they 'combine the comprehensiveness of concepts with the thorough-going definiteness of individual representations' (*FR* 39, p. 198). In their case, the universal content, as it were, individuates the individual, so that the Leibnizian principle of the identity of indiscernibles applies to them. Schopenhauer invokes in the same connection the Platonic notion, reported by Aristotle, of 'mathematicals', which are like sensible things in being many, but like Forms in being eternal; but he approves of this view only in connection with spatial figures, since in their case difference of place really does distinguish figures which are otherwise identical; so that the idea of a plurality of otherwise identical figures, such as triangles, does make sense. For this reason, the principle of the identity of indiscernibles really applies in this connection only to numbers. The number 12 is presumably the same 12 wherever we meet it; position in the number series (or temporal position if time were really relevant) distinguishes different numbers but not different instances of the same number. Schopenhauer adds that this is 'perhaps' the reason why '7+5=12' is a synthetic proposition as Kant maintained and not an identical proposition as '12=12' is. It is not altogether clear why he thinks that it does provide such a reason, nor does he explain what we are to do with arithmetical formulae containing more than one instance of the same number. Yet there may be some plausibility in the suggestion that while we may speak of the same number there is no room for the expression 'exactly similar number' — a fact that does not seem to hold good with geometrical figures.

There is one further point worthy of note in this section. Schopenhauer asserts that in Euclid it is only with the axioms that we appeal to intuition. The theorems are thought to be proved. Thus in Schopenhauerian terms they have logical truth, and it is this that receives a so-called demonstration. In that, however, their status as transcendental truths is not made clear. Hence, he says, in the demonstration we become convinced of the truth of the theorem, but we do not attain insight into it. What Schopenhauer says suggests that in this respect we are in the position of the boy at the end of the first stage of the geometrical example in Plato's *Meno* (at least on the standard interpretation of that dialogue, over which I have a certain scepticism). The boy is convinced of the truth of the answer to the question posed, but he does not see why it is true. Plato adds that the boy will get insight if he is put through the same questions many times and in many ways. Schopenhauer would not agree with that however (and it is the doubt which I also have as to why this should produce insight that is in part responsible for my scepticism about the standard interpretation of the dialogue). In consequence, he thinks that one gets a better conviction of Pythagoras' theorem if one is presented with a diagram in which the relations between the squares on the various sides of a right-angled triangle can be seen than through Euclid's 'mousetrap proof' (*FR* 39, p. 205, cf. *WR* I 15, pp. 72-3; *WI* I, p. 95). Unfortunately the diagram that he offers is of an isosceles right-angled triangle only, and the insight is thus restricted to that. In any case, to despise proof for not providing insight is to mistake the function of proofs. If they provide insight into the reasons why the truth so proved is a truth, this will be incidental only; the main function of a proof is to show that the truth in question is indeed a truth.

The principle of sufficient reason of acting — the will and motivation

If the third section of *The Fourfold Root* is brief, and in truth far too brief to do justice to the complexities of its subject matter, Schopenhauer could at least have pleaded in excuse that he was merely following out what Kant had had to say. The fourth section is just as brief, and in this case no such excuse is available. Moreover, in it the reader is brought up to the threshold of the central part of Schopenhauer's metaphysics. Unfortunately *The Fourfold Root* merely brings us to that threshold and takes us no further. The discussion in the fourth section is too brief in all conscience. Without reference to the main work the reader can scarcely gain an adequate grasp of what is said in this section. I shall, however, confine myself to the bare bones and reserve more detailed treatment until later when the issues can be given more extended treatment in the context of the second book of Schopenhauer's main work.

Schopenhauer says that for each individual there is only one object for this fourth class of objects for a knowing consciousness. It is the subject himself as subject of willing, this being the immediate object of the inner sense, so appearing only in time. This suggestion provokes certain immediate objections, some of which Schopenhauer does something to meet. First, is not the subject a knower too? Schopenhauer's answer is that he is, but there is no knowledge of knowing or of the subject as subject of knowing; or, to be more exact, there is no direct knowledge of these. One knows of one's powers of knowledge by inference from the very fact that one has certain kinds of representations. To know that one knows, Schopenhauer says, is just the same as to know (a claim that reveals yet again how much Schopenhauer identifies knowledge with consciousness). If one thinks that one has knowledge of oneself as a knower on the basis of self-consciousness, Schopenhauer's answer is that the condition of knowledge of representations can never itself stand as a representation.

In all this he rejects the idea that the knowing self can figure within our representations for very much the same reasons as Kant does. If the 'I think' accompanies all our representations, the 'I' as such does not figure as a representation. However, and here Schopenhauer differs crucially from Kant, the same does not apply to the self as willer; this one knows directly from self-consciousness. Hence he says that starting from knowledge one may say that 'I know' is an analytic proposition but 'I will' a synthetic one. (Whether that is a happy way of putting it given Schopenhauer's classification of kinds of truth is a question that I shall leave on one side.) In other words, one may have substantive knowledge that one is a willer, and that knowledge comes from inner experience directly. The identity of the knower with the known as willing is, he says, immediately given, but it is inexplicable, and whoever grasps the impossibility of explaining it will assuredly join him in calling it a miracle par excllence (κατ' ἐξχήν, to invoke one of Schopenhauer's characteristic Greek phrases).

How does all this fit in with the demand for a principle of sufficient reason, and how does that get application to this object? If — and this is perhaps the main immediate objection to what Schopenhauer says about this fourth class of objects for a knowing consciousness — if the subject of willing is the immediate object of inner sense, why does it need a ground and how is it to be thought of as having one? A preliminary question might be why there are not other immediate objects of inner sense, such as feelings. Schopenhauer's answer to this latter question is that all emotions, under which heading feelings in general are to be included, are states of the will. That is to say that awareness of them presupposes awareness of oneself as a willer. Whether that answer will do is a question that will have to be left until later. For the moment we can attend to the will alone and seek an answer to my first question — or rather questions, since I asked a double question.

The answer that Schopenhauer actually gives to the second part of that question is that to find the ground we shall have to look to motives. These were mentioned during the discussion of causality earlier, when it was said that causes function as motives in connection with human-beings and the conscious part of animal life, i.e. in connection with knowers. Thus for something to be subject to motives it must be a knower also. In the present section Schopenhauer says that motivation is causality seen from within, and it is in this sense that the principle of sufficient reason of acting appears as the law of motivation — in that every action is subject to

motives in this sense, such motives influencing the will. There are
many points of obscurity in this. We have not been told, for
example, what exactly is the relation between willing and action.
While motives are said to bring about an act of will they are also
said to explain actions, being in some sense their cause. The truth
is, although Schopenhauer does not say so here, and although the
answer emerges only relatively opaquely elsewhere, is that what
motives determine is what might be called the phenomena of the
will, our representations of what we do in willed action. ('Phenomenon of the will' is indeed the phrase that he himself uses in this
connection, e.g. in *WR* I 20, p. 106; *WI* I, p. 138.) This is in a way
evident in what Schopenhauer says near the beginning of *FR* 43,
p. 212, when he speaks of our regarding ourselves justified in
asking 'Why?' for every decision that we observe in ourselves or
in others. As far as we ourselves are concerned the reason is
required for what we *observe* through our inner experience. That
is why motivation is causality seen from within, and from this we
are supposed to get a special view of how causes work in general.
The *a priori* character of the principle of causality thus carries over
to motives too (although there are further considerations that
relate to this which I shall return to in chapter 5). Schopenhauer
indeed represents as the corner-stone of his whole metaphysics the
proposition that just as the law of motivation is related to that of
causality so is the fourth class of objects for the subject, and
'hence the will observed within ourselves', related to the first (*FR*
43, p. 214). The way in which it is the corner-stone of his metaphysics will emerge in due course.

There remains a great deal of obscurity about the place of the
will in relation to the principle of sufficient reason. In *WR* I 20,
p. 106 (*WI* I, p. 138) he says quite definitely that the will itself lies
outside the scope of the law of motivation and that what motives
determine is simply what I will on a given occasion. One might say
that they determine the content of the will on a given occasion,
what I observe myself as doing intentionally. Nevertheless, as he
says in *FR* 43, p. 213, the motive consists in a mere representation; hence the law of motivation, as a form of the principle of
sufficient reason still connects representations, even in this context. Schopenhauer's thesis is, once again, that such representations occur only subject to the conditions specified by the principle of sufficient reason in this form. It is thus quite misleading in
this context to make any reference to the will as the immediate
object of inner sense; that is neither here nor there as far as concerns the subject of this chapter. It is of course crucial, as will
appear, for Schopenhauer's general metaphysics, and it is no doubt

his desire to make some reference to that which brings about its inclusion here. It remains quite misleading.

Schopenhauer concludes the chapter with a section on memory considered as a means whereby the will is enabled to influence the knowing subject. I shall not comment on this, although it contains a curious warning against reading too many novels if we wish to preserve our memory — novels furnish too many representations without sufficient repetition among them! One further comment, however, is perhaps called for on the content of the chapter in general — one that connects up with what I have been saying about the misleadingness of Schopenhauer's discussion, but one that may have some general importance. I raised earlier the question why there were not other immediate objects of knowledge apart from the will, and I considered briefly what Schopenhauer has to say about feelings in that connection. Why, however, are not representations in general immediate objects of this kind? Do they not after all constitute a 'given'? The answer lies in what was said in the statement of the 'root'. No representation ever occurs by itself but always in such a way that it is conditioned by others; and that conditioning is not merely something that holds good of it in itself but is so for the knowing consciousness that has the representation. Hence what we know in any representation is itself conditioned and thus not truly immediate. (This is so despite what he confusingly says in *FR* 19, pp. 48 ff., as noted earlier, about the *immediate presence* of representations to the inner sense; but, as he goes on to say there, such representations are, even if complex, at any given time subject to the law of causality, and hence are not in the same position as the will. One might note also the qualifications put on the notion of sensations as immediate objects in *FR* 22, p. 121; they are immediate in a nonliteral sense.)

This last point is absolutely crucial for an understanding of Schopenhauer's position, and it equally explains the sense in which our awareness of the willing subject through inner sense is supposed to be immediate. It is not just that we are so directly aware of it; the knowledge that we have in being so aware of it is a knowledge of something unconditioned and is for that reason in itself unconditional. To be immediate in the full sense an object has to be unconditioned also. None of this is true of representations. For Schopenhauer, representations are not like Hume's impressions or later empiricists' sense-data, which (as Hume himself acknowledged) tend to be substantial entities in their own right. For Schopenhauer, no representation can exist in its own right, and there cannot be a world consisting of one representation. The situation is very different with the will, and that is all-important for his metaphysics.

General remarks and results

Schopenhauer has a concluding chapter which contains a number of heterogeneous remarks and two general results which he takes to emerge. It is perhaps best to deal with the latter first, since they have a connection with what I have just said. The first main result is that the principle of sufficient reason cannot, since it has its root in a knowing consciousness or intellect, have an application outside that context. In particular, it cannot have an application to the world as such; it does not, that is, apply to the thing-in-itself. There is thus no room for a cosmological proof of the world as such. This, Schopenhauer says, really follows from the fact that the principle of sufficient reason may be reduced to the fact that everything exists by reason of something else, but only in relation to objects of the intellect. The second main result is in a way the converse of the first. Just as the principle of sufficient reason can have no application outside the domain indicated, so that domain itself can have no general or absolute ground (and Schopenhauer makes some critical comments on Kant for speaking as if things-in-themselves count as a ground for phenomena in general). The only way in which there can be a ground for things is in one of the ways set out, and these apply to representations only, their ground being other representations. It is in this context that Schopenhauer makes the remarks that I mentioned earlier about what would be the case if someone were to imagine a new, fifth class of objects coming about. Once again, there can be no proof of the impossibility of this; it is simply that the framework that has been presented leaves no room for the intelligibility of such a suggestion.

For the rest, the chapter consists in the main of a series of remarks on whether the relation between ground and consequent involves a time relation, whether it can be reciprocal, and whether the series of grounds and consequents goes on *ad infinitum*. Not altogether surprisingly, Schopenhauer answers in effect 'Sometimes yes, sometimes no' to these questions, although he makes some interesting remarks along the way about the fallacies involved in thinking otherwise. All that remains is a section (*FR* 49, pp. 225 ff.) on necessity, in which he says that the term has no meaning other than the inevitably of the consequent when the ground has been posited. All necessity is thus relative and conditioned, and the idea of anything absolutely necessary involves a contradiction. In this spirit, and in line with what was set out earlier about kinds of truth, Schopenhauer distinguishes four kinds of necessity to conform with the four forms of the principle of sufficient reason — logical necessity, physical necessity, mathematical necessity and moral necessity. All these, it should be noted, refer to a kind of relation between ground and consequent — the necessity of something being the case when something else is the case — and so constitute a relative necessity only.

Schopenhauer's thesis is that it is this that necessity *means*, but it is doubtful, to say the least, whether that can be quite correct. It may be the case (and I think that it is plausible to think that it is in fact the case) that everything or every truth that is necessary is so because it is necessary to or because of something else. Indeed one might think that that is what Schopenhauer should claim to have shown. It is another matter altogether to say that 'necessary' has no meaning except in the constructions 'necessary to' or 'necessary for'. It is clear that Schopenhauer himself does not keep to that thesis. For example, at the beginning of *FR* 49, p. 225, the section in which he discusses necessity, he says that the principle of sufficient reason is the sole principle and sole support of all necessity. If that last use of 'necessity' were elliptical for something like 'necessity to whatever is the reason for whatever is in question', the claim would become truistical, and I do not think that Schopenhauer means it to be that. On the other hand, it is a conclusion of some importance that there is no absolute necessity and that nothing is necessary in itself. What Schopenhauer says does indeed give some plausibility to that thesis.

It is that last point which serves to sum up the value of Schopenhauer's discussion in *The Fourfold Root*, whatever one may think of the details and the presentation of them along the way. That discussion presents a kind of rationalism, in the form of a schema within which there is no room for mere contingency with regard to the objects with which it is concerned. It does this, however, in the context of a certain epistemology, and the conclusions are relative to that. Although this implies the idealism which emerges in full form in the main work, that idealism is not really made explicit in *The Fourfold Root*, and is certainly not argued for. What is implied and presupposed is a certain relation between human consciousness and its objects, and Schopenhauer tries to present to us for our acceptance (with an explicit abnegation of attempts at proof) a picture of the consequences of that relation for how those objects are to be regarded. In the light of all this Schopenhauer would claim that any attempt to portray an object which did not conform to the principle of sufficient reason in one of its forms of application would be unintelligible. Given the admitted impossibility of proof of this, one must treat the

argument as dialectical. Schopenhauer asks us to accept his conclusions as following from or at least conforming to our ordinary
conceptions of the world when construed in certain terms. He
does not, however, simply present the individual items with which
he is concerned *seriatim*. That is the great glory of his approach.
He unifies them in terms of the unifying schema that the 'root'
provides. Hence the importance of the book lies not in its distinction between four forms of the principle of sufficient reason,
but in the unification of these that the fourfold root provides.

To find it completely acceptable one would have to accept
the standpoint of the 'root', and thereby think it satisfactory
to take one's stand on the notion of a knowing consciousness,
a knowing subject, in relation to representations conceived as
its objects. I have not yet examined or even noted the arguments
for the idealism that that notion presupposes that Schopenhauer
came to bring forward in the main work. Apart from that, however, it is arguable[8] that the scheme begs the question by *assuming*
the ideas of an objective world and of truth, ideas which cannot
be derived simply from the standpoint of a single consciousness
and its objects. What right indeed has one to speak of that
consciousness as a *knowing* consciousness or to speak of the
subject of *knowledge*? These objections are, however, objections to the idealism, and although I do not think that Schopenhauer ever satisfactorily meets them, we still have to consider
the considerations that he raises on the other side. *The Fourfold
Root* remains in its outlines and general programme an impressive piece of work.

3

Schopenhauer and Kant

Schopenhauer's philosophical relations to Kant were very special. I said in my first chapter that it was Kant and Plato who were the great philosophical giants as far as he was concerned. Kant, however, was in a very different position in this respect from Plato. Schopenhauer quotes with approval on many occasions passages from Plato's dialogues or from Aristotle and other ancient commentators on him. He also adopts the Platonic Ideas in his own system, although with a certain ambiguity as regards their status, and he uses that notion in his treatment of art. It does not strike one, however, that Plato was someone with whom Schopenhauer felt that he was engaged in a dialogue. The position is very different with Kant.

There are constant references to Kant throughout Schopenhauer's writings — the great Kant who had, as far as Schopenhauer was concerned, seen the truth of transcendental idealism for the first time, and whose views had been cruelly neglected by subsequent German thought. Yet Schopenhauer is also extremely critical of Kant, and he devoted a long appendix to the first volume of his main work to an extensive criticism of Kant. He says in the course of this (*WR* I Appx., p. 437; *WI* II, p. 32) that the 'Aesthetic' of Kant's first *Critique* 'is a work of such supreme merit that it alone would have been enough to make Kant's name immortal'. He clearly does not feel the same about much else of the first *Critique*, although he obviously respected it, and he was particularly opposed to the doctrine of the categories. When it comes to Kant's ethical writings, Schopenhauer clearly thinks that the notion of the categorical imperative was an absurdity, even a contradiction. In connection with aesthetics he says that instead of concerning himself with the beautiful

41

itself Kant was taken by the nature of the *judgment* concerning it and so started only from the judgments of others (it being, one might say, for that reason all second-hand) (*WR* I Appx., p. 531; *WI* II, p. 154). Whether these criticisms are warranted is obviously a matter for argument, but they are not really a matter for present concern. Consideration of some of them will emerge from an examination of Schopenhauer's own views in the areas in question.

There are two aspects of Kant's thought and Schopenhauer's attitude to it that merit separate consideration, however, if only because they figure so largely in Schopenhauer's own positive thought. These are, first, transcendental idealism and the notion of a thing-in-itself, and, second, causality.

Schopenhauer thoroughly approved of Kant's critique of speculative metaphysics. That critique involved an attempt to set limits to human understanding or its possibility by an appeal to the constraining factor provided by its connection with possible experience. It is this appeal to possible experience as determining the limits to what the understanding can do that came in Kant's thought to constitute the meaning of 'transcendental' in his philosophy. Something is transcendental, as opposed to transcendent, when it relates to possible experience as its condition. Kant's philosophy is an attempt to lay down what the human mind contributes to the possibility of experience of the world, and to criticize those views which seek to establish truths on matters which lie outside what is a possible experience for a mind so determined.

One of the main features of that philosophy is what Kant called 'transcendental idealism'. To understand this it is necessary to contrast it with empirical idealism. The latter is the view that all the phenomena with which the human mind is acquainted are as a matter of empirical fact really experiences, sensations or ideas in that mind. The empirical idealist holds that the empirical facts of sense-perception show this to be the case and therefore suggest that what we ordinarily think of as reality, a world independent of our perceptions, is in fact a mere appearance. That this is so in the strict sense has been denied by some idealists of this kind, particularly by Berkeley who thought that his idealism was entirely coincident with common sense. It is, however, a coincidence that many have found unconvincing, if only because Berkeley's identification of things with sensations seems to make physical things less substantial than they are ordinarily thought to be. In a way, Kant took over the epistemological apparatus of the empiricists, with its reliance on the idea that sensations, impressions or representations are the stuff of perceptual experience. He added to this the idea that a condition of such experience giving rise to objective judgments is that the experiences should be brought under concepts according to rules contributed by the understanding. The possibility of such objectivity in relation to experience meant that one could meaningfully speak of an empirical reality, while recognizing that this was still confined to what experience provides. To say this is to assert a compatibility between an empirical realism and a form of idealism to be called 'transcendental'.

Such a view has it that empirically, having regard to what experience tells us, physical things are real (as compared with, says, dreams or hallucinations); but if we have regard to what is required for the possibility of that experience then we have to note that we are given only sensations or representations, even if these are organized in terms of certain *a priori* principles, some of which govern the form of those representations themselves and others of which govern their subsumption under concepts in judgment. Hence, for Kant, idealism is true if we consider matters from the point of view of the conditions of possible experience; but for actual experience physical things are real and in these terms a valid distinction can be made between them and appearances in the ordinary sense. None of this, however, applies to whatever is responsible in some way for our experiences and which may thus be said to underlie them — what Kant called 'things-in-themselves'. *A fortiori* since such things-in-themselves lie outside experience and outside the possible application of the understanding, we can have no positive knowledge of them or of the ways in which they do in fact underlie experience. Thus Kant provides in his terms a certain rationale for the supposed coincidence between idealism and commonsense, although, it may be thought, at a considerable cost. Nevertheless, the important thing about transcendental idealism is that supposed coincidence with realism, and to that extent with common-sense.[1]

Schopenhauer accepts a great deal of all this, though not the unknowability of the thing-in-itself (and that there is only one of these is something else that he thinks he can show). I shall leave until chapter 5 Schopenhauer's arguments concerning the thing-in-itself, and I shall leave until chapter 4 his own arguments for idealism. What he finds unsatisfactory with Kant is the details of the way in which transcendental idealism is worked out by him. There is, first, his criticism that what Kant attributed to the understanding ought largely to be attributed to reason, and his claim that Kant had misconstrued the notion of understanding by bringing judgment and concept use under it. That, however, might be thought to be little more than a verbal point, as long as the same operations of the mind go on, however described. Nevertheless, there are ways in which Schopenhauer does not agree even on that. I shall return to that point directly; it may be best to consider it in relation to its place in the structure of Kant's *Critique*.

The comment that I mentioned earlier on Kant's 'Aesthetic', with its treatment of space and time, indicates an agreement with Kant on this aspect of his scheme. The same is evident from what . I said in chapter 2 about the principle of sufficient reason of being, under the heading of which was presented in brief a largely Kantian account of space and time as *a priori* forms of experience. Schopenhauer repeatedly speaks with approval of Kant's doctrine of space and time, and his reaction to that part of the *Critique* requires no further comment here. The same is not true of the 'Analytic'. Schopenhauer will have nothing to do with the doctrine of the categories; and although, as he himself admits (*WR* I Appx., p. 452; *WI* II, p. 51), something like the unity of apperception exists in his account of the matter, in the form of the subject of knowledge, he will have nothing to do with the *words* 'unity of apperception', which he finds impenetrably obscure. Nor does he accept the more specific arguments for the principles of the understanding such as are to be found in the 'Analogies' of the *Critique*. In a sense, however, his dissatisfaction with the 'Analytic' stems from a more general feeling that Kant's account of the understanding was seriously wrong.

I said earlier that his objection to Kant's treatment of the understanding might be thought to be a merely verbal point. It is really more than that. Despite Kant's famous remark about intuitions being blind without concepts, and concepts being empty without intuitions, he does sometimes speak as if intuitions constitute a *given* in perception and as if these are then brought under concepts in judgment. Schopenhauer objects that some-thing's being thus given should be a matter for the understanding. That is the sort of thing that understanding something should amount to; in having that perception we have understanding of something. If it is then objected that this must presuppose a concept and its application to the thing, Schopenhauer replies that concepts are the work of reason and are abstracted from what we understand in perception. It follows that Schopenhauer has a quite different understanding of the notion of a concept from that of Kant. For Kant a concept was a sort of rule for ordering experi-ences; for Schopenhauer it is much more like a Lockean abstract idea, a form of understanding abstracted from the understanding that we have in perception. I made allusions in chapter 2 to the difficulties involved in any such doctrine of abstraction; exactly *how* perception involves understanding on Schopenhauer's own theory remains obscure, as it does in Locke's, to which it is in this respect most close.

Schopenhauer goes further than that, however, since he objects to Kant's whole account of perception itself. Sometimes, it must be confessed, Kant speaks of experiences, representations, *of* something, as if there is an object of the experience distinct from the experience itself; and, in speaking in this way, he does not mean by 'object' to be referring to a thing-in-itself. From the point of view of idealism there should be no such distinction between an experience and its object, and Schopenhauer wants to emphasise that point. For transcendental idealism objects are simply representations (*WR* I Appx., p. 444; *WI* II, p. 41). In Schopenhauer's eyes, Kant imports too much of the empirical realism, with its distinction between real things and mere appearances, into the transcendental idealism itself. For a strict transcendental idealism, which Schopenhauer thinks of himself as putting forward, reality consists of representations alone. Hence the first part of the title of Schopenhauer's main work — the world as representation.

Schopenhauer sees part of the trouble as due to Kant's failure to distinguish between sensation and perception. If Kant had recognized that distinction, he thinks, much of the apparatus of the 'Analytic' would have been unnecessary. Strictly speaking, what we are given through the senses are sensations only, these being available to the inner sense and involving the form of time only. Perception involves already a transition to representations as objects, and that transition involves in turn the understanding of such objects as the cause of the sensations in question, an understanding that can be *a priori* only, since there is no empirical basis for the transition. It involves, as we saw in chapter 2, the principle of sufficient reason of becoming.

I shall not repeat the remarks that I made in chapter 2 about this part of his theory; it remains an unhappy one. It is, however, due, at least in part, to Schopenhauer's willingness to look for and accept an empirical backing for a metaphysical theory. He criticizes Kant for not allowing that possibility (*WR* I Appx., pp. 426ff.; *WI* II, pp. 18ff.), and in that context he emphasizes the point that in his view what he calls the 'riddle of the world' is to be solved only by setting out the proper connection between inner and outer experience — between, in other words, sensation and perception. That distinction is an empirical distinction; that is to say that within experience we find distinct elements which can be categorized conceptually only under the headings of sensation and perception respectively. As an empirical distinction in that sense, however, it is not one that has a place within transcendental idealism as such; indeed, as I suggested in chapter 2, transcendental idealism depends to some extent on not making that distinction.

Thus, while it is one of Schopenhauer's criticisms of Kant that he in effect imports into transcendental idealism too much of the empirical realism, by making a distinction between representations and their objects, there is a sense in which he does something similar, even if he sometimes covers this up by speaking of a transition from representations of inner sense to representations of outer sense. There is, however, a difference between the two philosophers. The elements of empirical realism that Kant imports into his transcendental idealism are simply the way of thinking that such a realism presupposes — that our experiences are, at least when objective, experiences of objects. That might be thought unobjectionable; for does not Kant think that transcendental idealism is coincident with empirical realism. If there is a fault it is one of expression only. On the other hand, what Schopenhauer imports into *his* transcendental idealism is a certain finding that someone working within the framework of empirical realism might light upon — that there is a distinction between mere sensation and perception proper (and Schopenhauer thinks that there is a further distinction between the latter and thought, a distinction which, as we have already seen, he thinks that Kant blurs in what he says about concepts and judgment). Thus what Schopenhauer imports into his transcendental idealism is an empirically based finding, and that would be impossible unless metaphysics (as transcendental idealism surely is) could have an empirical backing or source. That Kant firmly disallowed.

In order to take a stand on the general issue it would be necessary to undertake a detailed examination of the notion of metaphysics. It is not clear how one could proceed over that without recourse to particular examples, to see how they work out. If one takes that attitude towards the case in front of us, it has to be said that Schopenhauer's use of the sensation/perception distinction is near disastrous for the reasons given in chapter 2. Even if our move from sensation to perception is based on a principle that is given *a priori* in a general way, i.e. on the principle, supposedly *a priori*, that a sensation must have a cause, such a principle has nothing to say about the particular cause in each case. Hence, if we are given nothing but sensations, there is no basis that is remotely adequate for the transition to perception. While it may

46

be the case that whenever we perceive such and such we have certain sensations, those sensations cannot be the epistemological basis for perception. Hence, in this case at least, Schopenhauer's use of empirical facts as a basis for his metaphysics — his particular version of transcendental idealism — certainly does not work out.

It is on this, however, as we saw in chapter 2, that he bases his claim for the *a priori* character of the principle of causality — the second point of conflict with Kant that I wished to consider. For his claim is that perception is not possible without this kind of transition from sensation as effect to its cause. Every representation of outer sense is thus dependent on a cause of this kind as its ground. Causality is thus, on this account, presupposed by perception and cannot be founded on it. It is hardly, in any case, a justification for the claim for the *a priori* truth of '*Every* event has a cause'; but if it were valid it would certainly show that the grounds for that proposition cannot be entirely empirical. Its validity, however, unfortunately depends upon an incoherent account of perception.

Schopenhauer's criticism of Kant on causality partly depends on his own view as set out. It also depends on his view of causes as concerned with changes of states of things and on the connection of this with the notions of substance and matter. Much of that, however, is to be found in Kant, if one puts the three 'Analogies' together. It may be more pertinent to consider Schopenhauer's comments on the details of Kant's argument in the 'Second Analogy'. The most well known criticism — that Kant's argument applies equally to the succession of day and night, in the case of which one does not think of the one as being the cause of the other — was primarily put forward as a criticism of Hume (*FR* 23, p. 127: *WR* II 4, p. 38; *WI* II, p. 209). Schopenhauer applies it to Kant simply in relation to the claim that he takes Kant to make, that the objectivity of a change can be known only through the apprehension of a causal connection; the point is that the succession of day and night is objective without one being the cause of the other. He sums up his view of the relations between Hume and Kant on these matters by saying that Hume thought that all consequence is mere sequence, while Kant thought that all sequence is consequence. The truth is, Schopenhauer thinks, that it is not sequence which is the basis for the ascription of causality, but change.

If that is true, it should follow that there is something wrong with Kant's argument in the 'Second Analogy', where he seeks to show that causality is a condition of objective experience by contrasting the two sequences of experiences derived from (a) perceiving a ship going down a river, and (b) perceiving the different parts of a house, where the sequence is dependent on the perceiver's choice of where to look. What Kant seems to have in mind in this is a contrast between a sequence of perceptions which are clearly perceptions of a set of events which are objective and a sequence of perceptions which are in some sense subjective. Unfortunately, as Schopenhauer rightly points out, the examples are insufficient to make the contrast. The sequence of perceptions of the house is still very different from a sequence of phantasms. Indeed, Schopenhauer points out, the sequence of perceptions of a house is still a set of perceptions of the positions of two bodies relative to one another, just as the perceptions of the ship are. What Kant fails to notice is the perceptions of the movements of one's eye in relation to the house, movements which are indeed the product of one's will but which are nevertheless for him an empirically perceived fact, just as are the movements of the ship in relation to one's body. In fact, Schopenhauer goes on to say, one could reverse the order of perceptions of the ship, just as one can reverse the order of perceptions of the house, if only one had as much strength to pull the ship up-stream as to alter the position of one's eye (*FR* 23, p. 124)!

There is something in these criticisms. It certainly cannot be the case that in all objective sequences each member of the sequence is the effect of that which precedes it. Whether Kant meant to say just that is arguable, since in the example of the ship he argues for the applicability of the principle of causality *via* the notion that the sequence, being irreversible, is rule-governed. That by itself does not entail that each event in the series is the cause of its successor. On the other hand, Schopenhauer himself insists that causality has a place in objective sequences, and indeed even in those sequences which we think of as due to chance, such as, to give his own example, my going out and being struck on the head by a falling tile. The succession as such may not be causally determined, but the individual changes that take place may be so determined, although it may be by other things. Schopenhauer's criticisms amount, therefore, to accusing Kant of being too preoccupied with temporal succession in the spirit of Hume. That is probably fair criticism. It remains true that it is to the details of Kant's argument that he objects, not his general conclusion.

Causality is, however, the only one of Kant's categories that does any substantial work in Schopenhauer's scheme. (It is of course the one that has received by far the greatest amount of attention in relation to Kant also.) That difference from Kant is, however, in large part due to the fact that the starting point for

Schopenhauer's argument is different from Kant's. Kant is interested in those concepts or categories that are presupposed in any judgment that purports to be an objective judgment about the world. Hence he starts from the notion of judgment. For Schopenhauer this is to start in the wrong place. He does not quite say about Kant's metaphysics what he says about his aesthetics — that Kant starts from the notion of judgment about the beautiful, not beauty itself, so concerning himself with people's judgments about the phenomenon, not the phenomenon itself. But he might well have said that sort of thing about Kant's general metaphysics. Kant starts from the fact that people do make judgments about the world, thereby bringing intuitions under concepts; some of those judgments are objective and the question is which and why. Schopenhauer's starting point is knowledge of objects, and because of that there is a sense in which objectivity is built into the starting point and does not have to be 'deduced'; knowledge cannot be other than objective. Hence, given the principle of sufficient reason, Schopenhauer's concern is with how that works for different classes of object of knowledge. Where that object is an item in the physical world, causality is the obvious candidate for the form that the principle of sufficient reason should take. It is indeed difficult to think what else might be relevant. Apart, therefore, from the intrinsic difficulties in Kant's table of categories and their 'deduction', there is no need, in Schopenhauer's eyes, to have reference for these purposes to anything except causality. For similar reasons he has no need of a transcendental deduction; the transcendental unity of apperception is, as he says, already there in his notion of a knowing consciousness, and he sees no need for a justification of that. To say that he is right would not be to depreciate Kant's enterprise. It is to say that it is different from Schopenhauer's own enterprise, despite some similarities which Schopenhauer duly acknowledges.

It is perhaps worth-while to elaborate further the differences which I have noted in the points of departure of the two philosophers, since the issue connects with the point which I made in chapter 2 to the effect that in *The Fourfold Root* Schopenhauer does not present a transcendental argument. Kant certainly did that. He based himself on a view of experience which he inherited from his empiricist forebears, especially Hume, whether or not he was reacting specifically to them. Hume had presented a view of experience such that it was impossible to differentiate between experiences so that some are seen as objective and others merely subjective. Hence, when it came to the question of our belief in the so-called external world, Hume could give no account, in the face of scepticism, of why we are justified in having such a belief. Indeed he repudiated any such suggestion, offering instead an account of what makes us have such a belief, as a matter of psychology. In that account the imagination played a large part. So it did also in Kant's account, but only as one part of a more general theory in terms of which he thought that the problem which Hume repudiated could be solved. In consequence, Kant started from the same view of experience as Hume, but saw the key to his problem in the notion of judgment and its conditions, a notion that was hardly recognized in Hume. The question then became one of what conditions had to be satisfied if such judgments, based in some way on experience, were to be considered objective and thus the source of knowledge. It cannot be said that the theory of categories, a central part of Kant's theory, does more in itself than set out necessary conditions for such judgments; it does not set out sufficient conditions. If Kant does more than provide necessary conditions (which, however valuable, cannot show that objectivity is possible − only *how* it is possible if it is), he does so, it is often claimed, in the course of his 'transcendental deduction of the categories'.

The general aim of Kant's transcendental arguments is to try to show that certain things are a necessary condition of the possibility of objective experience. Such an argument can, however, establish a relative necessity only − that certain things are necessary *if* objective experience is to be possible. It cannot show that the things in question are necessary in an absolute sense, or that objective experience is in fact possible, not at any rate by itself. To the extent that the Kantian 'transcendental deduction' goes beyond this, it does so by arguing that a position such as that of Hume, with its emphasis on the subjectivity of experience beyond which it despairs of moving, in fact presupposes for its intelligibility the very point that it despairs of showing. For, Kant thinks, and takes himself to show, that the very notion of judgment as applied to experience presupposes the idea of a subject of judgment whose experience it is and an object of judgment which the experiences are of. That certain experiences are merely subjective is thus something that one can make sense of only by contrast with experiences which are objective in this sense.[2] Whether such an argument can show that there actually are any objective experiences is arguable; it might be taken to show only that the notion of the subjective presupposes a contrast with the notion of the objective, so that the latter must at least be intelligible if the former is to be. That is not to show that there *is* any objective experience, although there might be further considerations concerning what would have to be the case for these things to be intelligible. To construe the argument in that way is to construe it as a so-called polar argument, or argument from polar opposites, and there are well known limitations on what such an argument can achieve.[3]

However that may be, it is only at this point that there is any suggestion in Kant's argument of going beyond a merely relative necessity. On the account of it that I have offered, it does that by seeking to show that a certain position is presupposed even by its denial — objectivity or its possibility is presupposed even in the suggestion that only subjectivity is possible. The argument is thus similar to Aristotle's argument for the principle of contradiction, as indicated in chapter 2, except that in Aristotle's case the opponent has merely to assert something to be shown wrong, while in this case the opponent has to take up a certain philosophical position. Thus, by its very nature, Kant's argument is weaker than Aristotle's. In both cases, however, the aim is to go beyond a merely relative necessity, whether successfully or not.

Schopenhauer, by contrast, starts from the position that Kant finds problematic, and thus for the same reason obviates any pull towards an absolute necessity. He starts from the fact of knowledge, asks what is involved in this and thus in effect asks also what is necessary to its possibility. I said in chapter 2 that I did not think that the argument in *The Fourfold Root* was a transcendental argument. I meant that that was not how Schopenhauer presents it. He could not, in any case, while remaining true to his principles, present it as an argument for the position that knowledge *is* possible, in an absolute sense. If all necessity is relative, so must be all possibility; something is possible only relative to something else. Hence there could be no question of an attempt to show that knowledge is possible just like that and without qualification.

Schopenhauer was indeed not greatly taken by the force of scepticism, and felt little need to combat it. In his main work (*WR* I 19, p. 104; *WI* I, p. 135) he says that the denial of the reality of the external world is 'the meaning of *theoretical egoism*', i.e. solipsism. In his view that is a position that cannot be refuted by proofs, even if its serious entertainment could only be the position of a mad-man. He characterizes it as a small, frontier fortress which can be by-passed, since while it cannot be taken its garrison will never sally forth from it. It is not, in other words, a position that one needs to take seriously, except for the sake of polemic, since polemical is all that scepticism is. The fact of human knowledge is for Schopenhauer, therefore, something that can be taken for granted; what matters is what it involves. There is no need for arguments of the kind that Kant seems to put forward in the 'transcendental deduction'. All necessity remains relative, and the same applies to possibility and contingency. Hence, despite his acknowledgment (*WR* I 7, p. 32; *WI* I, p. 41) that Kant's principal doctrine was 'in spirit' that the principle of sufficient reason has only a relative and conditioned validity, it is to all the sins of the acceptance of unconditioneds that he objects to in Kant — and that includes the categorical imperative. For the rest most of his objections are aimed at the details of Kant's architectonic, and they need not concern us here. Given the idea of a knowing consciousness, causality remains the only idea outside the 'Aesthetic' of the *Critique* that Schopenhauer thinks is needed — until, that is, he breaks Kantian principles altogether and makes the move to the identification of the thing-in-itself.

4

The World as Representation

When Schopenhauer came to publish the essays that constitute supplements to the main work in the second volume he divided those corresponding to the first book of *The World as Will and Representation* into two halves. The first half he entitled 'The doctrine of perceptual [or intuitive] representation' and the second half 'The doctrine of abstract representation, or of thinking'. These titles give a reasonably accurate idea of the content of the first book of the main work. Roughly a third of it is given up to expounding 'the world as representation' — Schopenhauer's idealism — and it leans heavily on *The Fourfold Root*. The remaining two thirds are given up to an exposition of the scope of reason as he sees that faculty, and to the relations between reason and the other faculties of the mind. It gives his view of logic and mathematics (an amplification of what was presented in *The Fourfold Root*); and it also offers some remarks on the nature of philosophy in general and metaphysics in particular. It says very little about science, although one of the supplementary essays gives a classification of the sciences. There is, oddly as one might think, a little about laughter and the ludicrous. It is in many ways a strange mixture, and many who come to Schopenhauer for the first time through it must think it a disappointing opening to what is after all the main work. On its basis alone the accusation that Schopenhauer was an unsystematic thinker might strike home. Does not the real meat lie in that first third, and is that not a disproportionately small amount of space to devote to it?

As criticisms of Schopenhauer's style of presentation of his views these comments are justified. The style of presentation arose, I suspect, first from the fact that he wished to assume *The Fourfold Root* as presupposed, and second from the fact that, like

Kant, he wanted to base his work and his view of the world on a scheme of faculties of the mind. In Kant's case that was part of his so-called 'Copernican revolution', according to which the main features of empirical reality were made out to be reflections of features of the human mind, rather than the other way round. That is to say that the scheme of faculties and the necessity of reference to it were part of the transcendental idealism. So it is for Schopenhauer also. He thought, however, that he had to put Kant right in various ways about it, and for that reason alone much space had to be given up to what is in many ways merely apparatus presupposed in his theory of empirical reality, rather than a truly constituent part of it.

Much of the first half of the first book therefore recapitulates and elaborates material already presented in *The Fourfold Root*; but although it recognizes the guiding principles of that work it does not follow them in its presentation in the same way. In the following I shall first set out (or recapitulate — for we have met much of it already) Schopenhauer's scheme of faculties. Then I shall set out and discuss the positive argument for his trans-cendental idealism with which the work begins (although they appear in great detail only in the second volume). I speak of positive arguments, since although transcendental idealism has been presupposed in the views so far surveyed, there have not really been any positive arguments in its favour. I shall finally pick out some of the issues that remain from the second part.

The scheme of faculties

The starting-point for Schopenhauer's scheme of faculties is the relationship between subject and object — something that is also the foundation of his transcendental idealism. Every subject constitutes a knowing consciousness of some kind, such that there are objects *for* it. Hence the scheme of faculties corresponds in a way to the scheme of objects for a subject. For Schopenhauer, unlike Kant, there is not even a *prima facie* division between perception and understanding, for the former presupposes the latter. It also presupposes sensation, which has, as we shall see, an ambivalent and awkward status. Reason is distinct from these but in a sense dependent upon them, so that to that extent Schopenhauer's account of reason is definitely empiricist in tone.

We may begin, therefore, with sensation. Schopenhauer repeats the remarks that he made in *The Fourfold Root* to the effect that sensation is confined to what is underneath the skin (*WR* II 4, pp. 37-8; *WI* II, pp. 208-9). It is in that sense a form of immediate consciousness of changes in the body (*WR* I 6, p. 19; *WI* I, p.24). This presupposes the ability of one body to act upon another so that changes result, but in sensation we cannot be aware of that fact. In consequence, when Schopenhauer goes on to say that the impressions produced in parts of the body by other bodies can be called representations, in so far as they exist for knowledge without bringing in the will *via* pleasure and pain, he has to make an immediate qualification. For he adds that while in a sense the body is immediately known in this way and is the immediate object for the subject, this is not so in the fullest sense; for the immediate object, properly speaking, is the other object acting on our own body. We *can* have knowledge of our own body as an object proper, but not in this way, not by sensation alone, but by some form of perception as with other objects. Such perception involves the work of the understanding, which takes the sensation as a datum, and by applying the law of causality perceives it as an effect, thus making possible a transition to the object which is its cause.

In discussing Schopenhauer's account of the same issues in *The Fourfold Root* I said that it was an unhappy theory if only for the reason that the mere application of the law of causality could only make the subject aware that the sensation was the effect of *some* cause; it could not make it aware of the exact cause and it could thus form no basis for the identification of objects in perception. It should be clear, from what I have said above, however, that there are other difficulties in the account as well. Schopenhauer seems to want sensations to constitute data, and thus be objects of knowledge in that sense, and yet not be immediate objects of knowledge proper. One might put the point by saying that for Schopenhauer a sensation is an impression of a change in one's body, but not under that description, not under that concept. Such an interpretation would make his account of bodily sensations similar to that put forward by David Armstrong in his book *Bodily Sensations*.[1] Armstrong characterizes sensations as impressions of something happening to the body; a pain, for example, is for him (although, it must be admitted, not exactly for Schopenhauer, for whom pains involve the will also) an impression of something wrong in the body. To have a pain, however, is not, and cannot be, to be aware of it under that description. For that to be the case we should have to presuppose in the person concerned an understanding of and application of other concepts which the mere having of a pain surely does not presuppose.

On Schopenhauer's account, however, the impression of the bodily change produced by other objects must surely preclude *as sensation*, not only an awareness of it as produced by other objects, but also an awareness of it as being in the body. That is to say that the impression of the change in one's body must not be an awareness of anything under that description. What then is the content of the consciousness, and how can it comprise a datum on which the understanding is to work?[2] When Thomas Reid, whom I mentioned in this connection in chapter 2, distinguished sensation from perception, he defined a sensation as an act of mind that has no object other than itself. For that reason alone a sensation could not for Reid constitute a datum from which perception was to be derived, and Reid never suggested that it could. That is not his account of the relationship between sensation and perception. He says, rather, that the former may 'suggest' the latter, and he seems to have in mind in this that the occurrence of a sensation is not only conceptually necessary for there to be perception but that it is also in some way causally necessary. To perceive something the person concerned must have a sensation or sensations (together with other things — concepts and belief), or else it does not count as perception. Equally the occurrence of a sensation may in certain circumstances and given the satisfaction of other conditions, such as those mentioned above, lead to or bring about a perception of an object.

The difficulty with Schopenhauer's account is that according to it the relation between sensation and perception is not a causal one, even if it presupposes the law of causality. For, the latter is a principle that the understanding invokes in order to make an epistemic move from the awareness involved in the sensation to that involved in perception. In consequence, the sensation must, in Schopenhauer's terms, constitute a representation, and he says as much. What then is its content? Even if the object of the sensation is in a sense the change brought about in the body the sensation cannot involve any awareness of the object under that description, or under any description that involves reference to the body, or indeed any body. In that case it is impossible to see how a sensation can function in the way that Schopenhauer wants it to function within his scheme.

It has to be said that Schopenhauer never seems to think of a form of awareness as such that it relates to an object under a description. To be aware of something in that way is to be aware of it as falling under a certain concept. On such a view to have the impression of something going on in one's body one does not have to be aware of whatever is going on under *that* description; but one does need to be aware of it under *some* description. Such a form of awareness of an object is thus concept-dependent. Not all forms of consciousness need be like that perhaps, but the consciousness of something that can function as a datum must surely be so. Schopenhauer, however, does not think in that way, and that fact reflects in part his view of concepts. He does not think that concepts are a function of the understanding so as to be involved in perception; they are a function of reason. He says indeed (*WR* I 8, pp. 38-9; *WI* I, p.50) that the understanding has one function only — immediate knowledge of the relation between cause and effect. Reason has similarly one function only — the formation of concepts. Animals have understanding, for they perceive things; but they do not have reason. They lack abstract knowledge and the abstract representations that go with that; that is to say that they lack concepts. Schopenhauer also connects this power of abstract thought that animals lack with the possession of language (*WR* I 8, p. 37: II 6, p. 66; *WI* I, p.47: II, p. 238), since, he says, a word is the necessary means of fixing a concept. It is language that establishes a connection between reason, the objects of which are universals having nothing to do with space or time, and sensuous consciousness which is tied to time.

It is clear that for Schopenhauer a concept is something like a Lockean abstract idea — a representation arrived at by abstraction from perception and to that extent second-order as far as consciousness is concerned. It is from this that memory proper (i.e. the recollection of things *as* past and thus presupposing a consciousness of a past and eventual future) is derived, as well as the capacity for further intellectual operations, such as judgment and inference. None of these things can be attributed to animals, whose knowledge is confined to what is immediate and cannot be mediate. Without necessarily embracing Schopenhauer's Lockean account of how such concepts come about, one might conceivably go along with the view that there is a form of abstract understanding of what it is for something to be X which could rightly be put down as a function of reason. If one were to reserve the term 'concept' for that form of understanding, that, however, would be a terminological point only. It would not obviate the necessity of distinguishing between that abstract form of understanding and the more concrete form of understanding that is involved in seeing something as an instance of X. That distinction is present in Locke's thought in the distinction between the abstract idea of, say, white, and the corresponding simple idea of white, and it is Locke's thesis that one acquires the former by abstracting from the instances of the latter all that is merely incidental to them, so that one comes to see what is essential to whiteness. On the other hand, one could not see something as white without, in Lockean terms, having the simple idea of white, even if one did not need the corresponding abstract idea. Hence the abstract idea simply consists of a more abstract understanding of what is already understood in some way and in relation to instances in having the simple idea. Schopenhauer, however, would have none of that. For him a concept must comprise a form of abstract knowledge, and there is nothing in his thought corresponding to a simple *idea*; what plays that role in his thought is a perception or representation.

For this reason, in discussing the idea of clear and distinct concepts he says that concepts can at best be distinct; only perceptions or intuitions can be clear. The distinctness of a concept is revealed not just by analysis of it into its components but by the verification of these in terms of clear perceptions or intuitions (*WR* II 6, p. 65; *WI* II, p. 237). If what is in our heads cannot be cashed in terms of perceptions what we have is not concepts but mere words (*WR* II 7, p. 71; *WI* II, p. 224). Hence a concept must not just be abstract, it must have been abstracted from and for that reason dependent for its real content on perceptions. What, however, does the clarity of a perception consist in? Schopenhauer says little enough about that, but we may presume that its clarity is a function of its representational capacity. In other words, its content is a matter of its quality as a picture. It is impossible not to conclude from this that Schopenhauer has been misled by the very terminology that lies at the foundation of his theory — the terminology of *Vorstellungen* or representations. The clarity of a picture as a picture is not something that we can take it to have independent of our understanding of what it is of and of its method of picturing. Analogously what we are presented with in perception is not independent of our more general understanding of the world and what it is to perceive it. One must conclude that perception presupposes some form, however minimal, of understanding in a wider sense of 'understanding' than Schopenhauer allows. His insistence on the intellectuality of all perception does not amount to that, but only perception's dependence on the principle of causality. If someone does not wish to use the term 'concept' for that wider form of understanding of which I have spoken, well and good, but its existence must be recognized all the same. It is not enough, as Schopenhauer does, to take the representational function of perception as a datum. He says in one place (*WR* II 7, p. 77; *WI* II, p. 252) that perception is not only the source of knowledge, but is itself knowledge *par excellence*. To say that is really to treat knowledge as a given and not something which, as is the case, has to be acquired.

Schopenhauer is not alone in this. He stands with all those philosophers who think of knowledge as given in experience, and not simply mediated by it, and who think that further knowledge can be acquired only if that is so. Schopenhauer, however, is, as we have seen, in far greater difficulty than the more straight-forward sense-datum philosopher, because of his distinction between sensation and perception as connected with his concep-tion of the role of the understanding in providing immediate knowledge of cause and effect in relation to the sensation and the object which is supposed to be its cause. Sense-datum philosophers have often found difficulty in setting out in express form what the content of a sense-datum is. If what I have said is right, however, the consciousness that is involved in the having of a sensation is not related to an object as its content. To think that it is is to think of it, to use Kant's terms, as a blind intuition. Given that, it can furnish no basis for the application of the law of causality, even if that could provide what it in fact cannot – knowledge of the precise connection between the sensation and its cause.

Despite all that, understanding and reason remain for Schopen-hauer the basic faculties. Understanding makes possible know-ledge of the world in perception. To say that is really just to say that perception of things is a form of understanding them which is not mediated by other intellectual processes which are the province of reason. Understanding covers in fact, however, any form of intuitive knowledge of an object or objects. Hence Schop-enhauer can attribute to it also sagacity and good sense, while its lack can constitute stupidity, which, he says, is dullness in apply-ing the law of causality! Defect of reason, on the other hand, is not that, but foolishness, silliness or even madness. Reason is concerned with truth, understanding with reality, and their forms of deception are error and illusion respectively (WR I 6, p. 24; WI I, p. 30).

Given the remark that I have already noted, that the one func-tion of the understanding is the immediate knowledge of cause and effect, one might sum up Schopenhauer's views on the under-standing by saying that its role is to provide representations of the world and thus direct knowledge of reality. It does this in so far as the representations that it produces presuppose an under-standing of them as the causes of the sensations which we have. That move to the perception of the causes of our sensations is not supposed to be inferential in any obvious sense of that word; yet it is not simply caused by the sensations either. Hence, while perception involves having representations of the causes of our sensations, and knowledge of that fact, it is a direct, intuitive knowledge all the same. It is difficult, if not impossible, to make sense of that suggestion.

A second gross difficulty lies in the point with which I began this discussion — that the sensations, while themselves comprising representations, seem inevitably to be representations without content. They are forms of consciousness of objects — the states of the body beneath the skin — without those objects being known under those or, as far as can be seen, *any* descriptions. Thus it is impossible to see how they can furnish data for the application by the understanding of the law of causality, even if the understanding could, simply through the general principle that every event must have a cause, provide the basis for a move from one particular kind of effect to one particular kind of cause. Hence within this second difficulty there are in fact two considerations: (1) There is no basis for the application of the law of causality; (2) Even if there were such a basis the principle of causality could not warrant a transition from that basis to something else as its cause unless the general form of the principle of causality could bring with it knowledge of particular causal connections — which it cannot.

The third major difficulty is that Schopenhauer offers no account of how representations can have content at all, relying simply on the idea that they are *representations*. He thinks that concepts, which might afford a basis for an appreciation of the content of the representations which fall under them, are not the function of the understanding at all, but of reason. To make this criticism, however, is to point to an omission on Schopenhauer's part rather than an incoherence, as is the case with the other two major objections. It is also not an objection to the idea of representations having content; it is an objection to Schopenhauer's theory on the grounds that it provides no account of how the representations can be seen as having content, and thus as constituting knowledge.

So much for the understanding. I have already noted the central points about the other intellectual faculty — reason — in contrasting it with understanding. Its one function, Schopenhauer says, is the formation of concepts, and for this purpose it has to depend on the representations that perception provides in order that concepts may be abstracted from them. Hence it is to that extent secondary, and animals have, by and large, no part in it (although Schopenhauer insists (*WR* II 5, p. 62; *WI* II, p. 232) that the law that nature makes no jumps has a place here as elsewhere, so that some animals show traces, although mere traces, of reason). I have already hinted at the difficulties in the idea that concepts are abstracted from perception. The fundamental objection is that perceptions must already have content if some form of abstract understanding of objects is to be abstracted from them, and that it is impossible for them to have content unless they presuppose in the perceiver a form of understanding of objects that might justifiably be called conceptual. Thus abstraction cannot be the process by which conceptual understanding comes into being in the first place, although it might be a process by which, in some cases at least, a form of abstract understanding comes into being from more concrete forms of understanding. That is to say that 'abstraction' might be the label which we might attach to our coming to see what is essential to a number of cases of a kind of thing; but even here the cases have first to be seen as such, and seen as cases of a *kind* of thing, and it is to be expected that if this deserves the name of a 'process' it will be guided by certain general principles of understanding. It is not to be expected that the process of abstraction, seen in these terms, will be a linear one from concrete forms of understanding to abstract ones. Nor can it be the process by which conceptual understanding comes into existence in the first place. Nevertheless, if considered simply as one way in which abstract forms of understanding come into existence, under the condition that some form of understanding already exists, it would be a mistake to reject it altogether.

It seems, however, that Schopenhauer does want it to have the kind of global role that I have rejected, and where I have referred to understanding he would refer to reason. Thus in effect he assimilates the process of concept formation to whatever operations may be performed with concepts or which are dependent on concepts in his sense. It is not only that reason's province is that of things somehow detached from reality because of their abstract and abstracted character; it is also that reason is not intuitive in the way in which he takes understanding to be. Yet Schopenhauer thinks of concepts as representations, even if of an abstract kind. His way of thinking is thus very much in line with that of the British Empiricists. The same applies to his claim that concepts must be cashed in terms of perceptions. He claims indeed that all truth and all wisdom lie ultimately in perception (*WR* II 7, p. 74; *WI* II, p. 248). It is an unfortunate fact that perceptions as such cannot be retained or communicated; hence the necessity for reason and concepts, although these can never produce entirely new and original knowledge.

One wonders at this what becomes of *a priori* knowledge in Schopenhauer's scheme of things. As far as concerns *a priori* concepts it ought to follow from his general principles that there are no such things. Curiously enough he seems to seek Kant's support for this point of view (*WR* II 7, p. 82; *WI* II, pp. 258-9), with the proviso that this does not quite hold of what he calls the subjective conditions of perception — the 'forms which lie predisposed in the thinking and perceiving brain as its natural functions'. (He adds that Kant's philosophy is in every way a continuation of Locke's.) The reference to the brain is something of a gloss on Kant, and Schopenhauer will, in any case, have nothing of the Kantian categories; it is simply that, as *The Fourfold Root* argues, there are ways, determinable *a priori*, in which representations must be organized if they are to exist at all (and these Schopenhauer puts down to the constitution of the brain). Thus, despite the reference to Locke, Schopenhauer is with Kant, as far as concerns *a priori* knowledge in general, over its limitation to the conditions for the possibility of perception. Yet he also seems to say that the same is true of *a priori concepts*, and it is not by any means obvious that Kant would agree. Anyone who holds that to have a concept is to have a form of knowledge (knowledge of what it is for something to be X) must take the same view of *a priori* concepts as he takes of *a priori* knowledge in general. That would make the distinction between different kinds of concept relative only — a matter of the degree of detachment from the conditions of perception, with the proviso that absolute detachment is impossible.

That is not, I think, Kant's view. It is, however, Schopenhauer's, and it is reinforced for him by his theory that concepts are derived from perception by abstraction. For that too has the consequence that there can be different degrees of abstraction from perception. Schopenhauer holds also that it is possible to get to a stage where reason is too divorced from perception, so that it becomes empty. It is, he says, the gift of only a few to be able to compare concepts with perceptions, and so have wit, the capacity for judgment, sagacity or genius (*WR* II 7, p. 72; *WI* II, p. 245). He adds that all original thinking is done in pictures or images, and is thus dependent on perception; although he adds the proviso 'unless it be in mathematics'. Abstract ideas that do not have perception at their core are like mere cloud shapes; there is nothing substantial about them. It is clear from this and from many other similar things that he says that he puts an immense weight upon perception, and upon intuitive forms of consciousness generally. There is a corresponding tendency to depreciate the power of discursive thought as such. I shall return to that point when I come to his treatment of the various sciences in the third section of this chapter. It is perhaps worth noting in passing, however, that in this area lies what Schopenhauer considers to be the source of the ludicrous and therefore of laughter. These arise, he thinks, from an incongruity between a concept and the real object (*WR* I 13, p. 59: II 8, p. 91; *WI* I, p. 76: II, p. 271). Schopenhauer gives examples to illustrate that thesis; they are scarcely more encouraging than other examples of philosophical theses about humour.

Schopenhauer's scheme of intellectual faculties (I have said nothing about the will) remains very simple. There is an intuitive faculty typified by and based on perception, and a more discursive faculty concerned with concept formation and different operations with concepts. They both have representations as their objects, although of different kinds. Although Schopenhauer insists that there are only four principles which form the objects of rational knowledge or reason — identity, contradiction, excluded middle and sufficient reason (*WR* I 10, p. 50; *WI* I, p. 65 — *WR* II 9, p. 103; *WI* II, p. 286 reduces these to the principles of excluded middle and sufficient reason) — there are otherwise comparatively few references to *The Fourfold Root*, let alone echoes of its structure. In particular one comes away with comparatively little sense of the conditioned nature of all consciousness of representations; yet this, as will appear, is an essential part of the argument for the identification of the thing-in-itself with the will. A little more emerges from the argument for transcendental idealism with which the work as a whole and the additional essays in the second volume in particular begin. The crucial step to the thing-in-itself, however, is set out in the second book, and presupposes *The Fourfold Root* more than the discussion in the first book.

Transcendental idealism

Schopenhauer opens his main work with the declaration that the world is my representation. It is put forward simply as a declaration, but nevertheless as a truth that a proper philosophical insight will be bound to recognize. It suggests a form of subjective idealism and Schopenhauer indeed acknowledges a number of precedents for it, including Berkeley. It turns out, however, to be a partial truth in two ways. First, there is the very important fact that there is another, and, Schopenhauer thinks, less obvious, side to the coin, which will become apparent only after a good deal of argument — that the world is also my will. That 'also' is of some importance; although Schopenhauer will argue for the identification of the thing-in-itself with the will, that does not do away with the fact of knowledge and its objects, so that the world remains as representation also. Second, the 'my' in these theses about the world must not be interpreted in such a way that they are taken to mean that the world is *my* representation or *my* will, as opposed to anyone else's. The idealism does not entail any form of solipsism.

Schopenhauer does not discuss the last point explicitly until the second book (*WR* I 19, p. 104; *WI* I, p. 135) where, as indicated in chapter 3, he dismisses what he calls 'theoretical egoism' (the thesis that, as he puts it, dismisses as phantoms any phenomenon outside one's own will) by saying that it is a sceptical position which cannot be disproved, but which can be ignored and by-passed like a small, frontier fort which may be impregnable but is such that its garrison will never sally forth from it. It is a position that no one could consistently maintain as a matter of serious conviction (shades of Hume!). If the world is my representation and my will for me it is so for you too. It is indeed representation and will *simpliciter*. Representations, however, exist simply as objects for a knowing subject and there is no object without a subject. It does not turn out to be quite the same for the will.

In his first book, Schopenhauer goes on to set out the essential correlation between subject and object, whereby representations exist only as objects for a knowing subject. This, as was the case in *The Fourfold Root*, is the point of departure for the inquiry, since, as Schopenhauer says (*WR* I 2, p. 5; *WI* I, p. 5), everyone finds himself as subject. He goes on to summarize the conclusions, but not the argument of *The Fourfold Root* — that every representation is subject to the principle of sufficient reason, and that representations are subject, as Kant maintained, to the *a priori* forms of space, time and causality (the last of which, in the interpretation that Schopenhauer puts upon it, brings in matter). All this is familiar from *The Fourfold Root*, to which Schopenhauer here makes frequent reference, and it is not necessary to go into the details yet again. Schopenhauer adds here, however, the important point that one should avoid attributing the relation between cause and effect, which must hold good of the changes that we find in representations, to the relationship between subject and object also. It is the supposition that there must be a causal relation between subject and object, Schopenhauer says, which leads to what he calls 'realistic dogmatism' (that there really is an object quite separate from the subject and the representations that exist for it) and scepticism (that we can never know of any real being that lies behind representations) (*WR* I 5, p. 14; *WI* I, p. 17). On the contrary, the only objects are representations, and these exist as objects for the subject, and never such as to be in a causal relation with the subject, as the other two theories suppose. Causality applies only to and within representations.

By contrast with these views, then, Schopenhauer insists that the only things that exist as objects for a subject are representations and that these therefore constitute empirical reality, i.e. reality as far as experience reveals it to us. Such a reality exists only for a subject, however, and for that reason it has transcendental ideality. Hence for the first time Schopenhauer asserts the Kantian coincidence between the empirically real and the transcendentally ideal (*WR* I 5, p.15; *WI* I, p. 18). What experience teaches us is real, but if we consider the conditions for possible experience we come to see that the experience is conditioned by the subject; thus the representations on the one hand constitute reality, but are on the other hand ideal. Idealism in the non-transcendental sense supposes that one can ask the question, as an empirical question, whether anything lies behind our experiences, and there results either the realistic dogmatism or the scepticism that Schopenhauer notes.

He goes on in the same section of the book to consider the question whether the whole of life might be a dream, and answers it along the same lines. He asserts that from the empirical point of view the only certain criterion for distinguishing dream from reality is the empirical one of waking up. Each form of experience, however, has its own continuity, so that from an external point of view there would be no difference between them. That, however, is not an empirical point of view, so that to raise the question in those terms is to involve oneself in a confusion between what Schopenhauer calls the empirical origin of the question of the reality of the external world and its speculative origin. From the latter point of view there really is no meaningful question, once given the terms of reference of transcendental idealism. (Although it has to be said that, as Schopenhauer himself points out, the Hindu notion of the veil of Mâyâ which he often invokes in connection with the world as representation is sometimes spoken of in terms of the notion of a dream; and he himself, in arguing for the idea of a thing-in-itself, says that we tend to think in asking whether the world is nothing more than mere representation that if it were it would pass us by like an empty dream. That notion of a dream, however, is just like an image, and he can invoke it because he thinks that there is something in the relationship between subject and object that tells us that the world is not merely representation. It does not follow that it is something causally responsible for representations, as the positions of dogmatism and scepticism that he is rejecting suppose.)

On the whole the position of transcendental idealism and its coincidence with empirical realism is just asserted in these opening sections of the main work. We have to turn to the first of the supplementary essays of the second volume for more elucidation and argument. It is perhaps interesting and significant that it was not until these essays that Schopenhauer felt the need to engage in substantial argument for his position; in the first volume he seems to have thought that he could largely take it for granted. The first of the supplementary essays is entitled 'On the fundamental view of idealism'. It begins with a very striking passage, which it is worth reading for its style alone. In it Schopenhauer presents a thumb-nail sketch of a somewhat materialist view of the world in which we live, and ends by saying that it has been shown by 'philosophy of more recent times', particularly Berkeley and Kant, that it is all a 'brain phenomenon', and so hedged about with different subjective conditions that its supposed reality vanishes. Once again it is worth noting that Berkeley and Kant are put together in their idealism, and that Schopenhauer refers to the brain in this context in a way in which neither of those philosophers would have done. The way in which Schopenhauer was prepared to put a gloss on their views in this connection reveals the extent to which he was willing, as they were not, to look for an empirical basis for his metaphysical view of the relationship between subject and object, which is all that we have been presented with so far. Later (WR II 1, p. 8; WI II, p. 170) he equates Kant's 'faculty of knowledge' with brain functions in a similar way.

Schopenhauer's argument, brief though it is, is in effect that since all consciousness of the world has brain functioning as its condition, it must thereby be a product of that brain functioning. Indeed he says explicitly (WR II 1, p. 4; WI II, p. 164) that the same brain function which produces an apparently objective world during sleep in dreams must have just as large a share in the production of the world of our waking state. But why must it? It does not follow from the fact that both sets of experiences have as a necessary condition the activity of the brain that both have this as their sufficient condition. Other philosophers have sometimes used in this context what might be called the argument from creeping assimilations. That is to say that they have assimilated cases where it is obvious that the experience is totally dependent on subjective factors, including, sometimes, factors involving our bodies, to experiences where *prima facie* that is less obviously so, and these in turn to even less obvious cases. There is nothing 'creeping' about Schopenhauer's argument involving brain functions, however; he seems to think that the very dependence of experiences on brain functions is enough to show their ideality. He did of course think that he had precedents for this view in Berkeley and Kant (indeed he suggests that the view goes back to Descartes); and he distinguishes Berkeley and Kant simply by saying that Berkeley confined himself to the ideality of objects in general, while Kant was concerned only with the 'way and manner' of objective experience (*WR* II 1, p. 8; *WI* II, p. 170).

In effect these are the only strictly positive arguments that Schopenhauer adduces for idealism, except perhaps that he insists with Descartes that all objects of certain and immediate knowledge must lie within consciousness, and he takes that as sufficient in itself to justify the conclusion that since philosophy must depend for its data on what is certain and immediate philosophy must be essentially idealistic. True philosophy must be idealistic, he says (*WR* II 1, p. 4; *WI* II, p. 165), if it is to be honest. By that token many philosophers, including Descartes himself, who have accepted the premise about all objects of certain knowledge but who have not committed themselves to idealism, have been dishonest. Perhaps that might be taken to be so if lack of logical rigour were to amount to lack of honesty. It is also possible, however, to dispute the premise that all objects of certain knowledge lie within our consciousness. Certainly that premise does not itself follow from any of the supposed facts about brain functions.

Schopenhauer also supports his position by a number of arguments designed to meet counter-arguments. There are two in particular in the opening pages of the first essay in the second volume. The first tries to meet the objection that it seems clear that an objective world would exist whether or not there were any knowing beings. (One might add, though Schopenhauer does not do so explicitly, that there surely *was* a world once before any knowing beings came into existence.) Schopenhauer's reply is similar to one used by M. Merleau-Ponty at the end of the chapter on 'Temporality' in his *Phenomenology of Perception* — that this suggestion contains a hidden contradiction. He says that if we try to *realize* the thought in question (or, to use the language of Husserl from whom Merleau-Ponty derives much, if we try to produce its fulfilment in terms of perception) a contradiction will appear. For if we try to imagine a world without a knowing subject, we come to realize that we are trying to imagine something which is the opposite of what we are in fact imagining; for what we are in fact imagining is indeed something dependent on a knowing consciousness — our own.

It is of course a truism that we cannot imagine anything without an imaginer existing. It does not follow from that that we cannot imagine a scene where no conscious beings exist.[3] When we imagine a scene we do not, in order to do this, have to put ourselves into the scene. Imagining a scene and imagining ourselves perceiving, imagining, thinking of . . . . . a scene are not the same things. It is not in any case clear why imagination has to be brought into the matter at all. The position under consideration is that a world devoid of conscious being is *thinkable*. It might well be argued, on the other hand, that that thought would be an empty one, and to that extent lacking a sense, if it were not possible to put flesh on it, so to speak, by saying what it would be like for such a world to exist. The process of putting flesh on it in that sense might well necessitate describing it in terms that are perceptual in that a full understanding of them would be possible only for a perceiving being. That is what the realization of the thought in perceptual terms that Schopenhauer mentions ought to come to; it may presuppose imagination, but it does not entail that in having the thought we are *ipso facto* imagining anything. Nor does it entail that what is being thought involves as part of the content of the thought the existence of a perceiver.

The second argument that Schopenhauer considers, the objection that he says is the principal one and the one that everyone thinks of, is that I am object for another and yet I know that I should exist whether or not that other has a representation of me in his mind. The same applies to all other objects since they stand to his intellect in the same relation that I do. Hence they too exist whether or not he has a representation of them in his mind. One may feel like adding 'and the same holds good whoever is the knower in question', but Schopenhauer does not explicitly come to that general conclusion in the argument that he is presenting for consideration and reply. In a way it is a matter of some importance that he does not; for his reply to the argument involves in effect a rejection of that general conclusion. For he takes to all intents and purposes the same line as Berkeley, saying that even if things could exist whether or not that other person existed, they could not exist if there were not someone, some knowing being, for whom they existed as representations. What Schopenhauer actually says is that the other being for whom I exist as object is not the subject in an absolute sense, but simply a knowing individual. Hence if he did not exist, that would not mean that the subject does not exist; I myself am that in the same way that every knowing being is. On the other hand, my person, in the only sense that that can exist as object for another, exists similarly for me — as an extended and acting thing, something that involves the body. This is, like every other body, a phenomenon of the brain, of mine if not of someone else's.

Schopenhauer's reply to the argument in question — that things could not exist if there were not some knowing being for whom they existed as representations — is a Berkeleyan, near-phenomenalist, one, and might be taken to imply that for a material object to exist is for it to be representation for some subject. Certainly Schopenhauer's general thesis might be summed up as he does in the first volume (*WR* I 7, pp. 29-30; *WI* I, p. 38) when he says that the principle of no object without a subject is one that makes all forms of materialism impossible. He adds that while we can speak of suns and planets without any eye to see them or understanding to know them the words are in fact a '*sideroxylon*, an iron-wood' (i.e. a contradiction). 'No object without a subject' is indeed his position; but that does not, strictly speaking, imply for him an ontology consisting of a plurality of subjects, for one of which objects must exist as representations, if not for others. In the passage which follows Schopenhauer's reply to the objection which we have been considering, he goes on to state in brief what is the core of his philosophy. Having set out the position that one's own person is split up into a knower and a known, subject and object, which are, as everywhere, he says, both inseparable and irreconcilable, he goes on to say that everything that exists simply as object for a subject may still have an *existence for itself*, such that no subject is required. Such an existence cannot take the form of extension and activity, but must comprise another kind of existence, as thing-in-itself, which cannot therefore be *object*. That, he says, is the real answer to the objection, and because of it the objection does not overthrow the truth that things can exist *as objects* only in the form of representations and for that reason only for a subject.

One might think that the objection had been supposedly met by Schopenhauer without that last point. It would, however, have been dealt with only by accepting, in effect, a world of Berkeleyan spirits. As Schopenhauer says elsewhere (*WR* I 17, p. 98; *WI* I, p. 128), we are not satisfied with knowing that we have representations and that they are connected in certain ways that conform to the principle of sufficient reason. We have the metaphysical urge to know, as he puts it, their significance, and so to pass beyond the veil of Mâyâ. Hence, like Kant, Schopenhauer finds

The Berkeleyan position unsatisfactory. While representations constitute empirical reality their transcendental ideality is for these philosophers not enough, even if it is fact. Even if one is not idealistically inclined, it is possible, on occasion at least, to get oneself into the frame of mind in which one may see the world as a set of what Schopenhauer calls representations, perhaps governed by a set of internal laws. Yet anyone in such a frame of mind is almost bound to ask the sort of question that Schopenhauer notes in the passage just referred to. If we were content with the idea that the world is merely representation, it would, he says, inevitably pass us by like an insubstantial dream or ghostly apparition not really worth consideration. Hence the urge to get at the nature of some form of metaphysical existence or being, which must inevitably be different from that of the objects that we ordinarily know about and which, according to Schopenhauer, exist only for a subject. In the end that will affect also our conception of the knowing subjects themselves and undermine the thought that in reality a plurality of such knowing subjects is even possible. In that event the conception of a world of Berkeleyan spirits becomes quite implausible.

Given all that we may wonder where those brain functions to which Schopenhauer appeals at the beginning of his argument can possibly come into the picture. They must have the status of objects for a subject like any other object which exists as extension and activity. Once again, however, that does not undermine their empirical reality, and Schopenhauer feels that there is no reason not to appeal to them in an argument which rests on empirical premises. The arguments for transcendental idealism, such as they are, have been a mixed bag. The initial, positive, argument, based on brain functions, was, even if invalid, meant to provide empirical grounds for rejecting the belief that we have access to a world of objects independent of ourselves. The premise, however, depends on the acceptance of the objectivity of certain representations — those which tell us of the functioning of the brain. Hence it presupposes the empirical reality of at least some representations. The subsequent argument does not, however, attempt to undermine the empirical reality of representations in general, as some sceptical arguments can be taken as doing. The argument does not use the supposed validity of certain forms of perception to undermine the validity of perception itself and in general. The argument is supposed to use the empirical reality of certain representations to show the transcendental ideality of all representations.

Is such an argument possible? It is difficult to answer that question in general, but there is certainly a gap in Schopenhauer's version of the argument, apart from the consideration that I noted earlier, that dependence on brain functions is not the same as being solely determined by brain functions. The gap consists in the fact that it does not follow from the fact, if it is one, that representations are always a function of what happens in the brain that they are always simply a function of the subject, as is implied by transcendental idealism. Whether that follows will depend on the relation between subject and the brain. For Schopenhauer, the brain must exist simply as object for a subject, as known for a knower, and these are, as we noted earlier, inseparable but irreconcilable. That, however, presupposes the transcendental idealism and cannot be used as a premise in an argument for it. It would not, in any case, be sufficient. Even if a brain, like any other material object, exists only for a subject, it is another question whether a subject always implies a brain. Schopenhauer believes that it does, but he has no real argument for it.

It is not implied by the other general principle — apart from that of no object without a subject — which he goes on to invoke in this connection. This is the principle of no subject without an object (*WR* I 7, pp. 31ff: II 1, pp. 14ff; *WI* I, p. 40ff; II, p. 178). Such a principle is too general to justify the claim that a subject always implies a brain. It is however perhaps worth considering for its own sake. When he discusses the first principle of no object without a subject he generally does so in the context of a discussion of materialism. For he thinks that realism as such (transcendental realism, as one might call it) inevitably leads to materialism, since such realism implies that empirical perception gives us things-in-themselves such that they are governed by material principles. It is not clear that this implication really holds good, since there might, for that matter, be spirits also who perceive those material things. The materialism follows only if one adds that what is given in perception is the one nature that exists. However that may be, Schopenhauer takes his principle of no object without a subject to be a refutation of materialism, and he takes his argument to show that materialism involves a contradiction. Whatever one may think of materialism, it is doubtful, to say the least, that Schopenhauer can be thought to have provided a refutation of it, given the difficulties with his argument. The second principle of no subject without an object is taken by him to refute the position diametrically opposed to materialism.

Such a position he takes to be embodied in the philosophy of Fichte, in that it attempts to construct objects from a subject; it is an idealism without things-in-themselves. It would not be profitable to go further here into Fichte's philosophy, for which Schopenhauer has not much good to say, except that it is the most consistent position at the opposite pole from materialism. Materialism either leaves out the subject or tries to construct it out of objects; Fichtean idealism does the reverse. Schopenhauer thinks that it can be refuted simply by arguing that a subject must already presuppose objects. 'A consciousness without object is no consciousness' (*WR* II 1, p. 15; *WI* II, p. 178).

There are perhaps echoes of the later philosopher, Brentano, in the assertion of that principle, but that very fact serves to bring out the underlying ambiguity there is in Schopenhauer's use of 'object' (*Gegenstand*). When Brentano maintained that every mental act has its object, he did not mean by 'object' material object. Brentano used the notion of an intentional object, something that was immanent in the act. Without going closely into that notion it can nevertheless be seen that the claim that there is no form of consciousness which does not have an object does not imply anything about the existence of objects except as objects *for* the subject of consciousness. The most plausible interpretation of the principles of no object without a subject and no subject without an object is that in which 'object' is taken in each case simply as an object *for* a conscious subject; and in that case the principle of no object without a subject, at least, becomes not merely plausible, but truistic.

That, however, is not really the interpretation that Schopenhauer puts upon the principles, and for that reason alone they remain problematic in his case. For he concludes his discussion of them in the second volume (*WR* II 1, pp. 17ff.; *WI* II, pp. 181ff.) with a curious brief dialogue between subject and matter, both of which make claims to the world, and end up by recognizing their status as inseparably connected and necessary parts of the whole. A page or two before that he asserts that the world as representation has two poles — the knowing subject simple without its forms of knowing, and crude matter without form. Both of these are unknowable and limiting cases; yet both are presuppositions of all empirical knowledge. They constitute the framework within which phenomena are to be seen and understood. They correspond to the two 'god-heads' of which the early Wittgenstein spoke (*Notebooks*, 8.7.16, p. 74) — the I and the world. But for Schopenhauer, it must be remembered, there is also the world as will, and once we have recognized that aspect of things the world as representation will come to look different as well.

72

Logic, mathematics, science and metaphysics

In being concerned with transcendental idealism we are in effect still concerned with the world as representation in so far as it is the province of the understanding. To consider what logic, mathematics, science and metaphysics are capable of is, Schopenhauer thinks, to turn to reason and to consider its possibilities and limitations. If the sole function of reason is, as he says, the formation of concepts, the various forms of knowledge which are founded on reason will be concerned with the different kinds of relation between concepts and in different degrees of abstraction from the conditions of perception. For concepts are in a sense representations, as Schopenhauer puts it (*WR* I 9, p. 4; *WI* I, p. 52); they are thus dependent on perception and understanding. Reason is, he says (*WR* I 10, p. 50; *WI* I, p. 65), of feminine nature; it is dependent on what it has received. Of itself there are only the forms of its operation, and what we can know of that is simply what is involved in metalogical truth — the principles of identity, contradiction, excluded middle and sufficient reason. For the rest logic is concerned simply with relations such as those of inclusion and exclusion between concepts, and it is on those relations that syllogisms are founded. Nevertheless, while logic is dependent on relations between concepts, which are themselves dependent on abstraction from perception, it can pass for a pure science of reason. For even if concepts in fact presuppose perception, it is possible to consider the relations between concepts in terms of their content in independence of their origins. Hence logic is as near as we can get to a pure science of reason.

That having been said, it is clear that Schopenhauer does not have a high opinion of logic as a discipline. He has little enough to say about it, and while he allows that it may have some theoretical interest for philosophy he goes out of his way to emphasise its lack of practical utility. Indeed he has a low opinion of deductive argument and proof in general, claiming that it merely makes explicit what we already know. Much the same is true in this respect of mathematics. Indeed at one place (*WR* II 12, p. 121; *WI* II, p. 308) he says that while logic and mathematics are the only completely certain sciences this is because they teach us only what we already know. For they make explicit through a system of judgments what is already known implicitly in the concepts which are their domain. Mathematics is in a sense less pure than logic since its content is derived from the intuitions that we have of spatial or temporal relations. Even here Schopenhauer seems to think that the role of proof is limited. As we saw in connection

73

with the discussion of mathematics in *The Fourfold Root*, Schopenhauer condemns Euclidean style proof because it does not give us the conviction of geometrical truths in the way that a more intuitive appeal to a diagram or example may do. He ignores the fact that that is not the aim of the proof. Nevertheless he evidently thinks that a science is to be judged by its ability to enable us to see a truth, and that clearly puts the emphasis on a form of intuitive understanding rather than systematic exposition and explanation. For the latter, he thinks, is merely a setting out of what we already know, and the acquisition of new knowledge depends upon, in effect, intuition.

There is some similarity between Schopenhauer's position in this respect and Aristotle's. For Aristotle also thinks that for knowledge proper we have to be got to see that such and such is the case. It is the function of induction to make that possible in the case of general principles by getting us to see what is implicit in cases or examples. (Schopenhauer himself seems to view Aristotle's account of induction in this way in *WR* II 9, p. 106; *WI* II, p. 290.) Demonstration is for Aristotle another way of getting people to see that something must be so, but it works by setting out the implications of other things that they know must be so. Moreover scientific knowledge is for Aristotle a matter of seeing not only that something is so, but also why it is so, in terms of its ground; and that is how it is for Schopenhauer too in connection with knowledge proper (rational knowledge, *Wissen*), of which the only true example is abstract knowledge — something that animals do not have since they are confined to knowledge of perception. (Schopenhauer indeed thinks that all error involves an invalid conclusion from the consequent to the ground — a thesis that forces him to say that mistakes in calculation are not errors but mere mistakes (*WR* I 15, pp. 79-80, cf. II 7, p. 89; *WI* I, p. 105, cf. II, 268). Despite this rather arbitrary assessment he has very interesting things to say about the part that satisfaction with words plays in perpetuating error (*WR* II 15, p. 145; *WI* II, pp. 340ff.)).

What Schopenhauer sees as the defect of intuition of whatever form is its lack, by itself, of communicability. That can be seen *par excellence* in what he offers as the true opposite of knowledge proper (*Wissen*) — feeling, completely non-abstract consciousness. It is its very lack of abstractness, its confinement to the immediate present that produces its defect as regards preservability and communicability. That is where knowledge proper scores because of its abstractness and generality, particularly of cource where words can fix the concepts in the way that Schopenhauer presupposes.

On the other hand, the greater the degree of abstractness, and the further it is from perception and intuition, the less is the true content of the knowledge. Thus although Schopenhauer thinks of logic as the only really certain science (mathematics being sometimes put in the same category, although it is dependent on intuitions of space and/or time) it has minimum content.

It is clear that Schopenhauer has little in any case to offer anyone who is interested in logic. His knowledge of the subject is confined to that of traditional logic, and he works almost entirely within its terms of reference. It is, he says, concerned with the technique of our own thinking, or rather perhaps, the rules of that technique, which we follow without having learnt them as such. Dialectic and rhetoric are connected sciences, concerned respectively with the technique of disputing with others and the technique of speaking to many. He has little enough to say about either of them, although one of the *Paralipomena* (*PP* II 2) offers a specimen of what is involved as technique in an art of disputation. It is, however, only a fragment and contains little that is fundamentally new to the subject. Schopenhauer excuses himself from going further into it by saying that he has decided that detailed consideration of tricks and stratagems is not suited to his temperament!

The judgment on what Schopenhauer has to say about logic can equally be applied to what he has to say about mathematics. We have noted already in considering *The Fourfold Root* his theory concerning the way in which arithmetic and geometry are based on the intuitions of time and space respectively. He adds (*WR* I 12, p. 54; *WI* I, pp. 69-70) that the considerations that he has adduced concerning reason and its relation to perception show that the abstract knowledge of space relations presupposes their translation into time relations. Numbers alone can be expressed in abstract concepts which correspond exactly to them. The fact that every number has a distinct identity seems clear enough. It also seems clear that any metrical relationships between parts of space or an extension presupposes the possibility of their expression in arithmetical terms (although this leaves out of consideration, naturally enough given the state of the art in Schopenhauer's time, purely topological relationships). It is less clear, however, how the fact or supposed fact that numbers alone can be expressed in terms of exactly corresponding abstract concepts fits in with the other supposed fact that arithmetic presupposes an intuition of time. Ought not the last 'fact' to mean that the concepts do not constitute a completely pure abstract knowledge, since they are conditioned by the intuition in question? To that extent they are in the same or a similar boat as all other concepts, even those which are conditioned by perception. There can on Schopenhauer's account be no pure *a priori* concepts, which do not have either perception or what amounts to the conditions of its possibility as their condition.

Apart from that issue and the scepticism, already noted, about the value of proof in mathematics when this makes no appeal to our intuition, Schopenhauer's treatment of mathematics comes to grips with few matters of detail. It seems that, like logic and the art of disputation, it was not really to his taste. The situation over science is a little more complicated, but the end result is much the same. Schopenhauer sees the method of science as largely hypothetico-deductive, so that one uses, as he thinks, judgment to arrive at a hypothesis and then sees whether its consequences fit the facts. Its aim is to establish connections between phenomena in terms of the principle of sufficient reason of becoming, i.e. in terms of causality. Induction is simply a matter of confirmation of hypotheses by reference to what is 'given in many perceptions' (*WR* I 14, p. 66, cf. I 15, p. 77; *WI* I, p. 87, cf. I, p. 102), and so works only within a general procedure that presupposes the putting forward of hypotheses. Such a conception fits at least one well-known view of scientific method in its most general form.[4]

A science can be more or less general in its subject matter and more or less connected with mathematical considerations. In that spirit Schopenhauer puts forward (*WR* II 12, p. 127; *WI* II, p. 317) a classification of the sciences, in which, apart from logic and mathematics the pure sciences *a priori*, the empirical sciences are arranged in three categories, according to whether the reason of becoming functions as cause proper, stimulus or motive. Within each category a distinction is made between the universality and the particularity of the science's subject matter, e.g. as between physics in general and astronomy in its particularity. This amounts to a distinction between general and particular forms of the physical, biological and human sciences.

Except for that little enough emerges from the main work concerning science. Once again it seems that Schopenhauer had little interest in the practice of science as such or in the details of its methods. Among the *Paralipomena* (*PP* II 6) there is an essay in which he goes through and states his own position on a fair number of scientific *ideas*. While he is sometimes misconceived about them, it is clear that he had a wide knowledge, gained largely from reading, of scientific ideas, and he was not afraid to pass judgment on them, especially in connection with the question whether they fitted into his scheme of things. The same emerges, as we shall see in a little more detail later, from his treatment of the will in nature. He was not, however, really interested in scientific practice.

A little more ought to be said at this point about the relation of science to the conception of the will in nature to which I have already referred, although some of the comment will have to wait until we have considered the treatment of the world as will. Science, like every form of possible knowledge that is dependent on perception, can be concerned with phenomena only. From a strictly philosophical point of view, Schopenhauer thinks, that will be found unsatisfactory. It presupposes the working of the principle of sufficient reason of becoming within phenomena, but it can say nothing about the basis of that principle itself. It cannot penetrate the veil of Mâyâ and cast light on the underlying reality. Yet when one has recognized the truth about that underlying reality some confirming glimpses of it can be derived from what science tells us. That is particularly the case where we are constrained to think in terms of forces working in nature, whether these be physical forces, or teleological processes discoverable within biology, or finally the moral purposes that may have a place in the human sciences. A force, Schopenhauer says, is not a cause; it is what gives to a cause its possibility of acting (*WR* II 4, p. 44; *WI* II, p. 217) and is known only in its manifestation (ibid. p. 54; p. 226). It is thus an explanatory concept meant to explain why certain kinds of causality take place. In that sense its invocation automatically takes us beyond phenomena. As we shall see, Schopenhauer identifies all force with the will, and the point of his book *The Will in Nature* is to set out the manifestations of it that can be detected in nature. Strictly speaking, however, it is not something that one can have any reason to speak of unless and until we have found a reason to think that we can go beyond phenomena at all.

To investigate *that* possibility cannot be the role of science, since science is concerned to answer the question 'Why?' in a way conformable to the principle of sufficient reason. Such explanations as it offers must therefore be relative, in that what happens, a change, is explained by relating it to something else. To go beyond that, which is the task of philosophy, and of metaphysics in particular, involves an account of the world in which nothing is presupposed. Hence, Schopenhauer says, philosophy cannot attempt to say where the world comes from or for what purpose it exists; it can really say only what it is (*WR* I 15, p. 82; *WI* I, p. 108). Nevertheless of course Schopenhauer thinks that in doing that his philosophy, at any rate, will satisfy the demand that human beings feel for an understanding of the reality of things. The seventeenth essay of the second volume of the main work consists of a long and fascinating discussion of man's need for metaphysics. Schopenhauer thinks of religion as a kind of popular metaphysics (cf. *PP* II 15 on that), but one which, unlike metaphysics proper, has its verification and credentials outside itself — in authority, revelation, or what have you (*WR* II 17, p. 164; *WI* II, p. 365). This view of metaphysics enables Schopenhauer to refer to man as an *animal metaphysicum* (*WR* II 17, p. 160; *WI* II, p. 359), an animal which has an urge to seek knowledge that goes beyond the possibility of experience. In fact, he claims, philosophy, like all other forms of knowledge, must be based on experience; it is 'nothing but the correct, universal understanding of experience itself' (*WR* II 17, p. 183; *WI* II, p. 390). In the comparable passage in the first volume (*WR* I 15, pp. 82-3; *WI* I, pp. 107ff.), he says that it is the complete summing up of the world in abstract concepts, and is in effect the making abstract of what we all know in particular.

It might sound from this as if he means to say that philosophy or metaphysics is merely the attempt to give the most general and abstract account of the world — and that would certainly fit in with certain conceptions of metaphysics, e.g. that *metaphysica generalis* that some scholastics found in Aristotle. In the context of Schopenhauer's thought, however, it has a rather more special meaning. He says (*WR* I 15, p. 82; *WI* I, p. 108) that it might be said that everyone knows without further aid what the world is 'for he himself is the subject of knowing, whose representation the world is'. People know this only in a concrete form, however, and it is the task of philosophy to raise to the abstract what thus comes under *feeling*. The snag with this is that strictly speaking it will in the end tell us simply that the world is representation. Schopenhauer is not satisfied with that, nor does he think that other philosophers should be. For him at least the world is also will, and although he thinks that that realization is also based on something that we are aware of in ourselves, it does require argument to get us to the final conclusion. If that is so, philosophy is not just descriptive; it depends on arguments, and we ought to be given some account of them. To disentangle Schopenhauer's own arguments for his final conclusion will be the task of the next chapter.

Before turning to that there remains to note one further thing from the first book of the main work. Schopenhauer considers logic, mathematics, science and metaphysics in the way that he does because they are all for him functions of reason, all in a sense consequences of the power that we have of forming abstract concepts. They are, however, all functions of the theoretical role of reason, and it would be a mistake to leave the impression that that is the only role that reason has. In the last section of the first book of the main work (*WR* I 16, pp. 86ff; *WI* I, pp. 110ff.) and again in the corresponding essay of the second volume (*WR* II 16, pp. 148ff.; *WI* II, pp. 345ff.) he has a little to say about practical reason, and he associates this with an interesting discussion of Stoicism. A prelude to that discussion includes a hot repudiation of the Kantian theory of practical reason, about which he has more to say in the appendix on Kant and in the essay *On the Basis of Morality*. His main point against Kant is that he is wrong to associate practical reason specifically with morality and that the foundations of morality cannot be located in any such faculty. I shall not discuss that claim here and now.

It is clear, however, that reason could nevertheless have some role in connection with action and the conduct of our lives that need not be specifically ethical. Schopenhauer suggests that it has such a role when action is not subject to motives in connection with perception or, as he puts it, the impression of the moment, but rather where the motives are abstract concepts. Practical reason has a place, therefore, whenever we act from abstract principles or in relation to goals or ends abstractly conceived. That is something that human-beings are capable of, but not animals. There does not seem to be anything very problematic about that idea, and there seems to be no need to enter into any elaborate discussion of it here. It leads Schopenhauer into a very interesting discussion of Stoicism, and of the Stoic sage in particular. He sees that philosophy, not as predominantly and essentially a theory of ethics, but as a guide to a rational life, given that its aim and end is happiness and peace of mind. While he admires Stoicism as an attempt to use reason for an important purpose, he thinks that in the end it reveals a contradiction in wishing to live without suffering and particularly in recommending suicide as part of the guide to blissful life. Schopenhauer's conception of the central fault in all this depends on considerations to which we have yet to come. The closing passage of the first book of the main work remains a very impressive piece of writing.

5

The World as Will

There can be no doubt that the second book of Schopenhauer's main work contains the most important part, or at any rate the most crucial part, of the argument for his metaphysical position. It contains what he frequently refers to as the transition from phenomena to the thing-in-itself. It thus represents the other side of the coin to which I referred in chapter 4. While it does that it cannot be denied that the world as will is the more important side of the coin. If there were no phenomena, he sometimes says, there would still be will; but not vice versa. The thing-in-itself provides a kind of explanation of phenomena, but not one that involves the principle of sufficient reason. It does not explain each phenomenon taken separately; it explains them taken as a whole. That is, of course, something that Kant thought could not be the case in any positive sense. For him the concept of a thing-in-itself was a purely negative concept, required in order to provide a basis for phenomena but not in such a way that it can furnish any positive principles of explanation of them. Schopenhauer expresses the same urge for a basis for phenomena, saying, as I noted in chapter 4, that if we thought that the world was merely representation 'it would inevitably pass us by like an insubstantial dream or a ghostly apparition not worth our consideration' (WR I 17, p. 99; WI I, p. 128). He also admits that we cannot get at what he calls the 'nature of things' from without, from representation; for the principle that governs representations, the principle of sufficient reason, has no application outside them. He thinks nevertheless that there is available a clue to the nature of the thing-in-itself (and why we must speak in the singular will appear in due course).

Unfortunately, while Schopenhauer sets out clearly enough the order that the argument for the identification of the thing-in-itself must take, and follows that order in his presentation in the first volume of his main work, he is less clear about the details of the argument taken in that order. He does, however, provide us with all the materials for a reconstruction of that argument. On the whole, however, he is most anxious to give us the fundamentals of what he considered as his great discovery, which is in fact the *conclusion* of the argument. Thus in the first of the supplementary essays of the second volume which concern this part (*WR* II 18, p. 191; *WI* II, p. 399) he says that he has really published the essential supplementary essay in the work *On the Will in Nature* (published in 1836 in between the first and second editions of the main work), and in the chapter entitled 'Physical Astronomy' in particular. When one looks at that chapter, however, it does not seem to provide anything in the way of an argument, but rather a fairly systematic exposition of the conclusions of such an argument. It deals in particular with the ways in which different kinds of natural phenomenon can be viewed as subject to the same principles, *mutatis mutandis*, as those which apply to the manifestations of our own will. It is therefore concerned in effect with the claim that an insight into our own nature is really an insight into the nature of reality in general.

The supplementary essay to which I have referred is entitled 'On the knowability of the thing-in-itself'. It might be thought that if there is indeed a connection between our own nature and reality in general then an establishment of that should do something towards showing that knowledge of the thing-in-itself is possible. It does not do enough, however. It does not do enough because it does not by itself show that either of these things — our own nature and reality in general — is more than mere representation. It does not show that they are the thing-in-itself. We need, that is, an argument to show that the world is more than representation, and it is not enough for that purpose to make reference to our (whoever the 'we' is) feelings that if it were just that it would be merely an insubstantial dream. It might be that such feelings are simply misplaced and superstition, to be dismissed à la Hume through a good meal and a game of backgammon. Is there a thing-in-itself at all then?

An answer to that question is possible at two levels. It might first be pointed out that Schopenhauer could simply have taken over the Kantian supposition of a thing-in-itself and assumed uncritically that there must be such a thing. While there is something in that suggestion, in that Schopenhauer was profoundly influenced in this respect by Kant, it cannot be the whole truth. There is therefore the second possibility that Schopenhauer thought that he had a very good reason for thinking that there was such a thing, as well as reason for thinking that he could, despite Kant, identify its nature. Is it possible indeed that Schopenhauer thought that the justification for thinking that the thing-in-itself is to be identified in such and such a way is itself the justification for thinking that there is such a thing at all? It is hard to see that he could have been right in so thinking, if he did, but I believe that this is in effect what his argument comes to. For the 'transition' to the thing-in-itself turns on an epistemological point which is satisfied, Schopenhauer thinks, only by the will. If the will is separated off for that reason from all other objects considered as representations, then at least it is not representation; there must therefore exist something which is not representation. It is, however, another matter to show that the will is for that reason the thing-in-itself, and it remains a question whether the epistemological point is enough in itself to justify the separation of the will from all that is representation. These are matters into which we must go, but it is as well, first to see how Schopenhauer presents the matter in the second book of the main work.

Body, will and agency

Schopenhauer begins section 18 of the main work by pointing out that no transition to the thing-in-itself would be possible if the investigator himself were no more than a knowing subject (or, as he tellingly puts it, a winged cherub's head without a body). A knowing subject *per se* is confronted with representations only, although, since he has an understanding, he takes these as organized and governed by the principle of sufficient reason, so that they conform to certain *a priori* principles without which, Schopenhauer believes, he would have no consciousness of objects. Moreover, Schopenhauer agrees with Kant, and asserts as much in several places, that a knowing subject can have no consciousness of himself as such; there are no representations of the self, as Hume also claimed. It is not necessary here to argue that point; within Schopenhauer's terms of reference it seems valid — there is no perception by way of representations of the self as such. Nevertheless, Schopenhauer claims (*WR* I 18, p. 99; *WI* I, p. 129), any investigator of the problem is, as he puts it, rooted in the world and find himself in it as an individual. That is made possible by the body, which provides a principle of individuation for the subject, and enables him to acquire knowledge of the world.

For the knowing subject as such his own body is simply a matter of representation, and as far as that goes it is an object among objects. If that were all there is to it, Schopenhauer claims, the movements of his body would be for him just like the movements of other bodies. It is true that they would in some cases follow on motives and would be seen to do so according to the principle of sufficient reason, just as the movements of other bodies are seen to follow on causes, stimuli, or in some cases motives. There would, however, be no special insight into the movements of one's body; one might put them down to a force or what have you, but that is all. *But*, Schopenhauer insists, that is simply not the case. One has a further insight into the movements of one's own body, or at least some of them — those which constitute actions. This can be summed in the word *Will*.

This is the crucial point. We have a special insight into our own bodily actions just because they are willed. That insight has to do with what later philosophers have called 'knowledge without observation' (Anscombe) or 'intentional knowledge' (Hampshire).[1] We know of our willed and intentional actions in willing or intending them and in so doing them, and not simply in what is thereafter available to perception or any other kind of observation. It cannot be said that Schopenhauer is altogether clear in exactly what the knowledge in question consists. On two points in particular, however, he *is* clear: (1) The knowledge that I have in an exercise of the will is quite different from any form of knowledge dependent on representation — it is for that reason direct and unconditioned; (2) An act of will is quite inseparable from an action of the body and knowledge of the body. (Indeed Schopenhauer says (*WR* I 18, p. 100; *WI* I, p. 130) that resolutions of the will in relation to the future are not acts of will at all but mere intentions that can be altered, deliberations of reason about what will be willed in the future.) 'My body and my will are one', 'My body is the *objectivity* of my will' — these are the sorts of slogan by means of which he sums up the situation (*WR* I 18, pp. 102-3; *WI* I, p. 133).

Schopenhauer also argues (*WR* I 18, p. 101; *WI* I, p. 131) that impressions on the body which produce pain or pleasure are affections of the will in what is its phenomenon, the body. They are thus not, strictly speaking, representations at all. They are not, on the other hand, mere sensations either, but, as he says, affections of the will. It is far from clear that this is right. It may be, as many recent philosophers have suggested, that pain involves not merely sensation but also wants, e.g. the want to be rid of the feeling — and *vice versa* for pleasure. A pain is not, however, just an impression on the body that we do not want and which is in that sense contrary to the will; it also has the quality of painfulness and that indeed is the reason why we do not want it. Thus a pain cannot be simply put down as an affection of the will; if it affects the will it is because of its nature as a sensation. Schopenhauer is once again unfortunately unclear on the notion of sensation.

The identification of acts of will and bodily action, on the other hand, has been hailed by some commentators, e.g. Gardiner,[2] as remarkably coincident with the kind of thinking about willing and acting that is to be found in the later Wittgenstein. So it is, but it presents certain problems for any attempt to spell out the nature of that direct and unconditioned knowledge which is said to be involved in the exercise of the will. Indeed in one place (*WR* II, 18, pp. 196-7; *WI* II, p. 406) — in, it is worth noting, the second volume — Schopenhauer puts a certain qualification on the proposition that we have an immediate knowledge of the will. He says that even in self-consciousness the 'I' is not absolutely simple. There is both a knower (the intellect) and a known (the will); the intellect is not known while the will does not know, 'although both flow together into the consciousness of one 'I'. In consequence, he adds in a telling phrase, 'the I is not *intimate* with itself through and through'; it retains an opaqueness. Nevertheless the inner knowledge is free from two conditions that obtain in the case of outer knowledge — it is not subject to the forms of space and causality. It is however subject to the form of time, so that everyone knows his will only in successive, single acts.

What does all this amount to? The assertion that one knows of the will only in successive, single acts is certainly consistent with the idea that we know the will only in bodily actions; for the latter can well be construed in terms of successive acts. On the other hand, the connection with the body that is involved in this must surely mean that there is a lack of immediacy in the knowledge that we have of the will. Hence there is a tension between the idea that the will and the body are one, with all that that entails about the conditions for knowledge of bodily action and hence of acts of will, and the idea that we have an immediate knowledge of the will and only of the will. For, just before adding the qualification about the inward perception of the will not being a case of wholly immediate knowledge, Schopenhauer has said that the will is the one thing that is known to us immediately and 'not, as everything else, given merely in representation'. The point is that if it were given to us in representation it would be conditioned by being subject to the principle of sufficient reason. What Schopenhauer has to show is that it is nothing of the kind. It is the necessary combination of will with intellect as a condition of any kind of knowledge or consciousness of it, and the dependence of each on the body in their different ways, that causes the trouble. An act of will, he says (*WR* II 18, p. 197; *WI* II, p. 407), is 'only the nearest and clearest *phenomenon* of the thing-in-itself'. But is it not the case that it is only in acts of will that we know the will?

There is a further point in this connection that I touched on when considering the brief account of the will in *The Fourfold Root*. That is that every bodily act is subject, *qua* phenomenon, to motives as its condition and is to that extent subject to the principle of sufficient reason. How does that fit in with the idea that there is an immediacy attached to knowledge of the will? What I think that Schopenhauer has in mind in all this, although he does not really succeed in saying it clearly, is that it is the *fact* of willing that is known immediately, but not *what* we will. Thus in performing some bodily action, in which alone the will can be known by us, we are conscious directly and immediately *that* we do it. That knowledge is not something that needs or could depend on inference. It does not follow from that alone that we know immediately what we do and why. What we do is for us a phenomenon and thus subject to at least the form of time, even when we are aware of it from the inside, as it were. (It is of course arguable that to some extent it must involve the form of space, since the action is bodily; but I shall let that point pass for the moment.) It is also the case that the action as phenomenon is subject to motives which constitute the 'why' of what we do. It is thus subject to the principle of sufficient reason, and can be known only as so conditioned. Hence even if we can know directly and in an unconditioned way *that* we are doing something, *what* we do cannot be so known. It will be known merely as representation and thus, like all representations, subject to causes as its condition. Others can see it as subject to causes in the ordinary sense, but we see our actions as subject to motives, causes seen from within. To know what we do, therefore, we must know the motives for our action.[3]

How far is this plausible? Is it the case that we know what we do only if and when we know why we do it? It might indeed be held that there are many actions that we perform knowing that we are doing them but not knowing why; to suppose otherwise would be to preclude the possibility of our making further discoveries about ourselves and the reasons and motives that we have for doing things, and surely that possibility exists. On the other hand, there is a sense in which in making those discoveries we also attain a new and revised appreciation of what we actually do. There are of course some objective descriptions of actions considered in terms of their effects on and interaction with the objective physical world. Hence some of the descriptions under which our actions are subsumed and must be subsumed turn on facts of that kind. If we have by an action of ours brought about the death of a living being it must be right to say that we have killed that being, and 'killing' is a correct description of what we have done as far as that goes. It is indeed arguable that *any* effect brought about by our action can properly be brought within a description applicable to that action.[4] There is nothing discoverable about our motives that could affect a description of that kind of what we have done. There are, however, other descriptions of actions of which that is not true, where a motive or intention is essential to the applicability of the description, e.g. murder. It is of course in connection with such descriptions that question of real discoveries about ourselves can arise. If we do something unintentionally, the recognition of the fact that we have done it can indeed be a discovery, but it is not a real discovery about ourselves in the sense which holds good of a recognition that what we have done involves a certain motivation and can be described accordingly. Hence there is indeed a sense in which to know what we do we must know the motives for our action — where 'what we do' involves a description that itself presupposes motives or intentions on our part.

Descriptions of actions that merely make reference to physical happenings or their effects, e.g. 'hitting' or 'killing' respectively, merely concentrate our attention on what happened in the world with the proviso that there was an agent responsible for it. Thus they link agency with objectively discoverable happenings, but they tell us nothing of the character of the agency in question. For this reason there is a very important sense in which a more adequate account of what is done is provided by a description which does bring in something of the action's motivation — a more adequate account of what is *done*. To do something under such a description is therefore to do it with a proper consciousness of what is being done, whereas to do it under a description which merely invokes a physical happening or its effects is not. In both cases, however, what the correct description is under which what we do is subsumable is something that is discoverable, even if not in the same way in each case. The correctness of a physical-happening description can be discovered by observation of the world itself, and this is as well done by others as it is by ourselves. The correctness of a description which presupposes a motivation cannot be so discovered, and although others can decide, sometimes better than we can, about the appropriateness of such a description in our case, they cannot do so by simple observation of physical facts. The possibility depends on a kind of insight into human motivation which would not be possible if we did not know from our own case something of what it is to do things from motives.

Schopenhauer's claim is that such insight is always, in his terms, a matter of representation, so that what we do in the sense that we have been concerned with is always and necessarily a matter for discovery in that way, although not by outward observation, as is the case with others. It follows from that that we cannot have knowledge in this way of what we do in advance of doing it, and only then by a kind of noticing, through a form of observational self-consciousness. As we have already seen, Schopenhauer indeed says that mere resolves of the will are, until they are carried out, mere intentions and 'therefore a matter of the intellect alone' (*WR* II 20, p. 248; *WI* II, p. 472). They can prove false for various reasons, including the possibility that we have wrongly estimated the effect of motives. In that sense a resolve of the will, as he calls it, is something like a prediction. A motive objectively considered is a representation which arises as a result of the brain's functions, which then act as stimuli in relation to the working of the rest of the nervous system and the contraction of the muscles. As a representation it presupposes intellect and knowledge. A resolve of the will is a kind of prediction of such representations, but knowledge proper has a place only in connection with the actual having of those representations, and is thus a function of self-consciousness. Hence, however much we may determine in advance to do something, we shall not know what we shall do until we are aware of so doing through representations.

All this may suggest a kind of automatism which we happen to catch going on in ourselves. That, however, is not what Schopenhauer intends to convey. To think that would be to suppose that the will directly manifests itself in the action and we then happen to notice that and the reasons for it from the inside, so to speak. The will does manifest itself directly in that way in those forms of living creature where there is no consciousness. The supposition which I am rejecting would be that we are like such living creatures with a form of consciousness added on. That, however, is not how it is for Schopenhauer. In the first place, the motives which determine actions as phenomena of the will are not simply those causes of our actions that we happen to be aware of, so that there may be other causes that we are not aware of and are thus not motives. There are no causes of *action* except those which appear in representation as motives; in this context causality and consciousness are essentially intertwined. (I think that it follows also that for Schopenhauer there can be no such things as unconscious motives, despite what is sometimes said about his anticipation of Freud. If he did anticipate Freud it was in other ways.)

The will, Schopenhauer says (*WR* II 20, p. 250; *WI* II, p. 474), objectifies itself directly in irritability, not in sensibility. Irritability, however, does not amount to action; it is evident wherever there is the possibility of response to stimuli. There is action only where there is also consciousness of what one is doing, and what action it is will depend not only on the general fact of agency but upon that consciousness. That is implied by what I said earlier about the individuation of action in relation to its possible descriptions. If what we do is dependent on what the motives are, and if motives presuppose consciousness, then what we do cannot be distinguished from what we see ourselves as doing. The consciousness involved cannot simply be added on to the doing.

We have in any case somewhat ignored the fact of agency itself, in connection with which knowledge or consciousness comes into the picture in a different way. For the fact of agency we know directly without reference to representation. Schopenhauer puts that in terms of the direct knowledge of the will as it functions within ourselves, and it is this which leads him to his metaphysical conclusions. Nevertheless, if that is set on one side, and one asks oneself what it is that he is trying to grapple with in the considerations which eventually lead him to his metaphysical conclusions, the only possible answer is that he is trying to grapple with the nature of agency. What exactly is that? Can action be construed simply as a set of events or occurrences? His answer to the latter question is clearly 'No', for in divorcing the will from representations he is construing agency as something quite different from phenomena generally. (Even if Schopenhauer is in the end to bring a much wider range of phenomena within the scope of the will than we should ordinarily do, agency is a more specific notion than that of the will so generally construed.) What, however, of the first question? How exactly are we to characterize agency?

Schopenhauer's answer is simply that it is something that we are directly aware of in ourselves, such that its phenomena again essentially involve a consciousness, though not a direct consciousness, of them; and it is to be called *will*. That is far from clear, but it can hardly be anything else; agency is not like anything else. It is, however, important to note the essential role played by knowledge, awareness or consciousness within the account. I said above that the notion of agency is a more specific notion than that of the will generally. One might say that agency is simply the functioning of the will as it appears within ourselves, except that that presupposes the notion of the will which was to be explained by reference to the fact of agency. In any case, in the context of agency the will is inseparable from the intellect, and it is because of that that we know of our identification with the will directly in the fact of agency. Although we may be identified with the will, however, we are not just will; we have bodies, brains, and thereby intellect, and are thus presented with the phenomena of the will's functioning. There could be no such functioning in the form that it presents itself to us if we were not knowing beings as well as willing ones. The immensely difficult task that Schopenhauer undertakes is to give an account, within his own terms, of what that means.

One of the troubles lies in that phrase 'within his own terms'. For although Schopenhauer takes pains to reject the suggestion, the will often sounds like an agency in its own right, and for that reason the terms which are invoked to explain agency might indeed be taken to presuppose that very notion. The identification of acts of will with bodily actions compounds that difficulty, since we then need to know what a bodily *action* is, as distinct from a mere bodily movement occurring in the body. We need also to know about the relations between such bodily actions and the movements that take place in the body — the muscle movements etc. That is a problem that is still with us, and it is clear that no simple identification of the two will do. For Schopenhauer that is so because of the special place and form that knowledge has in connection with action. He seems to me quite right in that, and he is to be applauded both for the suggestion and for the attempt to work out some of the details.

It might be thought that some of the difficulties would have been removed if he had concentrated on so-called mental action; for at least in that case we do not have the problem of the relation of action to the movements occurring in the body. Yet even here there is a problem about the relation of the mental action to such mental occurrences as take place, e.g. the relation of the thinking to the images etc. that occur.[5] Moreover the issue concerning the identification of the action and the part that recognition of motivation plays arises here too. Can one be clear about what mental act one is performing without having any consciousness of the reasons why, of the motivation for it? If not, it is not the fact of bodily movement as such that causes the trouble; it is the fact that action of whatever kind has a phenomenal side. We are not only aware directly of the fact of *doing* something; the doing also presents itself to us as a phenomenon, and it is in this form that it has for us an identity. Thus agency is a complex matter; there is what Schopenhauer wants to convey in speaking of will, but there is also the dual aspect of consciousness — one's consciousness of acting and one's consciousness of what action one is performing. The latter, but not the former, brings with it consciousness of the reasons for the action in question, and thus consciousness of its causes seen from within as motives. All that would apply even to mental actions if Schopenhauer is right, but with the bodily action on which he concentrates there is also the question of the relation between everything that I have just set out and the bodily occurrences themselves. Clearly that would involve some account of the relation between the brain and the rest of the body, as Schopenhauer sees (*WR* II 20, p. 251; *WI* II, p. 475).

Schopenhauer uses more than one image to try to sum up his view of the relation between the will and the intellect. Perhaps his favourite one is that of the will as a strong, blind man carrying the intellect as a sighted but lame man on his shoulders (*WR* II 19, p. 209; *WI* II, p. 421). That does justice to some of the things that he wants to say about the two. The will is efficacious, but blind and unknowing; the intellect is impotent, but knowing. In addition, although I do not think that Schopenhauer underlines the point, the strong, blind man could function in some way on his own, but that is not true of the lame, sighted man. The functioning of the will without the intellect is blind and irrational, but it is hard to speak of *functioning* at all in the case of an intellect apart from the will. On the other hand, the image scarcely does justice to the complex interrelationship between will and intellect in connection with agency.

Another image used by Schopenhauer (*WR* II 22, p. 278; *WI* III, p. 13) is that the relationship between the knowing and conscious ego and the will is that between the image in the focus of a concave mirror and that mirror itself. That simile is scarcely perspicuous. A few lines before putting it forward, Schopenhauer likens the 'I', the focus of the brain's activity in sensibility, to the focus of a convex, rather than a concave, mirror, on the ground that the focal point of a convex mirror lies within it, not without, as is the case with a concave mirror. The I or ego recognizes itself as identical with the will, or at least recognizes the will as its own basis; the will is in that respect something within. Strictly speaking, however, what we are aware of in that way is merely what Kant called the synthetic unity of apperception — the fact that all our intellectual activities presuppose an 'I', which is, in Schopenhauer's words, their focus. It is, he says, 'indeed simple, as an indivisible point'; it is not however a substance (a soul), but a condition or state of something that can be known only by reflection and indirectly — the will. It is in that sense that it is related to the will as the image in the focus of a concave mirror to the mirror itself. What we are aware of in self-knowledge as the 'I' is merely what the will brings to a focus at that point. It is thus conditioned and in a sense merely phenomenal. It is not either of these things in quite the same way that representations are; for the latter are in effect conditioned by the structure of the brain, while here we are really concerned with the conditioning of the brain itself and its functioning by the will. Once again the simile brings out the point that the intellect depends on the will and that the latter could exist without the former, but not vice versa. Moreover, as Schopenhauer goes on to make clear, the intellect, as a function of the brain, depends thereby on the whole organism, which is itself the objectivity of the will.

As noted earlier however, the will objectifies itself directly only in irritability, and that is manifest in organic bodies generally, where we do not speak of action. It is only where the organism has a brain that the notion of action gets an application. That means that action is inseparable from what is the brain's function — intellect, consciousness and knowledge. To understand action and agency we somehow have to understand how will, knowledge and bodily functioning are intertwined. It might be objected that exactly the same is true of bodily events themselves on Schopenhauer's way of regarding things. For are they not the objectification of the will in bodily form and such that they manifest themselves to the intellect in the form of representations? There is however a difference — one that I have been trying to bring out. There are indeed representations involved in action, in our knowledge of *what* we do, and these, like all other representations, are conditioned by being related to other representations in accordance with the principle of sufficient reason — in this case to representations that constitute motives, causes seen from within. That is possible only because in acting we are, so to speak, the expression of the will, and we have a direct access to the fact of that, in that we know *that* we act directly, without having to observe anything else which tells us that we do. It remains true that we should not have that direct access were not the other things true, i.e. in particular, were it not for the fact that *what* we do is accessible to our knowledge. If we were not knowing subjects we should not act either; we should, like the animals which have no knowledge, merely be responsive to stimuli. It seems to me that whether the facts are to be set out and explained in the way that Schopenhauer does, there is an important point in all this that he is trying to get at.

The thing-in-itself

It is a further question whether Schopenhauer's recognition of that point provides any grounds for the identification of the will with the thing-in-itself. I raised earlier the question whether Schopenhauer had any reason for that identification apart from his reason for thinking that there was a thing-in-itself at all, and we must now return to that question. It must be remembered that the only real premise for an argument for either conclusion that has emerged from the discussion so far is that we know of the fact that we act in a way different from the way in which we know anything else; or rather, and to be more exact, different from any knowledge that comes by way of representation. That means that the argument will be of the form: If anything is a representation it is known conditionally; we know that we act directly and unconditionally; therefore action as such cannot be a representation. That is a very base way of putting the argument, and I shall consider a somewhat different way of stating it shortly, which will do greater justice to the complexities of Schopenhauer's thought. It is, however, the argument that emerges from what I have said above, and the important question is of course whether it is valid. If it is, then once we accept that an action is a manifestation of the will, the same conclusion follows for that — the will is not a representation.

Some would say that the argument involves quantification into an intensional or referentially opaque context,[6] since the quantifier that is implicit in the words 'if anything' has as its scope something that receives an epistemological and therefore intensional predicate, 'known conditionally'. It would be unwise, however, to allow the question of the allowability of quantification into an opaque context to be all-decisive. A more important question is whether the argument is valid even if quantification into opaque contexts is allowed. As I have presented it the argument is not valid, since the fact that something is known in given circumstances in a certain way does not show that it is not identical with something that in other circumstances is known in another way; nor does it show that it cannot have properties possessed by something of that latter kind. Nothing, that is, follows directly from considerations about how something is known in certain circumstances.

It would be a different matter if in one of the premises at

least it were asserted that whatever is under consideration is knowable *only* in the way in question. If that were the case, it would normally be the case that the thing's knowability only in that way was due to some other factor, and the argument would then depend on that. As far as the first premise is concerned, Schopenhauer does presumably want to claim that we can know representations in a conditioned way only. The reason for this lies in the nature of the relation that exists between a knowing subject and its object. That at any rate was the claim made at the outset in *The Fourfold Root*, where it was said that nothing existing by itself and independent could become an object for us. The truth of that claim was said to turn on the nature of what it is for something to be an object for a knowing consciousness. Given that, the first premise of the present argument can be taken as claiming that representations are knowable in a conditional way only. The notion of a representation is indeed an intrinsically epistemological notion which, Schopenhauer has argued, can have only this conditional status. If that is acceptable (and it is of course a large question), it is enough for the formal validity of the argument that the second premise should state only that we *can* know that we act, when we do, in an unconditional way. That indeed he does show, and is all that he does show by way of a premise stated in modal terms; he does not show that we cannot know that we act, when we do, in another way also. It does follow from the premises so stated that the notion of an action is not that of a representation; action and representations cannot be equated. That, however, is not enough for his all-over purposes; for nothing follows from that about things-in-themselves or their identification, not even if we allow the move from action to the will. Indeed, to the extent that the notion of a representation is a purely epistemological notion the conclusion hardly goes beyond the premises — actions and the will are not known merely conditionally. We need at least the additional premise that anything that is not a representation is a thing-in-itself.

It is difficult to know how such a contention could be sustained. For Kant the notion of a thing-in-itself was largely, if not entirely, a negative notion, such that it was (almost) equivalent to the non-phenomenal. I say 'almost' and 'largely' because it also had the suggestion of 'beyond the phenomenal'. That is because of the transcendental idealism which is Kant's starting point. Given that view the notion of a thing-in-itself becomes the notion of whatever it is that is the ground for phenomena and is thereby responsible in some way for our representations. So it is for Schopenhauer also, except that he is not prepared to leave matters there as Kant was. Nevertheless, if we can know in an unconditional way that we act, when we do, and if that knowledge is thereby different from our knowledge of phenomena, it does not follow that in that we know of something *beyond* the phenomenal; at best we know of something *non*-phenomenal. Its actual relation to the phenomenal remains obscure. Hence it is only on the assumption that anything non-phenomenal must be beyond the phenomenal and in some sense responsible for it that we could have any reason for supposing that the thing so known and knowable constitutes a thing-in-itself. Such an assumption has not been justified, and, as far as I can see, is not justified by Schopenhauer. Hence it is that his arguments for the existence of a thing-in-itself and for its identification with the will come to the same thing. They are both incomplete and presuppose the truth of the unexamined premise that anything that is not a representation is a thing-in-itself. If that were allowed, then with the sub-conclusion that whatever we know when we know of ourselves as acting is not a representation, it would follow that in knowing that we know a thing-in-itself. But too much is left unexamined for such an argument to be persuasive.[7]

The will

It is a further step, which so far I have not made much of, to the conclusion that what we know when we know ourselves as acting is the will. In a sense that is a point of which too much should not be made. As far as the argument has gone up to this point it would probably be enough to say that what has been identified as the thing-in-itself is our acting, willing self. That would be, in Kant's sense, a noumenal self, but one which wills whatever else it does. Once that is given, however, and once given also the thesis that such a thing cannot have any of the characteristics of the phenomenal, it soon becomes apparent, as Schopenhauer in effect makes clear, that it will be an uncomfortable position, to say the least, to maintain that all that he means to identify with the thing-in-itself is our willing self. Such a thesis might indeed tempt us to think that what Schopenhauer wants to say is that the world of phenomena is the creation of our wills; the world is not merely ideal in the sense that it is constituted entirely of our representations, it is also our creation. Such a view would be an exemplification of what Freud called the 'omnipotence of thought'. It would, however, be a false interpretation of Schopenhauer, and he must never be interpreted along those lines. It suggests indeed the 'will to power' interpretation, which some have imposed upon Schopenhauer, but which is not his view at all. It is a less misleading interpretation to take the will as being for Schopenhauer a kind of force which permeates nature and which thus governs all phenomena. That is in fact the kind of view that emerges from *The Will in Nature*, to which, as I indicated at the beginning of this chapter, Schopenhauer refers as the necessary supplementary essay on this subject. Nevertheless, as I said then, that view is in fact the conclusion of a further argument which turns on the claim that an insight into our own nature is really an insight into the nature of reality in general.

We get part of the way in that argument if we accept the step that what we are aware of in our knowledge of ourselves as acting is, as will, a thing-in-itself, something noumenal in the sense that transcendental idealism brings with it. Being non-phenomenal this is not subject to the conditions of the phenomenal, and Schopenhauer wishes to add, cannot be. In particular, the will, as thing-in-itself, is not and cannot be subject to the conditions of space and time, and thus cannot be subject to what space and time alone make possible — plurality. It is not entirely clear why plurality can have no place without the forms of space and time. Even if we were to suppose that Schopenhauer was right in saying, with Kant, that arithmetical truths presuppose the form of time and that we could have no idea of what such truths presuppose — plurality — if we did not have an intuition of the form of time, it does not seem to follow that the concept of plurality can get no application outside the area where alone that intuition holds good. That would be so only on a verificationist view of the meaning to be attached to speaking of plurality, according to which it makes no sense to speak of plurality where the conditions under which alone the fact of plurality can be ascertained are missing. Such a thesis is, to say the least, far from obviously true, and if it is false there will be no objection, as far as that goes, to invoking the idea of plurality where the conditions of space and time have no place.

Kant was quite willing to speak of things-in-themselves and so to apply the notion of plurality beyond the phenomenal to the noumenal. Schopenhauer is not willing to do the same. In that, however, he simply presupposes that nothing that holds good of the phenomenal applies to the noumenal. He takes it to follow from that that there is not a plurality of wills; there is just will. He says that will is one, but not in the way that either an object or a concept can be one; it lies 'outside the possibility of plurality' (*WR* I 23, p. 113; *WI* I, p. 146). This is, as will appear, of fundamental importance for many other aspects of Schopenhauer's philosophy. It seems, however, that once again an epistemological point — that it is not easy, to say the least, to see how notions like that of plurality are to be given application outside the domain where the notions of space and time also have application — has been turned into a metaphysical point, that outside the domain of the phenomenal plurality has no place.

If there is no plurality of wills there cannot fundamentally be a distinction between your will and mine. What we are aware of in willing is, Schopenhauer claims, just will. Whereas every representation requires a ground according to the principle of sufficient reason, the will itself is groundless (*WR* I 23, p. 113; *WI* I, p. 146). It constitutes the metaphysical reality that underlies phenomena and is the force that determines that phenomena should have a course. By this Schopenhauer does not mean that the will determines directly *which* representations we have. As far as their course is concerned, those representations occur according to the principle of sufficient reason, due to the intellect. In the phenomena of the will, however, we have the most direct access to the will that the intellect can have, because of their association with the direct awareness of willing itself. Hence we have a kind of insight into the workings of the will through the medium of the intellect — the causes seen from within — which is parallel to what we can see of its workings in nature generally (where if we see causes it is from without). While, however, we are provided with that insight by the phenomena of the will, that will itself is not, and is not seen as, the cause of the course of our representations; it is the force that determines that there shall be a course to phenomena at all.

To the extent that we can see the will at work in our own actions we can see it in nature generally. What we are aware of in relation to our own will is literally the same thing, Schopenhauer thinks, as exists in relation to nature generally, but with respect to our own will we view it from within. Hence, although it is true that the will directly determines simply that we have representations, it indirectly determines through the intellect the kind of form that the representations take; and it is this, the fact that phenomena can be seen as governed by a force which is to be identified with the will, whether it is from within or from without, that reveals the parallelism between ourselves and nature in general. In other words, what Schopenhauer wants us to see is that the will is the metaphysical ground or basis of all phenomena, and that what we become aware of in ourselves as the phenomena of the will, the facts of motivation, is just a sample (though seen from within) of what holds good in nature generally. All of these things provide similar clues as to the nature of the underlying reality which, through the intellect, determines phenomena so that as representations they conform to the principle of sufficient reason. It is doubtful if there is in a strict sense an argument for this. Schopenhauer simply presumes that if we accept the point for one class of phenomena — the phenomena of our own will — we must accept it for phenomena taken generally, if there is no plurality of wills.

He also thinks, however, that once we have this key we shall be able to use it to unlock nature's secrets quite generally. That is the point of *The Will in Nature*, which in many ways merely elaborates things that are said in the main work, in e.g. I 23 and in several of the essays of the second volume that correspond to the second book of the first volume. He thinks that we can speak of the will in nature wherever, as I have already indicated, we are tempted to speak of force (*WR* I 22, p. 111; *WI* I, p. 145). That is most obvious in the case of biological phenomena, where the will to live might be thought most evident. Schopenhauer thinks that it accounts for the phenomena of teleology, wherever that appears, for instinct in animals, and nutrition and reproduction generally — the force towards survival either of the individual or of the species. He also thinks it evident in non-living things, wherever there appears to be the manifestation of a force accor- ding to a strict and immutable law of nature. Gravity, for example, is seen by Schopenhauer in that light.

The book *The Will in Nature* is an attempt to chart that sort of thing in various provinces of knowledge, not all of them obvious ones. Schopenhauer also draws on his very extensive knowledge, even if general knowledge, of both the sciences and other systems of thought, such as those to be found in the East, in order to seek confirmation, or at any rate parallels, for this way of thinking. It is not important for present purposes that we should go into the details of this. It is enough to note again that, once given the general principle, the explanations of particular phenomena in different domains come by recourse to varieties of causation — motivation in creatures which have consciousness, stimuli in animals where that does not apply and in other living things, and causation simply in entities which are non-living.

It is a striking synoptic insight, and once one gets into the frame of mind in which one can begin to see things in Schopen- hauer's way it can make a great deal of sense. To say that is not to say that it is true; it is to say that Schopenhauer presents us with a vision into which a great many things seem to fit once we begin to think in his terms. The key to that vision lies in the details which we have surveyed of the fact of agency and the argument which Schopenhauer takes to rest upon that. It is important in that respect to see that he is not simply setting out analogies between what is the case with agency and what is the case with the rest of nature; what is the case in these instances is really the same. It is not just that there is a similarity to be seen between agency and causation generally; and Schopenhauer is certainly not just saying that our understanding of causation rests upon our experience of agency, as many other philosophers have done. He is saying that we have direct awareness of the will only in agency, but just as our awareness of what we do is an awareness of representations conditioned, as with all representations, by others (in this case by motives), so our awareness of phenomena generally is an awareness of representations conditioned by others (in this case by causes), in accordance with the principle of sufficient reason. What we are aware of in each case is the same, and the governing principles are the same; such differences as there are arise simply from differences in the part played by intellect in the two cases, in relation to the will.

There is an interesting passage in that connection towards the end of section 24 of the first book of the main work (WR I 24, p. 126; WI I, p. 164). There he refers to Spinoza as saying that if a stone thrown and flying through the air had consciousness it would imagine that it was flying of its own will. Schopenhauer agrees but adds that the stone would be right! It is of course a fact that the stone does not have consciousness, and for that reason the relation of will to its action is not the same as its relation to action in conscious beings. Its action is not subject to motives, but only causes. If it were conscious, however, the causality would be available to its consciousness as motivation. It is important to see, therefore, that when Schopenhauer says that motives are causes seen from within he means what he says. In our consciousness of motivation we do have a peculiar insight into the workings of causality. Causality in general would not function without the will, but we are given a peculiar and definite insight into its workings through our awareness of motivation. It is in the area of our own action alone, however, that we have direct, or at any rate relatively direct access to the will itself, and it is only through that, Schopenhauer thinks, that we can have knowledge of the thing-in-itself.

As we have seen the will is blind. Hence while any individual act of a person or conscious animal has a purpose or end, willing as such has no end or purpose; for it can have that only in conjunction with the intellect (WR I 29, p. 165; WI I, p. 215). The intellect, however, is the tool of the will and in some sense its creation, in that the representations that are the intellect's concern must in the end be due to the underlying reality which is the will. Hence when Schopenhauer says that willing in general has no end in view he can also say that the only self-knowledge of the will is representation as a whole, the whole of perception; it is 'its objectivity, its manifestation, its mirror'. What it expresses is simply the will to live, the continuation of existence. That will to live is the only true expression of the world's innermost nature (WR II 28, p. 350; WI III, p. 107); and that too is simply our own innermost being (WR II 28, p. 352; WI III, p. 109).

This will be seen to have large consequences for Schopenhauer's ethics, and we shall return to those later. Much of it, however, turns on the characterization of the will that Schopenhauer gives in his exposition of that notion. The will is absolutely egoistic, he says (WR II 19, p. 215; WI II, p. 429), and thus directly opposed to morality. It is untiring and incessant (WR II 19, pp. 211, 215; WI II, pp. 424, 429), and the intellect is simply the bridle and bit to an unmanageable horse in that respect (WR II 19, p. 213; WI II, p. 426). There is indeed a curious passage in which he gives as an example of this the fact that in doing accounts we make mistakes more frequently to our own advantage than to our disadvantage (WR II 19, p. 218; WI II, p. 433). That, he goes on to say is just one example of the way in which the will promotes self-deception.

In general intellect is a mere tool of the will which is man's inner nature. High intellectual faculties, he says, have always been regarded as a gift and not really the man himself. No one, he adds, takes that view of moral excellences, although they too are inborn. 'Virtue expects its reward in the other world; prudence hopes for it in this; genius neither in this world nor in that; it is its own reward' (WR II 19, pp. 230-1; WI II, p. 449). That also introduces another idea to which we shall have to return, one which Schopenhauer makes much of in the Essay on the Freedom of the Will — that character is inborn, and constant and unchanging; for it too is an aspect of the will. There are qualifications to be made concerning that to which we shall return when we consider Schopenhauer's ethics. However, if we are fundamentally will there must, if that doctrine is to be given any content, be something about us that manifests itself as constant and unchanging in its nature, just as there must be something constant and unchanging about the nature of the world in general.

Or so Schopenhauer says. For it is not clear why the will's relation to phenomena of any kind need be more than formal — making possible the occurrence of phenomena according to principles that are discoverable through the key provided by the principle of sufficient reason in relation to representations. To be content with that, however, would be to revert to a Kantian conception of the thing-in-itself, as a 'something I know not what'. It would therefore be to ignore what Schopenhauer thought of as his great discovery, the identification of the thing-in-itself with the will, something of which we can be directly aware of in ourselves. To know that is at least to know that our nature, and therefore the real nature of things in general, comprises agency or will. It seems to me that the rest, or most of it, that Schopenhauer sees as attributable to that nature is a consequence of the suggestions implicit in his use of the term 'will' to sum up the fact of agency — given of course that nothing is to be attributed to it itself which depends on its connection with the intellect. It is that last fact that gives plausibility to the claim that its only real object or end is its own continuation.

Nevertheless the relation of the will as thing-in-itself to the phenomena which are the function of the intellect remains something of a puzzle, if only for the reason that the intellect itself is, as a function of part of the human or animal organism, in some sense an expression of the will's objectivity. Indeed in one place (WR II 20, p. 245; WI II, p. 468) Schopenhauer says that 'that which in self-consciousness, and thus subjectively, is the intellect, presents itself in the consciousness of other things, and thus objectively, as the brain; and that which is in self-consciousness, and thus subjectively, is the will, presents itself in the consciousness of other things, and thus objectively, as the complete organism' (and he italicizes the passage to emphasize the thesis, which he then goes on to discuss further throughout the chapter). The brain, however, is obviously just one part, even if an extremely important part, of the whole organism. Later (WR II 20, p. 255; WI II, p. 481) he says that the will objectifies itself most immediately in the blood, as that which creates and forms the organism and which maintains it in being. That remark only serves to emphasize the problem why the brain comes about at all. Once it exists, one can see why it is necessary for the continuance in being of the animal or human-being. But why does it come into being at all? Schopenhauer had of course no access to any theory of evolution of the kind that Darwin was to produce, and his physiological thinking is both second-hand and archaic. It is not clear, however, how a theory of evolution of the brain would have helped him in his underlying problem. For what we want to know is why the will takes the forms of objectification that it does at all, not why, given that it has some forms of objectification, it then goes on to have others. I do not think that there is any answer to that question to be found in Schopenhauer's philosophy.

In other respects the relation of the will to phenomena is rather like that of God to phenomena in other systems of thought. Schopenhauer says in one place (*WR* I 26, pp. 137-8; *WI* I, p. 179) that Malebranche was right in his view that every natural cause is in fact an occasional cause; it gives the occasion or opportunity for the objectification of the will in the way that it does. In respect of human action Schopenhauer sometimes speaks of motives influencing the will, or determining, or exciting it (especially perhaps in *FW*, ch. 3). Strictly speaking, however, that cannot be right, except in the sense that motives provide an occasion for the action of the will and so its objectification in a certain way. Schopenhauer often says as much (it is only the phenomena of the will which are thus determined). Once again, however, that leaves certain questions unanswered. If Malebranche is right, are the causes which are the occasion for the will's activity or agency independent altogether of the will? Or rather, is the fact that one thing can be an occasional cause of another just a brute fact, or do we in the end have to put even that down to the underlying reality which is the will? These questions take us back to the issues of the previous paragraph and receive again no answer.

There remains to mention one other topic that Schopenhauer, perhaps rather surprisingly, deals with in connection with the will. That is the notion of matter. In *The Fourfold Root* Schopenhauer explained matter as the perceivability of space and time, i.e. as that which makes occupiers of space and time perceptible (cf. *WR* II 4, pp. 44ff.; *WI* II, pp. 218ff.). It is thus the basis and form of causality itself; it is indeed causality in general and is in its nature activity. It can be thought only as that which makes perception of the spatio-temporal possible, and as such is not subject to causality itself and cannot be an object of perception. The notions of matter and force thus go together. The subsequent realization that what we see as forces acting in nature are really manifestations of the will leads also to the idea that matter (which, Schopenhauer says (*WR* II 23, p. 303; *WI* III, p. 46) Kant rightly reduced to forces) is also a direct manifestation of the will. It is, he says (*WR* II 24, p. 307; *WI* III, p. 51) 'that through which the *will*, which constitutes the inner being of things, enters into perceptibility, becomes evident, *visible*.' There is thus nothing to matter as such except the agency or activity which is responsible for the various causal connections that are evident among phenomena. Since, however, matter is not perceptible, it cannot

6

The Ideas

In section 25 of the first volume of the main work, towards the end of the book with which we were concerned in chapter 5, Schopenhauer suddenly and surprisingly introduces the notion of Platonic Ideas (for which he always uses the German 'Idee', never 'Vorstellung'). He does not do that in any academic way, as if the notion were simply part of the history of ideas. His invocation of Platonic Ideas is an essential part of his scheme. This has surprised most commentators, and the task of understanding what he has to say on the matter is made worse by the difficulty of assessing just what he took Plato to mean by that notion. *That* cannot be taken for granted, for, while Schopenhauer was well read in Plato and ancient commentators on Plato, such as Aristotle, and while he quotes passages that are meant to sum up what he is after, the exact status which the Ideas had for him may remain in doubt.

Did he, for example, really think that there was a separate world of ideal entities, distinct from the world of the senses, as Plato seems to have done? Such a conception fits rather badly with a point of view that is, in origin at least, Kantian (although he does try to argue (*WR* I 31, pp. 170ff.; *WI* I, pp. 220ff.) for a kind of reconciliation between Kant and Plato). Did he, on the other hand, think of the Ideas as Kantian 'ideas of reason', as some later, Kantian interpreters of Plato were inclined to do? What Schopenhauer himself says on the matter does not suggest so, since he speaks of the Kantian misuse of the word, and he quotes with approval a summary of Plato's views by Diogenes Laertius, which says that in Plato's view the Ideas exist in nature as exemplars and that other things are like them and exist as likenesses of them (*WR* I 25, p. 130; *WI* I, p. 169). Hence he appears

103

to regard them as prototypes or ideal patterns, and these he identifies with what he calls grades of objectification of the will.

It may be possible to get some kind of clue to his intentions from something that he says in *The Fourfold Root*. It may be remembered that in dealing with mathematics in that book he refers to what he calls, after Kant, *normal intuitions*, which 'combine the comprehensiveness of concepts with the thorough-going definiteness of individual representations' (*FR* 39, p. 198). These normal intuitions correspond to numbers, each of which constitutes a necessarily unique universal, such that there is no place for exactly similar 2s, only identity.[1] In dealing with this earlier I referred to the fact that he also invokes the Platonic notion of 'mathematicals', but only in connection with figures (shapes), not numbers. The implication is that what holds good with numbers corresponds more to what holds good of the Platonic Ideas themselves, and in a footnote to the passage Schopenhauer says that the Platonic Ideas may perhaps be described as normal intuitions which hold not only for the formal but also the material part of complete representations. He goes on, 'Hence they may be described as complete representations, which, as such, would be determined throughout, and yet, like *concepts*, would at the same time have to do with many things; that is to say as *representatives* of concepts, but ones which would be quite ade-quate to them. . . '. In other words, Schopenhauer is less concerned with the ontological status of the Ideas than with their logical character as representations. Hence, when he says that the grades of the objectification of the will are Ideas in Plato's sense, we are not meant to ask whether in that case they exist in another world or whatever. The real question at issue is their logical status as representations (or, as we might put it, the logical status of their content).

That is how it appears from what he says when he first mentions the grades of the objectification of the will (*WR* I 25, p. 128; *WI* I, p. 166). What makes it necessary to refer to grades is that some phenomena seem to manifest the will more than others. There is, he says, a higher degree of objectification of the will in a plant than in a stone, and a higher degree still in an animal. What he has in mind are the distinctions, now familiar, in his thought between inorganic phenomena, organic phenomena, and conscious beings, and the ways in which causality differs in respect of them. These distinctions, however, are in fact very broad ones, and the number of distinctions possible with respect to the gradations of the will's objectification are, he says, endless (*WR* I 25, p. 128; *WI* I, p. 167). These distinctions are in effect what *The Will in Nature* is concerned with, and Schopenhauer has also much to say about them in sections 27 and 28 of the first book of the main work. What makes it necessary or desirable, in his opinion, to identify these grades with the Platonic Ideas is something else again — a problem concerning the relation of the will to the phenomena in which it is objectified.

The problem is this. The will, being thing-in-itself, and thus not subject to the conditions of space and time, has nothing to do with plurality, and is in that sense one; it is one, however, only in that sense, as something to which the notion of plurality is, as he puts it, foreign. Hence there is an indivisible will on the one hand, and on the other a plurality of things in space and time which constitute its objectification. That plurality, however, can have nothing to do with the will, and in its objectification it is not *divided* among them. The will, he says, reveals itself just as completely and just as much in one oak as in millions even if at a particular grade (*WR* I 25, p. 128; *WI* I, p. 167). In consequence we can get at the inner nature of things by thoroughly investigating one thing. (He also says that it could be asserted that if, *per impossibile*, a single being were totally annihilated, the whole world would be destroyed with it; for the underlying nature of each being is the will. I shall return to that point in chapter 7.) It follows that any particular grade of the will's objectification is expressed in innumerable individuals. Hence, like a concept, it has to do with many things, as the note in *The Fourfold Root* has it. Yet, as a complete representation it must be determined throughout and so must in a sense constitute an individual.

When we speak of a grade of the will's objectification we must therefore have in mind a single prototype to which numberless individuals in space and time only approximate. In Platonic terms, the individuals are always becoming, and never are, while the grades of the will's objectification are fixed and cannot be subject to change. They are to that extent and in that sense Platonic Ideas. The problem in effect arises from the need, in Schopenhauer's thinking, for a link between the indivisible will and the plurality of individuals in space and time, given that they are themselves instances of various grades of the will's being. (The problem, although Schopenhauer does not mention it, is similar to one that confronted Plotinus in his attempt to state the relation between what he calls the One, which is an indivisible unity like Schopenhauer's will, and the particular instances of Forms that exist in the sensible world. How that works out is a complex story; but part of it is that the Forms are supposed to function as mediators.)

The grades of the objectification of the will are thus 'nothing but Plato's Ideas' not in a sense that brings with it any suggestion of a world distinct from this one, but in that our thought calls out for representations having the logical status of Platonic Ideas. They do not really correspond to *species*, for the Aristotelian notion of a species is one of something that is in some sense *in* the world of nature; it is the notion of a natural kind. Schopenhauer's grades of the objectification of the will are not *natural* kinds, for they do not exist in the world of phenomena; they are not representations of that sort. Schopenhauer indeed says (*WR* II 29, p. 365; *WI* III, p. 123) that species are the empirical correlates of the Ideas; species, he adds, are the work of nature, while genera are contributed by man and are mere concepts. Grades of the objectification of the will are not just *kinds* either, if that term suggests something that is merely universal in character and simply instantiated in a number of particulars — a mere class. There remains a gulf between particulars and grades of objectification of the will, just because the will has nothing to do with plurality. The grade of the will's objectivity which is the oak is *the* oak; not the class of oaks, but the prototype oak which no single oak tree in the world may quite match or live up to. It is an ideal entity, something that is both token and type.

Later (*WR* I 26, p. 134; *WI* I, p. 175), Schopenhauer says that a law of nature is the relation of the Idea to the form of its phenomenon, and that also brings out something of what is at stake. Laws of nature state what is the case with *the* heavenly body, *the* falling body, etc., and under ideal conditions. We may say that *a* falling body will fall with a certain acceleration, but we do not just mean by that that any token of that type will fall in that way under ordinary empirical conditions. Nevertheless we are concerned in such a case with something that is subject to the conditions of space, time and causality, which in Schopenhauer's view constitute the form of the phenomenon in question. Hence it is that a law of nature is the relation of the Idea to the form of its phenomenon. The law of causality, as he goes on to say, though obscurely, is 'the norm of the boundary points of those phenomena of different Ideas, according to which space, time and matter are assigned to them'. That account of the matter is far from perspicuous, and Schopenhauer's subsequent discussion does not really help, although he appears to have in mind the way in which causality plays a part in the individuation of phenomena. He has, however, said just before that every universal and original force of nature is in its inner nature an objectification of the will, if only at a low grade, and is thus an eternal Idea in the Platonic sense. The law thus sums up that force in relation to phenomena, and the use of the word 'norm' is significant, associating the law with an ideal state of affairs.

We could take the notion of ideals or prototypes in the sense which Schopenhauer has in mind without much real concern if it were possible to treat them merely as *entia rationis* — as fictions or conceptions introduced for explanatory purposes. They do not, however, seem to be merely that for Schopenhauer, even if the Ideas do constitute a class of representations which we have, and that is what causes the trouble in interpreting his views. The apparently sudden introduction of Platonic Ideas *seems* to bring in a piece of alien ontology — a realm of entities which seem to have little to do with the scheme of things that Schopenhauer has worked with so far. The fact that, as we shall go on to see, Schopenhauer also uses the notion in connection with aesthetics only adds to the sense of mystification; it does not lessen it, even if we can find something in common between aesthetic objects and the ideal entities of science. It is impossible not to think that in this respect Schopenhauer's wide-ranging historical knowledge is merely a hindrance or obstacle to our understanding. The problem originates, however, as I have tried to make clear, from the attempt to relate in thought a single will, in connection with which plurality is not only absent but does not even make sense, to a world consisting of a multiplicity of phenomena. The obvious logical model is the relation of a concept to its instances; but the will is not a concept. Equally the notion of a grade of objectification of the will cannot be interpreted in such a way that its relation to the phenomena in which it is realized is like that of a concept to its instances. As a type it has the kind of generality that a concept has; but it is an individual, an ideal individual, as well. The notion of a Platonic Idea is not far from that.[2]

In effect, therefore, Schopenhauer is saying that if we wish to understand how a single, plurality-less, will is to be related to a world of changing phenomena of various kinds in such a way that those phenomena can be seen as its expression or objectification at some grade or other, we must recognize those representations which he calls, after Plato, Ideas. It is important to see, however, that those Ideas do not constitute another item in his ontology apart from the will and representations. The sub-title of the third book of the main work makes that clear — 'Representations independent of the principle of sufficient reason; Platonic Ideas; the objects of art'. The Ideas are thus representations, i.e. objects for a knowing consciousness, objects for a subject (cf. also *WR* I 32, p. 175; *WI* I, p. 226).

Indeed in *WR* II 29, p. 364 (*WI* III, p. 122) Schopenhauer speaks of Ideas as having sprung from knowledge of mere relations. Both there and elsewhere (e.g. *WR* I 33, p. 177: 38, p. 197; *WI* I, p. 229: I, p. 254) he says that the intellect in its activity in the service of the will, i.e. in carrying out its normal function, really knows only the relations between things. Science differs from ordinary knowledge in this respect only in form, system and completeness. That this is so is in effect a consequence of the fact that knowledge of representations in the ordinary way is subject to the principle of sufficient reason. For such knowledge is conditioned and relates to an object only if given its relations to other objects in accordance with the principle. We know primarily and most directly the relation of objects to the will, in their role as motives; but we know also, though less directly, the relations of one thing to another, and that is the only way in which such things can be known. The implication of the remark that the Ideas spring from a knowledge of mere relations is that as representations they derive from ordinary representations and their conditions, but go beyond them in such a way that those conditions no longer apply.

The claim that the Ideas spring from knowledge of mere relations suggests that our access to them comes only from a kind of abstraction from phenomena and from the conditions under which alone knowledge of phenomena is possible. That indeed is what one might expect of ideals, although it is quite opposed to the kind of epistemological view that Plato himself put forward. Epistemologically, therefore, the Ideas will be secondary to other representations, and since the latter are in a sense secondary in comparison with the direct knowledge that we have of the will, the epistemological status of the Ideas might be said to be even tertiary. Schopenhauer does say (*WR* I 32, p. 175; *WI* I, p. 227) that if perception did not come about through the medium of the body, and if we were not in that way individuals, we should apprehend only Ideas and our world would be a *nunc stans*, i.e. eternal (for the Ideas are eternal, timeless, by contrast with their empirical correlate, species, which are merely sempiternal). That suggests the possibility of Ideas existing and being apprehended without the existence and apprehension of phenomena which the body makes possible. Schopenhauer does however refer to this as an 'impossible presupposition'.

Nevertheless, whatever the origins of our knowledge of Ideas, our actual knowledge of them must go beyond the sum of all relations and beyond the conditions that obtain for knowledge of mere relations. The grades of the objectification of the will which the Ideas comprise are, as Schopenhauer puts it (*WR* I 32, p. 175, *WI* I, p. 227), the most adequate objectivity possible of the will; and he adds that an Idea is indeed the thing-in-itself, only under the form of a representation. There are grades of this simply because the will manifests itself in representation in this way in various degrees. Phenomena are of course a more indirect and less adequate form of objectification of the will, although they reflect the more adequate objectification of the will to be found in the Ideas to the extent that they conform to them. In this way the Ideas function as a mediating link between the will, as thing-in-itself, and phenomena, because they constitute a unity within which there is an implicit plurality and form the model or pattern for countless individuals which, while belonging to the same species, fall short of the ideal which the pattern affords. They remain, as direct objectifications of the will, aspects of the will itself, only under the form of representation. It is because of that that our access to such representations is not subject to the conditions that representations in general must conform to, even if it is dependent on our having such representations in general.

Because of this also Schopenhauer can say (*WR* I 34, p. 179; *WI* I, p. 231) that in knowledge of the Ideas the subject ceases to be merely individual and becomes a '*pure* will-less, painless, time-less *subject of knowledge*'. Schopenhauer's view seems to be, there-fore, that even if knowledge of the Ideas is possible for us only because we are individuals who have representations in the ordinary way, it is possible for us in having that knowledge to free ourselves from our ordinary individuality. In that state, he claims (*WR* I, 34, p. 180; *WI* I, p. 232), the subject becomes object; he is no longer subject to the conditions of ordinary knowledge. Since, however, the object is what it is — an aspect of the will in effect — this means that in this state it is really a case of the will knowing itself. Hence anyone who becomes so lost in contempla-tion of nature that he becomes a purely knowing subject thereby becomes immediately aware that he is as such 'the condition, and so the support, of the world and of all objective existence'. He and the object are both will.

Whatever one thinks of the logical and epistemological status of the Ideas in Schopenhauer's system of thought, his identifica-tion of the Ideas with grades of the will's objectification makes this conclusion almost inevitable, although it is doubtful whether there is an argument in the strict sense for it. There is an obvious problem about how it is possible for someone to free himself or to allow his intellect freedom from the dominance of the will so as to contemplate the Idea without being subject to the usual constraints of the principle of sufficient reason and the forms and conditions that it presupposes. The result — that the subject and object are both will — makes the problem worse, since it now appears that the attaining of that state brings with it the realization that, so far from being free from the will, one is, along with the object, simply an objectification of the will, that one is indeed fundamentally just will. This is, in fact, the first of two paradoxes that Schopenhauer's treatment of the will involves. They both involve forms of the will denying itself. The second comes right at the end of Schopenhauer's argument, in the form of a supposedly permanent denial of the will by the will, through a form of asceticism (not, be it noted, in death, let alone in suicide, which, as we shall see later, Schopenhauer regards, surprisingly enough perhaps, as a form of the will affirming itself).

The contemplation of the Ideas turns out to be a more transitory phenomenon of the same kind, one which is mediated mainly by art. Schopenhauer refers to its connection with the denial of the will by itself at *WR* II 30, p. 369 (*WI* III, p. 129), but it is not in general something that he makes much of. In the main, he describes the knowledge of the Ideas and what that entails as something that occurs only when the intellect is strong enough to free itself from its subjection to the will. That, he says (*WR* II 30, p. 369; *WI* III, p. 129), is something that involves, as it were, the accident (intellect) mastering and abolishing the substance (will). That very metaphor, however, brings out the paradox that is really there. It is impossible to see why the will should make it possible for anything of the kind to happen. Indeed, why is there intellect and phenomena at all? It is of course true that for Schopenhauer the will is blind, so that no rationale for its activities is to be expected, but that consideration hardly helps us with the paradox.[3]

Aesthetic experience

One might think that there was no need for the paradox of the intellect abolishing the will to arise at this stage of Schopenhauer's argument. Whatever one thinks about the need, if that is what it is, to introduce the Ideas, that does not necessarily bring with it a will-less contemplation of them. It is impossible to avoid the conclusion that Schopenhauer had in mind some actual state of mind which might be recognizable by us, and saw it as fitting in this context. So it seems to be. The real importance for him of this kind of contemplation lies in its role in aesthetic experience, where it is exemplified by an interest-free form of apprehension which, in his view, works of art characteristically produce. Since it is interest-free, such a form of apprehension is free also from the demands of the will. Hence it is that the intellect may be supposed to have overcome or abolished the will in this respect.

Art, Schopenhauer claims, is the work of genius (at any rate in its higher forms), and it is the fundamental characteristic of genius (*WR* II 31, p. 379; *WI* III, p. 143) always to see the universal in the particular. It presupposes a greater measure of the power of knowledge than the service of an individual will requires (*WR* II 30, p. 370; *WI* III, p. 130). Thus genius can bring out what is essential in things, eliminating the inessential, by reason of an intellectual concern for those things in themselves. (Women, says Schopenhauer in one of his characteristic damning remarks which spring no doubt from personal factors but are also certainly culture-dependent, may have talent but never genius (*WR* II 31, p. 392; *WI* III, p. 159).) Even less is genius identical with madness, although Schopenhauer thinks that there is a certain empirical connection with it. He attempts to explain that fact by a theory which sees in madness a malady that concerns the memory. The madman is one in whom the thread of memory is broken, so that he fails to see the connection between the present and past events (*WR* I 36, p. 192; *WI* I, p. 249). This totally inadequate theory provides a point of connection with the genius who, according to Schopenhauer, also ignores knowledge of the connection between things, so seeing the individual thing in vivid isolation. Such a view fits well enough with Schopenhauer's general view of art, whatever its general validity.

The aim of the artist is, in Schopenhauer's eyes, to separate the Idea from reality or nature and to omit all disturbing contingencies (*WR* I 37, p. 195; *WI* I, p. 252). All willing, he says (*WR* I 38, p. 196; *WI* I, p. 253), arises from a deficiency and therefore from suffering; a wish fulfilled at once makes way for a new one. (This is a claim of doubtful generality, but is familiar enough in the history of thought.) The aim of the artist should be to produce will-less contemplation of what is essential to an object or objects, and Schopenhauer takes that to be contemplation of a Platonic Idea. A state of mind produced in this way will be one of peace of mind free from all suffering and pain, just because it is free from the will. Schopenhauer praises Dutch still-lives for their embodiment of this ideal in the depiction of insignificant objects (*WR* I 38, p. 197; *WI* I, p. 255), although he adds later (*WR* I 40, p. 207; *WI* I, p. 269) that they spoil things and reduce the work of art to the merely charming when they include depictions

111

of food! For these merely excite the appetite and thus arouse the will, as do nude or semi-nude figures. With food, however, it is all right if this is confined to fruit, since we can view that simply as a product of a plant without reference to its edibility! It may well be that many will find these observations less than encouraging, considered as part of a worked-out theory of art. What he has in mind as the aim of at least the representational arts is, however, clear enough. It is the presentation in visual form of an eternal object, or of what is as near as possible to it, in such a way that we have an apprehension of the corresponding Idea. That, Schopenhauer assumes, must emerge from a tranquil and peaceful mind, so that the viewer, even if he is not free from emotion himself, will take something from the artist, and even see force in the contrast between that peace and his own possibly turbulent state. It is, one might think, a very restricted, not to say passive, view of art.

Schopenhauer takes the visual arts as paradigmatic in this respect. Sight, he says (*WR* I 38, p. 199; *WI* I, p. 258), is the only sense which is in its own functioning 'absolutely incapable of pleasantness or unpleasantness of *sensation* in the organ', and it thus has no direct connection with the will. This explains the aesthetic importance of light and colour, light being, as he says in the same place, 'the correlate and condition of the most perfect kind of perceptual knowledge, the only knowledge that does not in any way affect the will directly.' By contrast, sounds can cause pain and can have a sensuous agreeability of their own, while the objects of the other senses are even more closely connected with the giving of pleasure and pain. Whether or not that is true – and it seems very doubtful as a generalization – Schopenhauer sees in it confirmation of the general thesis that the subjective side of aesthetic pleasure (the objective side having to do with the Ideas as objects of aesthetic contemplation) comprises delight from pure knowledge in perception apart from the will.

Despite his criticisms of Kant in the appendix to the first volume of the main work, and his assertion that Kant based his considerations on aesthetic judgment and less on any personal experience of an aesthetic kind, there is much in all this that Schopenhauer derives from Kant. It is thus no surprise that he goes on from a general consideration of the subjective aspects of aesthetic experience to consider the special place of the sublime in this connection. He sees the experience of the sublime in the contemplation of objects that are as a matter of fact hostile or terrible to the will. The awareness or representation of some feature of nature which is, or may be taken as, threatening to the individual — high mountains, storms, vast deserts — produces, so Schopenhauer claims, a state of exaltation. For, whereas in the case of the merely beautiful the state of contemplation, the pure knowledge, of the Idea is achieved without opposition, in the case of the sublime it is won only after a struggle, by a violent tearing away from the relations of the object to the will which are seen as unfavourable. Moreover, the exaltation has to be maintained, so that there has to be constant recollection of the will — not an individual willing as might be found in fear or desire, but human willing in general ' in so far as it has a general expression in its objectivity, the human body' (*WR* I 39, p. 202; *WI* I, p. 261). Hence for the state of exaltation that the contemplation of the sublime involves there has to be a constant awareness of the object as a threat to the will in human existence without its actually producing the fear or other emotion that it might well produce in a concrete situation.

Schopenhauer takes over from Kant the distinction between the dynamically and mathematically sublime — roughly the distinction between those cases in which the individual is confronted with an awareness of representation of immense forces in nature and those in which he is confronted with a situation in which he is seen as lost in some immensity — but he disagrees with Kant's diagnosis of those cases. He also adds (*WR* I 39, p. 206; *WI* I, p. 267) a section on the ethically sublime, although what he mainly has in mind here is the ethically sublime character — the man who, whatever the misfortunes of his life, looks less at his own fortunes than those of men in general. In this case sublimity seems to lie in the knower rather than in what is known, and it is less than clear that there really is a parallel between it and the aesthetically sublime.

All these considerations have to do with the subjective side of aesthetic experience. It would not be aesthetic experience proper, however, if that was all that there was to it. Schopenhauer thinks that an awareness of the Idea that is brought up by the perception of the aesthetic object is essential to the aesthetic experience itself. Hence in calling an object beautiful and thus an object of aesthetic contemplation we imply two things (*WR* I 41, p. 209; *WI* I, pp. 270-1): there is first the fact that we contemplate it as will-less subjects of knowing (the subjective aspect), and there is second the fact that we recognize the Idea in the object in question (the objective aspect). The latter works somewhat differently for the artist and viewer respectively, since the artist anticipates the beautiful *a priori* while the connoisseur recognizes it *a posteriori* (*WR* I 45, p. 222; *WI* I, p. 287). All knowledge of the beautiful is partly *a priori*, however, though not in the way that applies to knowledge under the principle of sufficient reason, for the *a priori* knowledge in question is that of an Idea. That Idea is in the object in the sense that it is the object's expression, 'its pure meaning, its innermost being, which opens itself up to me and appeals to me' (*WR* I 41, pp. 209-10; *WI* I, p. 271). Hence the particular spatio-temporal position that an object in fact occupies is irrelevant to its standing as an aesthetic object; what *is* relevant is the Idea which is its 'meaning' and which may be identical in different manifestations. This has obvious consequences for an assessment of different art-forms, to the extent that they differ in their dependence on spatio-temporal particularity.

For Schopenhauer it also has the consequence that *anything* can be regarded as beautiful, since everything is the expression of some Idea, of some grade of objectification of the will. He invokes again in this context the case of Dutch still-lives, as the presentation of quite ordinary objects as aesthetic objects. Nevertheless, one thing may be more beautiful than another, according to its ability to call out the purely objective contemplation that is necessary for aesthetic consciousness of it. That may be partly a function of the organization of the object, which enables it to do more to suggest the Idea than other similar objects do. Schopenhauer also maintains, however, that it may be due to the fact that the Idea itself that is suggested constitutes a high grade of the will's objectivity. Thus man is more beautiful than other objects, even if they too have their own characteristic but lower form of beauty. 'Human form and human expression are the most important objects of plastic art, just as human behaviour is the most important object of poetry' (*WR* I 41, p. 210; *WI* I, p. 272). Whether or not that is true, it clearly provides a principle of organization for a discussion of the individual arts, and Schopenhauer duly follows it. It also has the consequence, he thinks, that where the Idea is a low grade of the objectivity of the will the aesthetic experience will have more to do with the enjoyment of the pure, will-less knowing, while in those cases where the Idea is a high grade of the objectivity of the will the enjoyment will have more to do with the Idea contemplated (*WR* I 42, p. 212; *WI* I, pp. 274-5).

It is perhaps worth pointing out, finally, in connection with Schopenhauer's general view of aesthetics, that despite the very obvious debt to Plato that Schopenhauer owes and acknowledges in connection with the notion of the Ideas, his view of art is very different from Plato's. For Plato the artist is twice removed from reality, being concerned with copies of copies of the Ideas (or at least that is the view expressed in *Republic* X). According to Schopenhauer the artist is concerned directly with the Ideas themselves. That, however, does not have quite the same significance that it would have had if Plato had asserted it. For the Ideas are for Schopenhauer still representations and grades of objectification of the will in that sense. With one exception, as we shall see, the artist does not afford a direct contemplation of the reality that the will comprises — simply and at best a contemplation of a grade of the will's objectification. Nevertheless, as I have been at pains to insist several times, it is difficult to think that for Schopenhauer the will was the only reality. The world is representation as well as will, and if the will is nevertheless the underlying reality it remains a profound mystery why it manifests itself as representation. The existence of art, like our own existence as knowers, is part of that mystery. All this makes Schopenhauer's view of art very different from that of Plato, despite the common reference to Ideas. For Schopenhauer, Plato's views on art are simply to be set down as one of the greatest errors of a great man.

The individual arts

At the end of section 42 of the first volume of the main work (*WR* I 42, p. 213; *WI* I, p. 275) Schopenhauer announces his intention of going through the arts one by one. The following sections carry out that intention, but they are organized in terms of Schopenhauer's view of the different grades of Idea that are involved in each case. Hence the order presupposes Schopenhauer's metaphysics. There is a further discussion of some of the arts, following the same order, in the second volume (and it is perhaps interesting that the essay on music, essay 39, is explicitly entitled 'On the metaphysics of music'). There is also a briefer discussion of similar themes in the *Parerga and Paralipomena* (*PP* II 19).

It is perhaps no surprise to find that architecture is treated first as the lowest of the arts. It is concerned, Schopenhauer thinks, with bringing to clearer knowledge Ideas such as those of gravity, cohesion, rigidity and hardness — the properties of stone, what he refers to as 'the dullest visibilities of the will' — although he also brings in the part that light 'which is in many respects their opposite' plays in our consciousness of architecture (*WR* I 43, p. 214; *WI* I, p. 277). The aesthetic material of architecture is, he claims, to be found in the conflict between gravity and rigidity, the aim being, as he puts it, to deprive these indestructible forces of the shortest path to their satisfaction. Thus the beauty of a building is to be found in the evident suitability of each part to the stability of the whole. This Schopenhauer thinks to be best manifested in column and entablature, where the relation between support and load is most obvious (*WR* II 35, p. 411; *WI* III, p. 182), and his ideal architecture is thus to be seen in the architecture of the Greeks. (He admits however that this is less obvious from the inside of a Greek building, where the flat ceiling may seem depressing, in comparison with the interior of a Gothic building (*WR* II 35, p. 418; *WI* III, p. 192). But the exterior of a Gothic building suffers from the opposite failing.) It matters too what the building is built of; for our knowledge of the materials determines our view of the building's suitability for fulfilling the criteria of the balancing of load and support. He thus goes so far as to say that no architectural work, considered as fine art, can be made of timber (*WR* I 43, p. 215; *WI* I, p. 278). It is stone that constitutes the proper material for architecture. (One wonders what he would have made of steel girders and reinforced concrete on the one hand and Norwegian stave churches on the other.)

It is an austere view of architecture, according to which suitability to purpose is all important, and from which all embellishments are to be excluded.[4] Ornamental work, he says, belongs to sculpture rather than to architecture. On the other hand, it is not to be denied that architecture is influenced by considerations of utility also. The purpose which I mentioned above is the purpose of balancing load and support, but buildings are of course put up for various human purposes. Schopenhauer thinks that these have nothing to do with architecture as fine art, although he admits that architecture would scarcely maintain itself merely as a fine art unless it had other uses (*WR* I 43, p. 217; *WI* I, p. 281). It is this which distinguishes it from what he thinks would otherwise be a sister art — the artistic arrangement of water in fountains, lakes etc. — where the governing Ideas are those of gravity and fluidity. Moreover, while regularity and symmetry contribute to architectural beauty they are not indispensable, as is evidenced by ruins which may still be beautiful.

There is also the other factor mentioned earlier — light — in that the visual beauty of a building is affected by the way in which its parts interfere with or reflect light; it follows from this that an aesthetic consideration that is relevant to architecture is the suitability of the building to the predominant light and the climate generally. On that Schopenhauer is sound enough, but his preoccupation with ancient Greek architecture and his antipathy to forms of architecture, such as the Gothic, which have as an aim the concealment of the main properties of the material is clear. Also played down, except perhaps as unfortunate necessities, are the more human aspects of architecture. In dealing with music (*WR* II 39, pp. 453-4; *WI* III, p. 240) Schopenhauer quotes the remark, which he at least attributes to Goethe, that architecture is frozen music, but he says that this applies only to outer form, in e.g. the analogy between rhythm and symmetry. It would be ridiculous, he says, to put 'the most limited and feeble of all the arts' on the same level as that which, as we shall see, he puts at the top of the list.

After architecture, the material of which consists of forms of matter such as stone, the next art to be considered should be concerned with the next grade of the will's objectivity above inorganic matter. It should therefore be concerned with 'vegetable nature' (*WR* I 44, p. 218; *WI* I, p. 282). There is artistic horticulture, but Schopenhauer thinks that the beauty to be found in it is mostly due to nature, and that since nature tends to work against it through the inclemency of the weather the art achieves very little. (There is nevertheless in the second volume (*WR* II 33, p. 404; *WI* III, p. 175) an interesting comparison between English and French gardens, in the former of which art is concealed as much as possible, while in the second, Schopenhauer says, only the will of the possessor is mirrored!) While therefore vegetable nature offers aesthetic enjoyment everywhere without art, it figures as art, Schopenhauer thinks, mainly in the art of landscape painting. Of that he has little to say except that in it the objective side of aesthetic enjoyment tends to balance the subjective. With animal painting and sculpture there is a further increase on the objective side. Schopenhauer sees the depiction of animals as the depiction of a kind of willing uncontrolled by thought, so that we are interested not only in their form but in their action and position. It is difficult to know whether that is true.

It is in art concerned with human form that Schopenhauer sees the highest visual art, since it is concerned with the highest grade of the will's objectification in its most complete form. Once again it is clear that it is Greek art that Schopenhauer sees as the acme as far as sculpture is concerned. In that art, he says (*WR* I 45, p. 225; *WI* I, p. 292), it is beauty and grace that is the main thing, and he clearly thinks that it is form that determines this. Character of mind, which can be represented only by facial expression, is, he says, really the province of painting. In this context Schopenhauer offers in section 46 his solution to the problem discussed by Winckelmann and Lessing, why in the Laocoön group sculpture Laocoön does not cry out. His answer is that shrieking is something the presentation of which lies outside the province of sculpture; his mouth, if open, would be one 'endeavouring vainly to shriek'. Hence the artist has had resort to every other expression of pain, but not that. A voiceless shrieker in stone, he says, would be ridiculous, although it is possible to paint singers or other musicians if this does not involve in the painting too great or violent a movement of the mouth or other part of the body. While all this is clearly consistent with Schopenhauer's general view of sculpture as concerned with form, it seems very questionable.

Schopenhauer goes on to consider historical painting, which he sees, as one would expect, as the attempt to portray the inner meaning of an event. The nominal or outward meaning of a picture, which is added, he says (*WR* I 48, p. 231; *WI* I, p. 299), only as a concept, is quite different from the inner meaning which is one side of the Idea of mankind. The historical event is chosen, or should be, only for its suitability for expressing that eternal aspect of the Idea. In that light Schopenhauer goes on in the next section to elaborate further on differences between Ideas and concepts, maintaining that the latter are 'eternally barren' in art (*WR* I 49, p. 235; *WI* I, pp. 303-4). In the light of this he goes on in the next section again to condemn allegory and symbolism because of their dependence on conceptual understanding, adding only that the situation is quite different in poetry, since there the concept is the material, which is not the case with painting and sculpture. In poetry too, however, the aim remains that of revealing the Ideas.

Poetry can be concerned with Ideas of various grades but is preeminently fitted to reveal the highest grade of Idea — that of man. Schopenhauer thinks that in this respect it compares very favourably with history, of which he has in general a rather slight view, claiming that much of it, and indeed all except what is universal in it, is merely subjective. He does, however, allow history *something* (*WR* II 38, p. 445; *WI* III, pp. 227-8), saying that what reason is to the individual history is to the human race; it is what enables the human race to attain a rational self-consciousness beyond the present. The poet, on the other hand, is concerned to present through concepts and descriptions the Ideas that he has already perceived. While lyric poetry may have something of the subjective about it, the higher and more objective forms of poetry, the romance, the epic and drama, and above all tragedy, have as their main aim the objectification of the Idea of man. In tragedy in particular the antagonism of the will towards itself is most completely expressed at the highest level of objectivity. Thus while Schopenhauer goes along with Aristotle's conception of tragedy as concerned with the universal and history as concerned with the particular, the universal that tragedy presents in his view is the real nature of man as an objectification of the will.

So far, what has been most evident about Schopenhauer's survey of the arts is the extent to which they are presented in such a way as to conform to his metaphysical preconceptions. One might indeed say that they have been made to fit those preconceptions. Schopenhauer's aesthetics is not something pursued for its own sake and in its own right; it is part of the metaphysics. Once given the original conception of art as concerned with the aim of affording contemplation of the Ideas, the details of the particular art forms are considered in such a way as to fit that conception and with that aim alone. Little attempt is made to test the validity of the theory, however many confirming instances are offered. With music, however, which has generally been the test case for aesthetic theories, and a test case on which such theories have often foundered if presented in a quite general form, Schopenhauer has the courage to face up to the fact that it does not fit the conception of art so far presented. For unlike the other forms of art considered up to this point (though perhaps unlike also some styles of art that have been pursued since Schopenhauer's day) music is not characteristically representational.[5] It is certainly not easy to see how it can be thought of as presenting an Idea in the way that may at least seem feasible in the case of the other arts. Indeed Schopenhauer is very critical of composers, such as Haydn in *The Seasons*, who have attempted a representation of nature in music. What then is the aim of music?

Schopenhauer's answer to that question is that music is not, like the other arts, a copy of the Ideas, but is a copy of the will itself. It passes over the Ideas and is thus independent of the phenomenal world altogether, and 'in a way could still exist even if there were no world at all' (WR I 52, p. 257; WI I, p. 333). Indeed there is an analogy between music and the phenomenal world itself, in that they are both, though different, expressions of the same thing — the will (WR I 52, pp. 257-8, 262; WI I, pp. 333, 339-40). For this reason, Schopenhauer thinks that a certain similarity of structure is to be found between music and aspects of the phenomenal world. Music is, he says (WR I 52, p. 262; WI I, p. 339), a universal language 'which stands to the generality of concepts approximately as these stand to particular things'. The suggestion is not altogether clear. Schopenhauer seems to have in mind the idea that aspects of music express in a universal or general form what lies behind the generality that conceptual thinking abstracts from phenomena. He says (WR I 52, p. 263; WI I, p. 340) that the relation could be expressed in the language of the scholastics by saying that concepts are *universalia post rem*, while music yields *universalia ante rem* and reality yields *universalia in re*. In other words, music expresses in universal form the aspects of reality as will which objectifies itself in Ideas.

It is for that reason that we can find in music parallels with various grades of objectification of the will. That is why, Schopenhauer says, music seems to disclose to us the secret meaning of any situation to which it is suited. He adds (*WR* I 52, p. 262; *WI* I, p. 339), 'Moreover, to the man who gives himself up entirely to the impression of a symphony, it is as if he saw all possible events of life and of the world passing by in himself.' There is however no real likeness between the music and those events. There are perhaps similarities between this claim and Mahler's assertion that a symphony must be a world, although there is much in Mahler that I suspect Schopenhauer would not have approved of. The composer of whom Schopenhauer speaks with most approval is Rossini, on the grounds that his music speaks its own language 'so distinctly and purely that it needs no words at all' (*WR* I 52, p. 262; *WI* I, p. 338). This may seem a strange judgment today, although the emphasis on melody in Rossini fits in with the emphasis that Schopenhauer puts, as we shall see, on that. Also, despite the fact that Rossini's music was mainly written for opera, which Schopenhauer despised for its impurity (rightly in my opinion!), it might well be said to speak for itself; it is naive in Schiller's sense. It is reported that Wagner, who was considerably influenced by Schopenhauer's ideas, sent him a copy of the libretto of *The Ring*, and that Schopenhauer received it rather coolly. It is legitimate to wonder what he would have made of the music when it was written. What too of subsequent developments in music? What for example would he have made of Webern, and post-Webernian music?

The parallels that Schopenhauer sees between music and the phenomenal world are reflected in such considerations as that in the ground-bass may be recognized the lowest grades of the will's objectification (*WR* I 52, p. 258; *WI* I, p. 333), and that the higher notes, considered as harmonics, can be regarded as arising from the bass-notes as all the bodies and organizations of nature arise out of 'the mass of the planet'. The intervals of the scale can be regarded as parallel to the definite grades of the will's objectification. Above all, melody reflects 'the reflective life and endeavour of man'. 'It relates the most secret history of the will illuminated by reflection, it portrays every impulse, every effort, every movement of the will, everything which reason brings together under the wide and negative concept of feeling, and which it cannot further take up in its abstractions' (*WR* I 52,

p. 259; *WI* I, p. 335). Or as he says later (*WR* I 52, p. 264; *WI* I, p. 342) parodying Leibniz, 'Music is an unconscious exercise in metaphysics in which the mind does not know that it is philosophizing'. He goes into some considerable detail in setting out these parallels, which may or may not be found convincing. Some of them are certainly relevant only in relation to features of the musical language of Schopenhauer's time, and would have to be modified if subsequent developments in music were to be taken into account. It remains a courageous attempt to fit music into his scheme of things, with the recognition that music is a difficult case for an aesthetic theory. If many aesthetic theories have foundered on this rock, Schopenhauer's theory at least attempts to take it into account. It is the culmination of his treatment of the world as representation. With music we go direct to the will, and it provides a fitting transition to the last stage of Schopenhauer's inquiry.

Before turning to the will, however, it may be useful to look back again at the status of the Ideas in the light of the whole discussion. What science and art might be seen as having in common, if Schopenhauer is right about their aims, is a concern with what essentialists would call 'the essences of natural kinds'. They are not concerned merely with the superficial aspects of the world that the senses immediately tell us about, not with, for example, the many aspects that men present to us, but with *man*. This is the case despite the fact that both art and science must depend on what the senses tell us. Such an essentialism is no doubt Aristotelian in its impulse. The origins of Schopenhauer's way of thinking are, however, Platonic and for that reason he goes beyond what I have just said. But any reason for going further must depend on factors extraneous to the way of thinking about science and art that I have mentioned. For that way of thinking simply appeals to essences which may not be immediately apparent in the flux of phenomena but which science and art may make more obvious to us.

Some things that Schopenhauer says — for example his talk of the Ideas springing from knowledge of mere relations — seem to reflect that way of thinking alone. But he does want to go further, and what he takes to be differences between science and aesthetic experience confirm him in that. Nevertheless, I suggest that the only reason that he has for appealing to Platonic Ideas as such is the necessity of attempting to say something about the relation of the will as thing-in-itself to phenomena, given the supposition that those phenomena reveal grades of something reflecting will. That whole attempt is in fact incoherent. Kant was surely right;

be set down as another piece of evidence for the thesis that the real nature of things is the will. The notion of matter that Schopenhauer employs is, like Locke's 'substance', simply that of whatever is responsible ultimately for the representations that we have. It is thus equivalent to the notion of an underlying reality, and it is no surprise that it comes to be identified with the will.

Schopenhauer's conception of the will presents us, as I said earlier in the chapter, with a striking synoptic insight, whether the argument that leads to its identification with the thing-in-itself is valid or, as it surely must be, invalid. It is clear that once he got the idea he saw signs of its exemplification in many aspects of the world. The world as will has a considerable grandeur. The world as will does not, however, get rid of the world as representation, and although there could be the former without the latter, but not vice versa, it cannot be said that as things are there is just the will. But why things should be as they are, why there is a world as representation at all, remains something of a mystery. It is that same mystery that allows Schopenhauer at the end of the book the idea of an escape from the will in its very denial. The denial of the will through a form of contemplative asceticism that Schopenhauer suggests there is a permanent denial, an escape from the conditions imposed by the will altogether. It is a denial of the will by the will's turning on itself. That paradox is yet to come in my discussion, but in the next book Schopenhauer offers a rather more temporary escape from the will in art, or at any rate in certain forms of it. That is the second aspect of the world as representation.

once given the notion of a thing-in-itself there is no way of spelling out the relation between it and phenomena, and Schopenhauer's claim to find evidence of the nature of the thing-in-itself in phenomena is just illusion. (It should be noted, however, that this is a different matter from the question whether the initial *argument* for the identification of the thing-in-itself is itself valid.)

Once given the attempt to spell out the relation between the thing-in-itself and phenomena there immediately arises the secondary problem how a plurality-less will *can* manifest itself in phenomena. If the idea of grades of objectification seems (and perhaps only seems) to provide a way in which the will can, when objectified, manifest plurality in a countless number of grades, that does not in itself explain the relation of the will to the kind of plurality manifested in phenomena proper; for every grade is exemplified in numerous instances. The Ideas are supposed to fulfil that role; for while they comprise a plurality in that each constitutes a grade of objectification of the will they also contain an implicit plurality in themselves in their applicability to a plurality of instances. They have to do the latter, however, without being merely concepts. Apart from any incoherence in that suggestion, an incoherence that lies at the heart of the notion of a Platonic Idea,[6] the suggestion that the Ideas do in fact succeed in performing a mediating role between the will and phenomena is another illusion. Many philosophers have appealed to intermediate objects to connect two extremes of this kind,[7] but something that is intermediate does not necessarily mediate. That holds goods with Schopenhauer's Ideas also.

It might be said that what I said about science and art three paragraphs ago might allow a Schopenhauerian aesthetics to exist in independence of any reliance on the notion of Platonic Ideas. No doubt something would remain in that event, and many of Schopenhauer's observations on particular aesthetic issues are of interest in themselves. It has to be said, however, that in the main Schopenhauer's aesthetics is dictated by his metaphysics and stands or falls with that. Such must remain the final judgment on it.

7

Ethics

The last book of Schopenhauer's main work is by far the longest. The supplementary essays in the second volume are also long, although not greater in number than those which go with the other books of the first volume. Moreover, Schopenhauer opens the fourth book of the first volume (*WR* I 53, p. 271; *WI* I, p. 349) with the assertion that the last part 'proclaims itself as the most serious'. Yet, with the possible exception of the final paradox of the will's denial of itself, it could for the most part be set down as a natural corollary of what has preceded it; and even the paradox of the self-denial of the will has been met before in its echo — the will's making possible the intellect's freedom from itself in artistic contemplation. Indeed, Schopenhauer repeats near the beginning of the fourth book (*WR* I 53, p. 272: 54, p. 285; *WI* I, p. 350: p. 368) the remark made in his preface that the whole work is simply the 'unfolding of a single thought'. On the other hand, Schopenhauer's concern for the subject-matter of the fourth book — ethics and practical issues generally (for it is under that heading too that the topic of the will's denial of itself is eventually reached) — is revealed not only by the length of the discussion there, but also by the two essays *On the Freedom of the Will* and *On the Basis of Morality*, not to speak of one or two shorter pieces in the *Parerga and Paralipomena*.

Schopenhauer begins with a kind of summary of what is to come, after first tilting at the idea of moral principles and the notion of an 'ought' in general as well as that of an 'unconditioned ought' in particular. (All such Kantian ideas come in for more extended criticism both in the appendix to the first volume of the main work and in the second chapter of *On the Basis of Morality*.) The basis of it all is the will's affirmation of itself, under which,

123

Schopenhauer is careful to point out, death itself must be subsumed since the end of the phenomenon which the individual is by no means entails the end of the thing-in-itself, to which in fact neither the notion of transitoriness nor that of permanence can have any application. Life as *we* know it is willed by the will with knowledge, in that that is how willing manifests itself in us, but it is so willed in any case. Yet it is through knowledge that the affirmation of the will-to-live, that precise form of willing, comes to exist in us. The opposite of that, which Schopenhauer finally comes to — the will's denial of itself — starts similarly from knowledge (*WR* I 54, p. 285; *WI* I, p. 367), though not, he says, an abstract knowledge but a living knowledge. It does that because a knowledge of this kind of the inner nature of the world serves as a 'quieter' of the will, when phenomena no longer function as motives. The details of that, however, come many pages later. Immediately Schopenhauer deals with the notion of 'freedom', since it is a cardinal point of doctrine that when the will denies itself it does so freely. What does that mean and how does it relate to the individual's own supposed freedom of will?

Freedom of the will

Schopenhauer's most extended treatment of the notion of the freedom of the will is to be found in the prize essay which he entered for the competition organized by the Norwegian Scientific Society in 1839 (and which he won, as was not to be the case with *On the Basis of Morality*, submitted to the Royal Danish Academy of Sciences in the following year). The essay *On the Freedom of the Will* was meant to answer the question set — whether it is possible to prove the freedom of the human will from its own self-consciousness. To this Schopenhauer answered by giving a resounding 'No'. There is no such thing as what he called *liberum arbitrium indifferentiae* — an absolutely free will. Schopenhauer carefully analyses what is at stake in that suggestion, and sets against it his own view of necessity as expounded in *The Fourfold Root*, according to which actions are determined by motives. There is, he says (*FW*, pp. 36-7), a relative free will made possible by deliberation, which brings about a relative freedom from an immediate determination to action by those objects perceived as present and as motives for the will. Immediate action, that is to say, may be put off by deliberation. The thoughts that the deliberation produces still function as motives, however, so that there is even here no final freedom from the causal necessity that motives provide. It is at least in part this relative freedom, however,

124

that people confuse with real, absolute freedom.

In a more particular way Schopenhauer tackles the problem in the second chapter of the essay by analysing what is at issue in a manner which is more than reminiscent of the approach adopted later by G.E. Moore, when he suggested that to say that someone could have done otherwise is to say that he would have done otherwise if he had chosen.[1] In a similar way Schopenhauer insists that it is true that 'I can do what I will', but adds that this means only 'If I will this, I can do it' (FW, p. 18). The judgment is thus entirely hypothetical and depends on whether there is in fact any alternative to my willing the thing in question. Moore was similarly to raise the question whether, given the analysis of 'could have done otherwise' in terms of 'would have done otherwise if he had chosen', the person concerned could have so chosen. Schopenhauer insists that it by no means follows from the truth of the proposition that a man can do either of two opposed actions if he wills it that he can in fact will either. The proposition that 'I can do what I will' is, he insists, a tautology and quite irrelevant to the real problem of the freedom of the will. Later, in the next chapter, he is to maintain, within the terms of his own theory as already noted, that the will is always determined by motives, so that there is no such thing as the complete freedom of the will that is generally sought and is supposed to reveal itself in self-consciousness. All that reveals itself is the empty 'I can do what I will'.

Whether that proposition is quite so empty as Schopenhauer supposes is a matter for argument. It does not, it is true, offer the complete and absolute freedom that Schopenhauer encapsulates in the phrase *'liberum arbitrium indifferentiae'*, according to which the will is supposed to be uninfluenced in any direction and in that sense 'indifferent'. That is the position that libertarians or indeterminists in this area of thought demand, but it is far from clear that it is required for any ethical purpose. Schopenhauer himself insists that, if someone protests that he can do this or that or that, it is just as if water spoke to itself saying that it can make waves or rush down a hill or plunge down as a waterfall or rise into the air as a fountain etc., while doing none of these things at the moment (FW, p. 43). In other words, these are all physical possibilities or alternatives, but that is all. The realization of each of these possibilities requires a cause. The same thing is true of a person and in this case which possibility will be realized will depend on which motive is operative. So, Schopenhauer claims, if a man puts a loaded pistol to his head, thinking that he can shoot himself with it, the least important thing in the situation is the pistol as mechanical instrument. The most important thing is whether there is present a motive strong enough to overcome the love of life (*FW*, p. 44).

It does seem true that when we say that we can do this or that or that we do generally mean that these possibilities exist for us, and we can do any one of them if we so will. If someone insists that we have free will does he want more than that? It is clear to Schopenhauer that some people at least do want more than that, and he is surely right in that. It may remain the case that, as Aristotle in effect suggested, the paradigm instance in which we think of someone doing something unwillingly, against his will, and therefore without freedom of will, is that in which alternative possibilities do not exist for him — when, for example, he is being physically propelled. It might be said that even here it could have been the case that he did something else. That, however, is beside the point. The fact that something else could, logically, have been true of him does not entail that it was physically possible to do something else; perhaps he just *could not*, physically, do those other things.

Schopenhauer would insist that the same applies to *any* action once the necessity of its causation is recognized. There is, however causation *and* causation, and it is not clear that being subject to a motive as cause is enough to rule out freedom of choice. To that Schopenhauer would agree, but he would insist that it amounts to a relative freedom only. It is still the freedom of 'I can if I will'. That may be agreed while insisting that it is enough to warrant the attribution of responsibility. In a way, Schopenhauer agrees even to that, but his account of that responsibility merits examination. In effect he claims that to be concerned with that is to be concerned with the *person* and his *character*. A casual examination of what Schopenhauer says on these matters might suggest that he is one of those philosophers who claim that for an act to be free it must emerge or arise from the person's character. This is not really so. In Schopenhauer's view, a person's acts do arise from his character; but to say that is to say that they arise from his nature, and what that nature is, from an empirical point of view, is revealed by what motives he responds to. That in turn is determined in accordance with the principle of sufficient reason. Schopenhauer invokes the scholastic formula *operari sequitur esse* (*FW*, pp. 59, 74, 98), interpreted as saying that everything acts according to its nature. But the nature, the character, that we are concerned with at present is simply that which is revealed empirically in what motives call out what acts, and this implies determinism, the kind of necessity that the

126

principle of sufficient reason entails. It is not at this level therefore that Schopenhauer sees any reconciliation between freedom
and necessity. As the closing words of the essay *On the Freedom
of the Will* indicate, freedom is for Schopenhauer, as it was for
Kant, transcendental.

Before considering that idea we must review at rather greater
length what Schopenhauer has to say about character and its
relations *via* motives with action. I have so far left without
comment the determinism that Schopenhauer sees in the
operation of motives. As he puts it (*FW*, p. 98), a man at all times
does only what he wills, but he does that necessarily. Deliberation, in which lies the relative freedom already referred to, serves
merely to make clearer to us what we will, what *are* the motives
on which we act. In my 'Schopenhauer on action and the will' I
have emphasized the continuity between this doctrine and the
contemporary view that actions may and do have as their cause
some combination of belief and desire, provided that one sees
also the essential part played in it all by agency. That part does
not, however, preclude the view that when we act what we do is
in some way subject to causes, even if it complicates any account
of the level at which such causes operate. I see therefore no reason
for rejecting the idea that even in the realm of action causality
is all-pervasive and all-operative, even if a proper account of the
way in which this relates to action is likely to be complicated —
more complicated than the simple account which declares that we
do what we believe will bring about what we want.

Schopenhauer's acceptance of the doctrine that we always do
what we will, and his treatment of it as a truism, seem to imply
on the face of it that simple view. That is so even when it is
glossed by his acceptance of the fact that we do not always act
on the motive which is immediate; for even in such cases, he
believes, we still act on the strongest motive, even if it requires
thought for it to be apparent to us that this is it. Whether that is
true as a fact of empirical psychology seems very doubtful, and
the same applies to the doctrine that we always do what we will
if, once again, it is treated as a putative empirical fact. If, on the
other hand, it is a truism, that is because of some special meaning
to be attached to 'will', and that will make it not only, as Schopenhauer says, irrelevant to the question of the freedom of the will,
but also not something to be confirmed or falsified by reference
to any facts of human psychology. Although Schopenhauer says
on occasion that it is a tautology, the truth is that its backing is
to be found in his case in his metaphysical theory, as enshrined
in his treatment of the principle of sufficient reason.

Given that, and given the determinism as regards motives that follows from it, a man's character will indeed be evident in what motives he responds to. It does not follow from that alone, however, that he will always respond to motives of the same kind. Schopenhauer's affirmation of the dictum *operari sequitur esse* suggests that he will, and there is indeed a certain plausibility in the view that what a man is will determine how he acts, given that suitable motives present themselves. Cannot people change however? Schopenhauer thinks not — not as far as their empirical character (that character that reveals itself in the response to motives) is concerned. He is quite adamant about that (*FW*, pp. 51ff.: *WR* I 55, pp. 293ff.; *WI* I, pp. 378ff.), and he seeks a kind of empirical confirmation of the principle by reference to examples. Above all, however, he thinks or seems to think that the position in question follows from the necessity, on his view, that human-beings should each have a distinct nature. To suppose the contrary and to accept freedom of the will in that sense would, he says (*FW*, p. 60), be to suppose an existence without an essence. Character is thus, in his view, inborn and constant.

Cannot people change? Only, Schopenhauer thinks, in respect of knowledge, not in respect of will. Thus, repentance, for example, never involves a change of will, only a change of knowledge (*WR* I 55, p. 296; *WI* I, p. 382). I can repent of what I have done, but not of what I have willed. The change of knowledge which this involves (if one *can* so speak of a change of *knowledge*, rather than change of consciousness) is really a clearer insight into what I really will. Many will no doubt think this an inadequate view of the situation; there can be changes of heart, not merely of self-awareness. Once given the notion of an unaltering will, however, no other view is possible for Schopenhauer. He does allow something that he calls 'acquired character' (*WR* I 55, p. 305; *WI* I, p. 393) but he adds that this is really 'the most complete possible knowledge of one's own individuality'. Such a view clearly follows from what he has said about the only alteration possible being in our consciousness or knowledge of our will. The man who has acquired that knowledge of himself will carry out methodically and deliberately 'the unchangeable role' of his own person. He will thus be able to be more consistent in his life, but he cannot alter what he fundamentally is. The acquired character is thus important, Schopenhauer says (*WR* I 55, p. 307; *WI* I, p. 397), 'not so much for ethics proper as for life in the world'.

Schopenhauer sums this up by invoking another Latin tag — *velle non discitur* — taken from Seneca. Most people are ignorant of themselves and their true nature. It is theoretically possible for them to learn what this is and so acquire a kind of self-knowledge. To the extent that someone does this he reveals an acquired character, a greater consistency in following out what he really is. So much he can learn, but he cannot learn to will other than what he does. That is constant. Apart from the evident fact that Schopenhauer was immensely impressed by what he took to be the *fact* that people do not fundamentally change, one may still wonder about the basis for the claim that willing is constant, especially as it reinforces even more the determinism that Schopenhauer sees as holding good with respect to human actions. He appears to think that the basis for the claim lies in the fact that there must be a single nature to a human-being if there is to be a constant response to motives, as implicit in the dictum *operari sequitur esse*. But even if that implies that a human-being must be born with some nature, it may be concluded that that nature remains constant only if the response to motives remains constant. It does not appear, however, that that is a necessary implication of the principle of sufficient reason as applied to motives. It would follow only if, given that something is a motive, it must always be so; but that is the very point at issue. It is not enough, as we have already in effect noticed, that it should be the case that if something is *seen* as a motive it must always be so seen; for Schopenhauer admits that one can be wrong about one's motives and that this is the basis of the idea of an acquired character. Hence for the constancy of the empirical character it must be the case that for any individual what constitutes a motive must always do so. The only other consideration that Schopenhauer has at his disposal is the view that except in the sense in which motives influence the will (and that is really something about the will's objectification) nothing can affect the will itself. Hence no changes can be produced in that.

Does that entail that the will is unchanging? We are in effect concerned here with what Schopenhauer calls the 'intelligible character' (*WR* I 55, p. 289; *WI* I, p. 373: cf. *WR* I 20, p. 106; *WI* I, p. 138), taking the idea and its contrast with that of the empirical character from Kant, as he acknowledges. The intelligible character is, according to Schopenhauer, the will as thing-in-itself 'in so far as it appears in a definite individual in a definite degree', and is to be regarded as 'an act of will outside time'. This is a very difficult idea, since one would have thought that the will as thing-in-itself must be the same wherever it is objectified, except in respect of grade of objectification, and cannot provide a basis for any distinction between *individuals*. We saw in chapter 6 that there was a problem for Schopenhauer in the expression of the relation between the single, indivisible will and the multi-plicity of individuals in which it is objectified, and that the Ideas were introduced as something of a mediating link — each Idea constituting a grade of objectivity of the will to which individuals of the corresponding kind approximate. Schopenhauer invokes the notion of the intelligible character in that same context (*WR* I 28, pp. 155ff.; *WI* I, pp. 203ff.). The problem that he is explicitly concerned with is how to express in his terms the 'fittingness of the organic products of nature' (*WR* I 28, p. 154; *WI* I, p. 201). That is to say in effect that he is concerned with an aspect of teleology. He says that this fittingness may be of two kinds — an internal one in the relation of the parts of the organism to the maintenance of the whole, and an external one in the relation of the organism to the rest of nature in respect of the maintenance of the species or nature in general. As far as concerns the internal fittingness he emphasizes the differences that may exist in the relations that obtain between different grades of the will's objecti-vity, i.e. Ideas, and their phenomena. In the lowest grades the Idea may retain its unity in the phenomenon, while in the higher grades this unity may require in the phenomenon 'a whole series of states and developments in time'.

The problem here is clearly one concerning the relation between the Ideas and their phenomena, just as there was a problem about the relation between the will and its grades of objectification, which the introduction of the Ideas was supposed to solve. The problem now before us seems to be one concerning what we have to look to in a given phenomenon to see it as the expression of a single Idea — given the fact that phenomena of a single type may be variable. Schopenhauer answers that it depends on the type of phenomenon. Those that are the expressions of the lowest grades of objectivity of the will may take a single form which is varied only by accidental factors. By contrast, for something to be seen as the expression of the Idea of a plant there is no such simple consideration; for plants take various forms and have vary-ing histories. Hence we have to look at its total development over time. In the case of animals we have to take into account not only that but the actions in which their empirical character is expressed, although this is the same for the whole species. In the case of man, the empirical character is peculiar to each individual, and the intelligible character which lies behind that empirical character 'coincides with the Idea'.

If we are to take this seriously, it implies that every human-being comprises a distinct type, if he is considered over his whole life-time; he is thus unique even if there are aspects which he shares with other members of the species. While two animals might in principle have the same life-history in its essentials (i.e. ruling out accidental factors), that cannot be the case with human-beings. Schopenhauer seems to think this obviously true, so that the principle of the identity of indiscernibles applies in a pure form here, if nowhere else. Later (*WR* I 28, p. 158; *WI* I, pp. 206-7) he repeats the statement saying that the character of each individual man, to the extent that it is individual, can be regarded as a special Idea 'corresponding to a peculiar act of the will'. (The suggestion has an obvious application to pictures of individuals, given Schopenhauer's view of art, but it does not appear that he makes a great deal of it.)

What this rather opaque discussion seems to come to is the following. If our problem is what we have to look to in a given phenomenon to see it as the expression of a single Idea, we have first to see what gives individuality to a given Idea, what ultimately distinguishes one Idea from another. Schopenhauer views this, in accordance with his view of Ideas as *grades* of objec-tification of the will, as a function of the complexity of organiza-tion of individuals corresponding to each Idea. Such a complexity is itself a function of how it can be thought of as involving parts related to the whole by a relation of fittingness (and also, Schop-enhauer believes, as involving a similar relation to the rest of nature). This is the internal and external fittingness which was mentioned earlier. If we were to try to individuate Ideas according to grade we should therefore have to proceed on these principles. But Schopenhauer believes that those principles would lead to the conclusion that the empirical character of each human-being is such as to correspond to a distinct Idea, and not to the same Idea as that of other human-beings as is the case with animals. The intelligible character of each individual man, which is expressed in phenomena as the empirical character, has therefore the status of an Idea — it is itself individual while corresponding to a complete concept, as one might put it. It is in this sense that the intelligible character, while being will as thing-in-itself 'in so far as it appears in a definite individual in a definite degree', can by itself provide a basis for distinction between individuals.

The question is what justification Schopenhauer has for this view. The answer seems to be 'None'. It is a premise of the argu-ment that individual human-beings are unique, not merely in the sense that they constitute distinct individuals differentiable in space and time, but also in the sense that they have distinct and unique characters in a way that is not true of any other beings. Schopenhauer really offers no justification for that claim, and it is not even very clear what its cash-value is. The claim that each human-being is unique has often been made, but it is hard to give sense to that claim by reference to the supposed fact that each human-being has a distinct character. That each human-being is a distinct and unique act of creation has often been put forward as a theological dogma, it being implied that this is so in a way that does not apply to other things; apart from a theological context it is difficult even to give sense to this. It is perhaps significant that Schopenhauer speaks of the character of each individual as a special Idea 'corresponding to a peculiar act of the will'.

Whatever may be thought about all this, it is in the reference to the will in the form of the intelligible character that Schopenhauer, like Kant, sees in the end the reconciliation between freedom and necessity. For, according to him, the only real freedom, apart from the relative freedom that we find in the consciousness of our ability to reflect on our motives, is a transcendental one, attaching to the will alone. Thus he asserts (*WR* I 55, p. 286; *WI* I, p. 369) that the will as such is free, not being subject, like phenomena, to the principle of sufficient reason. It is free, simply in the sense that 'it is not determined as a consequent through a reason' and so 'knows no necessity' (*WR* I 55, p. 287; *WI* I, p. 369). It is for this reason that he asserts (*FW*, p. 98) that freedom does not lie in the *operari* but in the *esse*. He adds that it is for this reason that the consciousness of self-determination and the like which accompanies our actions, and which makes them *our* actions, is in the end not deceptive. Even if all our actions are necessarily dependent on motives, the ultimate source of our agency is not so dependent, and we are conscious of that implicitly. Freedom is transcendental in that way.

Such freedom, we may think, has nothing to do with the freedom that we presuppose in individuals when we attribute responsibility to them. But, as we have seen, for Schopenhauer, to attribute such responsibility is to say that their actions arise from their character, and that is both unique to them and undetermined by anything else. Hence even if all our actions are necessarily subject to motives, they are somehow expressive of that character. Hence, given the argument about the individuality of the intelligible character and thereby of the empirical character which is its phenomenon, Schopenhauer is not subject to the criticism that the will which is said to be free has nothing much to do with us. It might still be thought, however, that the *sense* in which the will is free is still one that has nothing much to do with *us*. To make reference to that free will is surely to say no more, in connection with us, than that when we do things we *do* things; it is to point once again to the peculiarity of agency. But it is compatible with the claim that when we do things what we do is always subject to motives. That is enough, I think, to warrant attribution of responsibility and therefore of morality. It seems to me largely a matter of taste what one calls it in relation to the idea of the freedom of the will, in the sense in which that idea is generally construed.

The basis of morality

Schopenhauer was the only contestant for the prize offered by the Danish Royal Society of Sciences and was nevertheless refused the prize. When he published the essay along with that on the freedom of the will, he sought to justify himself against the decision of the judges. There is little point in going into the details of the wrangle. There can in fact be little doubt that in most respects the judges were muddled over the import of the question which they had set (the details of which Schopenhauer gives along with his essay and the text of the judges' report), and they were equally muddled in most respects in the reasons that they gave for their decision. (The reason for my qualification 'in most respects' will appear later.) They declared that Schopenhauer had not discussed the connection between metaphysics and ethics except in an appendix, although, as Schopenhauer insisted, it is far from clear that the question set asks for that. No doubt, as they themselves hinted, what they objected to most was the terms in which Schopenhauer discussed the views of other philosophers. He provides in the essay an extensive criticism of Kant's ethics. The criticisms are severe indeed, but Schopenhauer, as I have insisted throughout, had a profound admiration for Kant. The criticisms of Fichte and Hegel are in a different spirit and different style, and the judges no doubt took exception to them.

The criticisms of Kant are detailed. I shall not go into them, although they are predictable for anyone who knows Kant and knows Schopenhauer's general line of thought. The main objection that Schopenhauer has is to the whole attempt to provide an *a priori* basis for ethics. At the conclusion of the chapter on Kant (*BM* 13, p. 130) Schopenhauer asserts categorically that there is no other way to discover the foundations of ethics except the empirical. We must start from those actions to which we do undoubtedly attribute moral worth and attempt to discover the motives that lead men to such actions. It is worth noting how parallel this is to Schopenhauer's attitude to Kant over knowledge. In chapter 3 I pointed out that, by contrast with Kant in

133

an important sense, Schopenhauer starts from the fact of knowledge and asks what makes it possible; he does not think that we
can derive that fact from any superior principle. The same is true
of his attitude to ethics. There is no hope of deriving the fact
that we hold certain things as of moral worth from any superior
principle either. We should ask instead how it is possible that we
should hold such things as of moral worth.

Schopenhauer seems to think, however, that that is not altogether different from asking how it is possible that we should
do those things to which we attach genuine moral worth. Indeed,
in his comments on the judges' decision (*BM*, Preface, p. 6), he
says that the source and basis of morals cannot be different from
that of morality itself (where by 'morals' he seems to mean
'moral philosophy'). It is far from clear why that should be so.
Schopenhauer thinks that the actions to which we must attribute
genuine moral worth are those of 'voluntary justice, pure philanthropy, and real magnanimity'. Is it the case that in showing how
such actions are possible we shall show also how it is possible
that we should attach genuine moral worth to them?

Schopenhauer's strategy in chapter 3 of the essay is to start
from the claim that 'the chief and fundamental motivation in man,
as in animals, is egoism' (*BM* 14, p. 131). It is to be noted that he
does not say that this is the only motivation, but that it is the
chief and most fundamental one. Indeed, he says later on (*BM* 16,
p. 145) that there are three, but only three, fundamental motiva-
tions for human actions — egoism, malice and compassion. It is
compassion that he sees as the only genuine moral motivation, and
it is that which makes possible virtues such as those of justice and
philanthropy (*BM* 17, p. 148). (Characteristically, he adds that
women are less good than men at justice but better at philanthropy!) So the answer to the question how these virtues are
possible is that despite the generally overriding force of the
motivation towards egoism there is as a matter of fact compassion also. As we have already seen, however, Schopenhauer
appears to think that this too is the answer to the question how it
is possible that we should think of these virtues as of genuine
moral worth. That should mean that it is because we have compassion, or rather because there is such a thing, that we see the things
that are derived from it as of genuine moral worth.

Schopenhauer offers (*BM* 16, pp. 141ff.) what he claims as a
proof that compassion is the only true moral motivation. This
'proof' has as one of its premises the statement that egoism and
moral worth exclude each other, and in the previous section
(*BM* 15, p. 140) he has already concluded that the criterion of

moral worth is the absence of all egoistic motivation. That should mean that we think of something as having moral worth only when it goes beyond mere egoism; the next question would then be how going beyond egoism is possible and the answer would be 'Compassion'. But the claim that the criterion of moral worth is the absence of egoism is not, strictly speaking, an answer to the question how it is possible that we should think of virtues such as justice and benevolence as having genuine moral worth, unless this simply amounts to the banal argument: Justice and benevolence exclude egoistic motivation; any action that excludes egoistic motivation, and only such an action, is of genuine moral worth; so justice and benevolence are of genuine moral worth. I call such an argument 'banal' because, although the conclusion does follow from the premises and thus gives us reason for accepting the conclusion if the premises are true, it is not really directed to the question how it is *possible* that we should think the conclusion true. Moreover no reference to compassion directly bears on the question how it is possible that we should think the second premise true. Hence it is less than clear, to say the very least, that what shows moral action to be possible, in showing that justice and benevolence are possible, shows also the possibility of our attributing genuine moral worth to actions of those kinds. Thus, despite Schopenhauer's remarks to the contrary, there may have been some sensitivity to some such point in the judges' rather confused remarks on his essay. The question of the foundation of ethics is not the same as that of the foundation of morality.

When commenting on the judges' remarks in the preface to the essay, after the point already referred to — to the effect that the source and basis of morals cannot be different from that of morality itself — Schopenhauer goes on to say that the source of morality must be the ultimate ground for all good conduct. Later (*BM*, Preface, p. 7) he says that the problem set requires us to look for 'a *real ground of all morality, and therefore of a ground of knowledge of morals*'. It might justly be said that what he himself produces is a source of morality in the sense of how it is possible that such things as justice and benevolence should come to be; but he does not produce a ground of morality if that implies anything about the justification of or reason for such courses of action. Moreover, the only sense in which what he has in fact produced as the ground of morality is also thereby a ground of knowledge of morals is that unless there was sympathy or compassion there would be no action of genuine moral worth (defined as non-egoistic action), and unless there was action of genuine moral worth there would be nothing to be known which would deserve the name of 'knowledge of morals', i.e. ethics.

I have laboured this point because I think it important to be as clear as possible what Schopenhauer's ethics come to. His rejection of Kant is not simply a rejection of Kantian answers to ethical questions; it is also a rejection of Kantian questions in this field. For Schopenhauer, unlike for Kant, the question 'What is *moral* conduct?' is very simple and very simply answered. It is conduct that does not spring from an egoistic motivation. Schopenhauer does face the possible objection that malice does not spring from an egoistic motivation, but he answers by saying simply that actions that arise from malice are morally bad and thus do not have moral *worth*. Actions that arise from egoism are as such neither good nor bad. But there is no attempt in Schopenhauer to explain, let alone justify, the claim that it is a concern for others that is fundamental to morality as we understand it. That this is a fact about morality is simply assumed.

However that may be, Schopenhauer's appeal to sympathy or compassion is not just an appeal to the fact that people, or some people at least, do feel for others. For sympathy, as he sees it, involves a kind of identification on our part with others, so that their interests become in a sense ours. This, he says, is possible only through the kind of *knowledge* that I have of these others; hence that knowledge mediates between the interests of others and what is the fundamental motivation that governs me – egoism. That way of putting it may, however, be misleading, since, strictly speaking, egoism implies a concern for my own interests, my own will, as opposed to those of others, while the effect of sympathy is to remove that contrast with others. For that reason, Schopenhauer can speak of egoism, malice and compassion as motives more or less on a level, such that different people can be influenced by one or other of them to different degrees.

It remains true that compassion or sympathy receives an explanation through identification with others in a way that malice does not. Although Schopenhauer does sometimes connect malice with egoism, he does not explain it entirely in its terms, nor indeed in any other way. Malice and egoism, he says, have in common the fact that those influenced by them are very much conscious of their difference from others, and it is the opposition to that which sets compassion apart from the other two. It does appear, however, that Schopenhauer feels that compassion needs explanation, while the other two do not. If, however, it is egoism alone that is the chief and fundamental motivation, there is something theoretically unsatisfactory in the idea that compassion requires an explanation but malice does not. Behind it all lies, no doubt, the idea that the will is aggressive in its self-affirmation, but that is not enough to account for a malice which is not at bottom concerned with self-interest. There is a lacuna in Schopenhauer's theory at this point.

So far the account of the basis of ethics, whatever this amounts to, has been supposedly empirical. Schopenhauer added an appendix to the essay, attempting to spell out the metaphysical basis for these empirical facts, as he took them to be; but the main account of this kind comes in the main work, with the idea that compassion arises from the insight that we have, although often obscurely, that others differ from ourselves only phenomenally. In reality, he claims, there is no such difference; we are all the thing-in-itself. In the main work, however, all this receives a larger context. The will, he says, is always striving; any obstacle constitutes suffering, and since all striving springs from want or deficiency and dissatisfaction there is suffering as long as there is satisfaction. No such satisfaction is more than temporary; it simply leads to further striving and further suffering. Moreover, as knowledge becomes more distinct and consciousness is enhanced so suffering becomes more apparent and pain increases. All life indeed is suffering (WR I 56, p. 310; WI I, p. 401). Pain is the positive state, satisfaction the negative. Optimism is not only thoughtless, is also a wicked way of thinking since it involves a 'bitter mockery of the unspeakable sufferings of mankind' (WR I 59, p. 326; WI I, p. 420).

Schopenhauer goes into considerable detail and at considerable length in this account of things, emphasizing also the ways in which people attempt to excite the will (one minor example of which, he says, is the practice of card-playing 'which is in a very peculiar way the expression of the wretched side of humanity' (WR I 57, p. 314; WI I, p. 406)). But the will affirms itself even in the phenomenon of suffering. The world is as it is because the will 'is such a will as it is' (WR I 60, p. 331; WI I, p. 427). Hence the will bears the suffering also. That, Schopenhauer claims, is a glimpse of eternal justice — an idea to which we shall return.

Given this background, Schopenhauer can turn to the notions of right and wrong and all that he takes to follow from them. In his view it is the notion of wrong that is the positive idea. Wrong, he says, (WR I 62, pp. 334-5; WI I, pp. 430-1) arises from the overriding of another's will through the self-affirmation of one's own and has its clearest and most complete expression in cannabilism. The sense of wrong arises from the knowledge that the other's will is in reality the same as one's own. The notion of right and that of a right are by contrast negative notions, the latter based, in respect of property, only on the elaboration and adaptation of what one acquires — only on what is made of it through one's own powers — there being being nothing else to the thing that confers a right except the affirmation of the will in respect of it. Once again, however, it is difficult to see where the specifically moral notions come from in all this. It is easy enough to see that the affirmation of one's will in respect of another may lead to doing him harm; it is not clear why, on Schopenhauer's terms, this is to be called 'doing him wrong'.

In the course of his discussion of these matters Schopenhauer sets out five points of the doctrine of right (*WR* I 62, p. 347; *WI* I, pp. 447-8). They are (1) the explanation of the real meaning and origin of the concepts of wrong and right (origins perhaps, but meaning or significance?); (2) the derivation of the right to property; (3) the derivation of the moral validity of contracts (the breaking of a contract being seen as a form of lie, which is itself an extension of one person's will over another); (4) the explanation of the origin and purpose of the State (for which Schopenhauer, like Hobbes, finds the moral basis in the notion of a contract); and (5) the derivation of the right to punish (the purpose of which Schopenhauer sees as deterrence, but only in the context of a law, i.e. when the punishment is inflicted in fulfilment of a law (*WR* I 62, p. 348; *WI* I, p. 448)).[2] This doctrine of right is, he says (*WR* I 62, p. 342; *WI* I, p. 441), concerned with doing, not suffering, and that is what makes it a chapter of morality. The working out of that chapter would 'have as content the exact definition of the limit to which an individual can go in the affirmation of the will already objectified in his own body, without this becoming the denial of that very will in so far as it appears in another individual'. Political science is by contrast concerned with the suffering of wrong, the State not being an institution for promoting morality but for preventing as far as possible the suffering of wrong.

Schopenhauer's theory of morality and the State is indeed very Hobbesian, since it is based on the idea that egoism is the dominant motivation. It is Hobbesian also in the attempt to found morality on self-interest, except for the wider view of the self entailed by Schopenhauer's view of the merely phenomenal nature of distinct wills. Wrong is just a matter of an individual will being overriden by another, and a doctrine of right is simply one concerned with the limits that should be put on that, given that there is in the end and in reality no difference between wills. For Hobbes morality was a matter of 'convenient articles of peace', based on the realization that people were supposed to have, that unbridled egoism simply leads to perpetual war. The realization that Schopenhauer thinks is there is more profound, even if a philosopher such as Hobbes would have thought it mythical; it is, as Schopenhauer puts it (*WR* I 63, p. 353; *WI* I, p. 456), that everyone has all the sufferings of the world as his own. It remains, however, as difficult as it is with Hobbes to see how true morality can be based merely on such considerations, how we can get a moral 'ought' from the 'is' of self-interest, even given the wide concept of the self that is implicit in Schopenhauer's view. His view of morality reduces itself in the end to one based on prudence, but with the important qualification that the removal in reality of all differences between wills provides.

That, however, simply gives rise to the problem why a state of affairs in which the natural affirmation of the will produces suffering should exist at all. Why does the will objectify itself in that way? It is with this problem that the notion of eternal justice is reintroduced. Ordinary justice is a matter of the law and what that entails. Punishment in accordance with it, Schopenhauer insists (*WR* II 47, p. 596; *WI* III, p. 412), is aimed at the deed not the person (the aim, as already indicated, being deterrence). He takes it to follow that the *apparent* suffering involved in the punishment should exceed the actual suffering, but that 'the pledge must be appropriate to the worth of that for which it answers', so that capital punishment is a necessary institution, everyone being justified in demanding as a pledge the life of another in return for or as the guarantee of the security of his own (*WR* II 47, pp. 597-8; *WI* III, p. 413). This concern of temporal justice with the future, as indicated by punishment's supposed role as deterrence, is not possible with eternal justice which 'rules not the State but the world' (*WR* I 63, p. 350; *WI* I, p. 452). In the case of eternal justice the 'punishment must be so joined with the offence that the two are one' (*WR* I 63, p. 351; *WI* I, p. 452). This is a very difficult notion. Schopenhauer appears to want not only to emphasize the point that sufferings are inevitable (they 'are as they are because the will so wills', as he says in the same place) but also to insist that they are in a sense right. 'In all that happens or indeed can happen to each being, justice is always done to it. For it is its will; and as the will is, so is the world' (*WR* I 63, pp. 351-2; *WI* I, pp. 453-4). The last remarks seem to suggest again that what happens in this way is inevitable, but why *right*? (Although it must be remembered that for Schopenhauer right is simply the putting a limit on the infliction of wrong in the context of the self-affirmation of the will.)

Later (*WR* I 63, p. 354; *WI* I, pp. 456-7) Schopenhauer says that the man who has grasped and comprehended eternal justice must see that the difference between the inflicter of suffering and the sufferer himself is only phenomenal. He goes on, 'Deceived by the knowledge bound to its service, the will here does not recognize itself; seeking increased well-being in *one* of its phenomena, it brings about great suffering in *another*'! As a result it 'buries its teeth in its own flesh' and reveals a 'conflict with itself which it bears in its inside'. To say this is to say again that the suffering and the return for suffering is inevitable; it *must* happen with a will concerned with self-affirmation in relation to phenomena such as the world reveals. Why it should be so remains quite unclear. It is of no real help to be told that the will is deceived. Why does that have to be so? There is no real answer to the question in Schopenhauer, except for the appeal to the idea that there is a sort of justice, a natural justice, in it all.

We only have to consider the fate of human-beings, he says (*WR* I 63, p. 352; *WI* I, p. 454), their misery, their wretchedness and death, to see what they are worth, morally considered. The world is in this sense the tribunal of the world. Elsewhere (*WR* II 48, p. 604; *WI* III, p. 421) he says, while admitting that the terms of reference are mythical, that original sin is really our only true sin, and that is constituted by existence itself. For our existence is the result of the will's willing, and that, given our real identity with it, is and must be our sin too. It is a sin because the necessary result of the will's objectification in human form is the doing of wrong — the overriding of the will of others. Hence what Schopenhauer is trying to point out is that it is a *necessary* result of the will's objectification in the form that that takes that suffering occurs. Since it is a *necessary* result, that suffering can be regarded *sub specie aeternitatis* as its own reward, its own punishment — hence eternal justice.

It is given to a few only, Schopenhauer thinks, to see this clearly, but he adds that the doctrine of the transmigration of souls is the same view in a mythical form. Here again, therefore, he sees a profundity in eastern religious thought, which he takes to be the source of the doctrine of the transmigration of souls, with its corollary that suffering inflicted in one life must have its expiation in another (though with the opposite corollary also that there is the possibility of the attainment of Nirvana). There is a splendid passage in the same place (*WR* I 63, p. 356; *WI* I, p. 460) in which he says, having pointed out that Pythagoras and Plato admired the myth, 'We, on the other hand, now send to the Brahmans English clergymen and evangelical linen-weavers, in order out of sympathy to teach them better and to point out to them that they are made from nothing, and that they ought to be glad and thankful for it. But what happens is just as if we were firing a bullet at a rock.' (It is perhaps worth noting that it is from sympathy that this is supposed to be done; it is presumably at once both the result of a kind of perception of our identity with them and also a case of the will's being deceived through imperfect knowledge!)

Whatever one may think of all this as a mythical expression of a philosophical truth known only to a few, it is one thing to see it in the context of the metaphysics as a necessary truth; it is another to see it as *justice*. The inevitable and the necessary are represented in these or similar moral terms in early Greek thought. In Parmenides' poem, for example, it is *Dikē*, avenging justice, who guards the doors to the way of truth, the following of which leads the philosopher to see what is necessarily so. It is perhaps more surprising to find that Schopenhauer is so willing to speak in these terms. It is, however, to go to the other side of the coin, a particularly notable example of his tendency to naturalize moral terms. Wrong just *is* suffering caused by the self-affirmation of one person's will; justice is its inevitable comeback. That, Schopenhauer wants to say, is as true on the cosmic scale as it is on the individual human scale. The only way out of it is the grasp of the metaphysical truth that our differences as individuals are only phenomenal and not real. The ordinary case of compassion involves an obscure and partial realization of that truth.

There are, of course, cases outside human affairs where the will, considered in Schopenhauerian terms, can be regarded or seen as affirming itself against itself as objectified in another phenomenon. Any clash of forces would constitute such a case, let alone conflicts between living organisms unguided by knowledge. Do these constitute injustice, and an injustice which brings along with it its own justice? If these are cases where the will 'does not recognize itself', they cannot, surely, be cases where this happens because the will is 'deceived by the knowledge bound to its service', since these are phenomena which do not involve consciousness or knowledge. It might be argued that these phenomena are nevertheless such that in reality they are all a matter of representation — that from the point of view of transcendental idealism they can all be regarded as phenomena of the human brain — and that it is in its objectification in those representations that the will goes wrong; for it is blind and it is only in its connection with its objectification, the intellect, that both knowledge and error come into question. To emphasize that aspect of things, however, would merely compound the difficulties of interpretation. I have stressed all along that within Schopenhauer's system there is no real explanation why the will should objectify itself in the way that it does; hence there is no explanation why there is even such a thing as the human brain, and for that reason too there is no real explanation why there is consciousness and knowledge. It is just a fact, a brute fact, that it is so.

There is an even greater difficulty in seeing why the will should bring about a set of representations the content of which is inevitable conflict and suffering. Considered at the empirical level, however, the differences between human-beings seem obvious, and if one accepts that egoism is the fundamental motivation (and it often looks like it) suffering seems inevitable too. That will indeed be a cosmic necessity — justice, if you will. One can also understand, without thereby necessarily accepting, the claim that it is imperfect knowledge, the failure to see that we are all really one, that explains why egoism is not transformed into a single affirmation of the will in which there is no conflict, and why compassion is the best that can be achieved towards the insight that that is how it ought to be. That form of explanation is not available, however, for other conflicts within nature which do not involve knowledge or consciousness in whatever is the source of the conflict.

Moreover, we seem here to be up against one of the perennial difficulties that arise in connection with the 'problem of pain' — why does pain exist? Schopenhauer's answer to that question is somewhat different from that which is sometimes given in theological contexts — that pain is the inevitable result of our free-will. In the first place there is for Schopenhauer no such thing as free-will in that sense. Secondly, within the context of his metaphysical theory the question 'Why is there suffering?' cannot be answered simply by reference to the supposed fact that suffering is caused by one person affirming his will against that of another with imperfect consciousness of what that involves. There are other sufferings that are caused by other aspects of nature's workings. In the end Schopenhauer can offer no explanation of that; it just is so. To say that the will is blind says no more than that.

Virtue

I said earlier that Schopenhauer's conception of morality as such was very simple. In a sense he agrees with Kant in thinking that to be moral is to have a good will, but that, for Schopenhauer, means abstaining from egoism because of a compassion for others (this having as its rationale the real identity that exists between ourselves and others). It is perhaps of interest that in discussing ethics so far Schopenhauer has moved from an attempt to set out both the empirical and the metaphysical explanation of the possibility of concern for others, via a consideration of the doctrine of right, to the conception of eternal justice. It is only after that that the subject of virtue and goodness is considered. Right and justice, one might say, precede, in order of explanation, virtue and the good. That is understandable in view of Schopenhauer's view of human-beings and of egoism as the fundamental motivation. For it is egoism that leads to suffering and to the need to prevent it as far as possible by means of the institutions of justice. Goodness as such must on that account be a rarer phenomenon.

If that is a pessimistic view of human-beings, it fits in with what must have been Schopenhauer's natural tendency to pessimism (something that has often been seen as the key to his philosophy — though it cannot be its rational basis). It also fits in with the apparently rationally based thesis that egoism, the self-affirmation of the will, is the fundamental motivation.

Schopenhauer moves to the doctrine of virtue and the good via a brief consideration of two phenomena which he thinks reveal a consciousness of eternal justice, if only as an obscure feeling. They are the phenomena of (a) the desire for revenge, and, more particularly, the satisfaction that retribution of that kind may produce in others, even those not directly concerned, and (b) the self-sacrifice, even to the point of the sacrifice of one's own life, that a man may sometimes, though rarely, engage in to put right an outrage (something that Schopenhauer thinks is especially to be found among Spaniards). The latter arises from a deep consciousness that the person in question has that he himself is the whole will to live; he wants the outrage never to occur again because he wants to keep the Idea of man pure. What is common to these two phenomena is the fact that what is carried out is in a sense a form of punishment, although one that lies quite outside the province of ordinary punishment, since it has nothing to do with the law and the institution of the State. Moreover, the satisfaction that the onlooker gains in the first case and the self-sacrifice that occurs in the second have nothing to do with any egoistic motivation; nor on the other hand do they have to do with compassion, let alone malice. They involve, Schopenhauer thinks, a sense of eternal justice.

The ordinary man is not like that. What then does ordinary goodness consist in? What, in other words, is virtue? Schopenhauer tries to answer these questions via a consideration of the meanings of 'good' and 'bad' themselves (*WR* I 65, p. 359; *WI* I, p. 464). It is perhaps no surprise to find him seeking certain parallels between *good, beautiful* and *true*. It will be remembered that in *The Fourfold Root* Schopenhauer explained truth as the reference or relation of a judgment to its reason or ground. Hence, on this account the concept of truth is an essentially relational one; or at any rate if one says of a judgment that it is true (without further qualification) that second-order judgment and the concept that it invokes will be relative only. There cannot be any such thing as absolute truth. In a way, the same sort of thing holds good, on Schopenhauer's view, of the beautiful. In that respect Schopenhauer refers for confirmation (*WR* I 65, p. 360; *WI* I, p. 465) to the whole of his third book. I do not know that there is any statement there that explicitly says that the concept of the beautiful is relational or relative. That is nevertheless implicitly his view, since the beauty of anything is constituted by its fitness to express the corresponding Idea, so that the object can be said to be beautiful only in relation to that. Analogously Schopenhauer now says that the concept of *good* is essentially relative, denoting the *'appropriateness of an object to any definite effort of the will'*. We call something good, that is, to the extent that it is agreeable to our will, and bad if it is not. One thing may be in that sense good for me but bad for you, and that indeed, Schopenhauer thinks, is the only sense that the words have. Absolute good, he says a little later, is a contradiction, since *good* is always relative in this way. It is not so much that if someone calls something good he means that the thing in question is agreeable merely to *his* will; but if something is good it is always good to or for someone, some will.

In the case of none of these terms is Schopenhauer very alive to the question whether what he says about them constitutes their meaning or merely the criteria for calling something true, beautiful or good. He *says* that he is concerned with their meaning, but it is not evident that he is conscious of the distinctions that a more sophisticated view of the matter would involve. What he says seems to suggest, however, a naturalistic theory about the meaning of 'good' of the kind that relates the thing called 'good' to human wants; only, in his case, there is always behind it all the idea that individual wants are merely phenomenal and that there is a single will there in reality. What however follows from all this about what constitutes the good man? In fact one gets from Schopenhauer no recipe for virtue. He rejects, as he has done elsewhere, any suggestion that he should lay down moral precepts or principles as others have done, saying 'I have no 'ought' or law to hold before the eternally free will' (*WR* I 66, p. 374; *WI* I, p. 483). All he can do is to lay before people the theoretical truth which is expressed in the *Veda* : *Tat tvam asi* ('This art thou'); or, in other words, the doctrine of the single underlying will.

The good man will be one who, sensitive to that knowledge, makes himself agreeable to the wills of others simply because he makes less of a distinction than is usual between himself and others. Hence, Schopenhauer says (*WR* I 66, p. 374; *WI* I, p. 483), he 'lives in a world of friendly phenomena; the good of any of these is the same as his own good'. The bad man by contrast pursues simply what he himself wants, seeing no relation between those wants and what others will. Somewhere in between there is the just man who never, in affirming his own will, goes to the length of denying the will of others; hence he respects rights and the like irrespective of whether there are any sanctions imposed by the State or any other authorities of that kind. Up to a point he recognizes his own will in that of another, since he will never harm that other. His position is, however, negative by comparison with the man of virtue, in that only the latter so recognizes his real identity with others as to have a positive attitude towards them. That attitude is that of love, but 'all love (ἀγάπη, *caritas*) is compassion' — to invoke the words with which Schopenhauer concludes this section, claiming that they are paradoxical but true (*WR* I 66, p. 374; *WI* I, p. 484).

It is not altogether clear why Schopenhauer sees those words as so paradoxical, although they are that in the wider context which presents compassion as a form of identification with others; for the force of that, as I have suggested before, is to link compassion with an enlarged form of egoism. Schopenhauer uses the dictum as the first step in setting out the last stage of his ethics as he sees it — that in which the requisites for salvation are set out. Before turning to that, however, we must attend to one or two other elements in his account of virtue. Schopenhauer describes in glowing colours the lot of the bad man, but it is entirely what we should expect from the identification of badness with an affirmation of the will regardless of others and the suffering that this brings in its turn. Schopenhauer rejects the idea that has often been put forward by moralists and moral philosophers — the coincidence between virtue and happiness — if that latter notion has anything to do with the satisfaction of the will to live, with well-being in that sense. The bad man, who seeks the satisfaction of his own will alone, is not only subject to the miseries and sufferings that arise from intense willing itself — the want that

such willing stems from, the lack of real and permanent satisfaction, and so on; he is also subject to bad conscience, the pain of
which is due to (a) 'the merely felt knowledge of the merely
phenomenal character and nothingness of the forms of representation that separate individuals' and (b) 'the self-knowledge of one's
own will and its degree' (WR I 65, p. 366; WI I, p. 473). One
might think that a very loaded account of what conscience comes
to, and one might also think that the claim that the bad man is
inevitably subject to a bad conscience requires further justification. By contrast, Schopenhauer suggests, the good conscience of
the good man arises from the same recognition, now more explicit,
of 'our own being-in-itself, even in an alien phenomenon' (WR I
66, p. 373; WI I, p. 482). It produces a state in which 'the heart
feels itself enlarged, not contracted as with egoism'. As a result the
knowledge that the good man has gives him a certain serenity,
even though his knowledge of the lot of human-beings generally
cannot make his disposition a cheerful one.

To be good is therefore to be loving; to be loving is to be
compassionate; to be compassionate is to see the identity of one's
own real self with that of others. To see *that* one needs to pierce
the veil of Mâyâ and recognize in truth the single will as the
thing-in-itself underlying the multiplicity of phenomena. In
the light of this highly theory-laden account of virtue it is no
surprise to find Schopenhauer rejecting moral dogmas and the
like. He admits that they can influence *conduct*, by providing
motives for the will; but they do not influence, not can they
influence, the moral disposition itself that virtue consists in.
'Willing cannot be taught' (*Velle non discitur*) is the slogan that
Schopenhauer invokes yet again in this context. Virtue is
dependent on knowledge, but not a knowledge of principles or
dogmas.

The question remains whether a virtuous disposition is something that can be acquired, and whether in particular anyone can,
by listening to Schopenhauer, acquire a virtue that he does not
already have. Schopenhauer's views about the constancy of
character suggest that he cannot. Once again '*Velle non discitur*'.
Schopenhauer explicitly says (WR I 66, p. 370; WI I, p. 478)
that the theoretical account that a philosopher provides gives
only the concept of the knowledge in question; it finds its expression in words, not deeds. In other words, philosophy provides
only a theoretical account of what the knowledge consists in;
it cannot provide the knowledge itself. It must, he says, *dawn*
on each of us, and that, as he says later (WR I 70, p. 404; WI I,
p. 523), is what the Church calls *an effect of grace*. It depends, in

other words, on how the will turns. It is not perhaps a comforting doctrine.

Salvation

Schopenhauer's ethics, one might think, is too metaphysical. It says little enough about moral reasoning and the application of that to conduct. It depends on what is after all a rather simple-minded dichotomy between self-regarding and other-regarding attitudes, between egoism and compassion. It says very little about malice, or about particular virtues and vices. The doubts that I expressed earlier about Schopenhauer's claim that the basis of ethics must be the same as the basis of morality itself seem in the end well-founded. What he seems to be concerned with throughout even in the metaphysical context, is the question how morality is possible. Given the assumption that being moral consists fundamentally in being non-egoistic, the problem becomes simply how *that* is possible. Schopenhauer's solution comes through an appeal to the knowledge that he claims to be the foundation of compassion. It might rightly be said that there is more to ethics than that. In contemporary ethical discussions, for example, there tends to be argument between those who favour utilitarianism and those who favour a more Kantian approach. Schopenhauer has next to nothing to contribute to such a debate.

The last part of the main Schopenhauerian argument, with its emphasis on a form of salvation, might be thought to have more to do with religion. Schopenhauer does indeed invoke religious parallels to his thesis, particularly Buddhism. Nevertheless, he regards his thesis as a strictly metaphysical one. Schopenhauer had a comparatively low opinion of religion as such, despite what he saw as the influential character of religious ideas. In a sense he thought of religion as a poor man's metaphysics (*WR* II 17, p. 164; *WI* II, p. 365: cf. the dialogue in the essay on religion in *PP* II 15, pp. 324ff.). While therefore he speaks of salvation — the penultimate essay in the second volume of the main work is entitled 'The Road to Salvation' ('Die Heilsordnung') — it is not a salvation of a religious kind nor one, strictly speaking, to be attained by anything corresponding to a religious practice. The denial of the will to live which lies at the root of this salvation comes, he says (*WR* I 68, p. 378; *WI* I, p. 488), from the same source as 'all goodness, love, virtue and magnanimity'. The transition to the discussion of the denial of the will comes via a further elaboration of the dictum that ends section 66 of the first volume

(WR I 66, p. 374; WI I, p. 484) — 'All love (ἀγάπη, caritas) is compassion'. Whatever paradox there may be in that dictum is said to be removed by making the familiar distinction between *eros* and *agapē*; the former amounts to selfishness and it is only the supposedly legitimate identification of love with *eros* that produces the belief that there cannot be the compassionate form of love which is *agapē*. It is perhaps difficult to see why this needed so much emphasis; the phenomena of love are notoriously manifold.[3] As if to accentuate that point there is in the same chapter a curious account of weeping, which Schopenhauer sees as sympathy with ourselves (WR I 67, p. 377; WI I, p. 486: cf. WR II 47, p. 592; WI III, p. 406).

However that may be, for an assessment of Schopenhauer's 'road to salvation' we have to start from the compassion which is for him the source of virtue and goodness. That compassion is, as we have already seen, based, according to Schopenhauer, on an insight into the real unity of things in the will as thing-in-itself. It involves what he calls (WR I 68, p. 378; WI I, p. 488) 'the penetration [or 'seeing-through'] of the *principium individuationis*', so abolishing the distinction between our individuality and that of others. Schopenhauer goes on to say that when this direct knowledge of the one will that manifests itself in different phenomena is present in a high degree of distinctness, such a man will take upon himself the pain of the whole world. 'Everything lies equally near to him'. In this state the knowledge becomes the 'quieter' of all willing. 'The will now turns away from life; it shudders at the pleasures in which it recognizes the affirmation of life' (WR I 68, p. 379; WI I, pp. 489-90). There is thereby reached the state of 'voluntary renunciation, resignation, true calm, and complete will-lessness'.

Schopenhauer says that the phenomenon by which this becomes manifest is the transition from virtue to asceticism (WR I 68, p. 380; WI I, p. 490). The point is that while in ordinary virtue there is a perception, however obscure, of the real unity of things, the virtuous man is still controlled by the ordinary circumstances of life and there is, because of the will to live and the way that this works itself out in the body, a continual temptation to fall back into the natural, egoistic ways. Asceticism, involving chastity, fasting, and a general denial of the body's needs to the extent that they involve a definite expression of the will, entails going beyond anything that virtue can attain. It involves a renunciation of one's true nature and therefore a denial of the will itself. Such a man, Schopenhauer thinks, will eventually cease to will at all. If death comes through such a way of life, it will not merely be the case, as with ordinary forms of death (which I shall discuss further in the next chapter), that the phenomenon of the will comes to an end; it will not merely be the case, that is, that the world as representation ceases for the person concerned, leaving the will itself still in existence. In the case of the ascetic, governed by knowledge of the true reality and unity of things, the phenomenon has already been weakened by the withdrawal from life and what that entails. Hence in this case 'this last weak bond also is now broken; for him who so ends the world has ended at the same time' (WR I 68, p. 382; WI I, p. 494).

This whole doctrine is an exceptionally difficult one, but nothing perhaps is more difficult than the last suggestion that for the man who has achieved salvation in this way the world ends in a way that is different from that which is involved in ordinary death. In the case of the latter Schopenhauer's view is clear in at least one respect. Death is the ceasing to exist of the phenomenon; it is the end of consciousness, of knowledge, and of all that that entails. Hence the will can no longer have expression or objectification in the life of that human individual. The will does not thereby cease to exist itself, nor does its expression; there are other forms of objectification among phenomena. Since the real nature of the individual was really identical with that will, there is a sense in which, although the individual identified in terms of phenomena ceases to exist, as will he does not; although there would in that case be nothing to identify him as *him*. But Schopenhauer seems to suggest that when salvation is achieved not even that is true. The will literally denies itself and there remains literally *nothing*.

I shall have more to say about ordinary death and its connection with time in the next chapter; what I have said so far is meant merely to provide a background to a possible understanding of this special event — the denial of the will by itself. I say 'possible understanding', since it is far from clear what actual or real understanding of it is available. Schopenhauer provides a rich survey of religious and mystical beliefs that connect salvation with forms of asceticism and see that salvation in a form of nothingness. It is of course the Buddhist conception of Nirvana which provides the most obvious parallel, and Schopenhauer contrasts Buddhism to some extent with Brahmanism, suggesting that the former's asceticism does not, as the latter's does, involve extreme and unnecessary self-mortification. He also emphasizes parallels between these eastern forms of thought and practice and those aspects of Christianity which appeal to mysticism and asceticism — quietism in particular — criticizing Protestantism for its rejection of these things. He sees, however, a difference between the philosopher and the mystic, in that the latter, as he puts it, 'begins from within, while the philosopher begins from without' (*WR* II 48, p. 611; *WI* III, p. 430). The philosopher's approach, that is, is necessarily theoretical, arriving at his conclusion from a theoretical account of the world, while the mystic's approach is intuitive, starting from inner, but inexpressible, feeling or experience. His words, such as they are, have to be taken on trust and asceticism is simply the method of arriving at the goal.

For Schopenhauer, asceticism is not quite that; for the denial of the will, which is the goal, comes also through *knowledge*. It is the knowledge of the real nature of things in the definite form that involves a penetration of the *principium individuationis* that provides the road to salvation. That is why it is a more permanent form of the same thing that is evident, on Schopenhauer's view, in artistic contemplation. Asceticism is simply the way in which that knowledge as a quieter of the will becomes manifest. There is even, according to him, a second-best way of achieving the same end (and he uses in that connection the Platonic phrase *'deuteros plous'* – the second-best way of voyaging that Socrates mentions in the *Phaedo*). This is suffering itself. The will is broken by extreme suffering, and the man concerned is purified by it, undergoing a change and rising above himself. This, Schopenhauer suggests (*WR* I 68, p. 392; *WI* I, pp. 506-7), may indeed be the most common way in which men achieve salvation, and one that may take place only at the approach of death itself.

This salvation is evident in a form of peace and tranquillity in which a denial of the will is recognizable, however it comes about. In order for it to come about, however, it is not enough that one should have simply a general knowledge of the metaphysical nature of things, not even that form of knowledge of it that is involved in virtue. For in that state the person concerned is still subject to the demands of the will, particularly in respect of his own body; and it is that which needs to be stilled. That is why the real knowledge of the unity of things, and the true acceptance of the sufferings of the world as one's own, must, if it is to have the upper hand, involve the quieting of the demands of the body; so it must involve either asceticism or, as a second-best, purification through suffering. It is nevertheless knowledge that lies at the heart of it, in Schopenhauer's view. The will itself cannot be abolished by anything else except knowledge (*WR* I 69, p. 400; *WI* I, pp. 517-8). Yet it is only as a result of this combined with asceticism (or perhaps again purification through suffering) that the will ceases to exist in a given individual. Suicide, as I shall indicate in the next chapter, does not involve that and is in fact a form of the affirmation of the will, not a putting an end to it. It follows that if there are instances where, as it appears, the will does deny itself, then since the will is all that the underlying reality consists in, the result can only be that nothing to which I have already made reference — at any rate if the notion of the denial of the will is to be taken literally.

That suggestion is perhaps not particularly difficult to understand, at any rate in the formal sense; the rejection of the underlying reality by itself could only result in nothing. The major difficulty — the one that I mentioned earlier — is how we are to understand the words 'for him who so ends the world has ended at the same time' in a sense that marks off ascetic death from ordinary death. Once again perhaps there is no insuperable difficulty if we restrict ourselves to a formal understanding. The difference lies in the following. Since I am identical with the single underlying will, in ordinary death when I die I go on in the same way as I really am now — as that will — but without the phenomena which now go with me; hence ordinary death is simply the ceasing to exist of one set of phenomena — those that, as things are, go with me now. By contrast, in ascetic death nothing goes on that has any real connection with me. Those words do not, however, mark any difference in the phenomena from the point of view of the person concerned; the phenomena cease to exist for him in both cases. Nor of course do they mark a difference in how it must seem to others. What is left by way of phenomena is for them the same in both cases — the corpse.

What then does Schopenhauer mean, apart from these considerations, in saying that *for him* who so ends the world has ended at the same time, since in both cases the world ceases for the individual concerned, even if there is a sense in which we might see it as intelligible that there is something left for the *will* (if one may speak in that temporal way) only in ordinary death? The answer must surely be that there cannot be anything that he can mean *apart from the considerations that I have mentioned* — except perhaps this, that the person who faces an ascetic death has the intellectual assurance, if Schopenhauer is right, that when phenomena cease for him, then even though the body (a form of objectification of the will although a lowly one) remains, there is no possibility of the will objectifying itself yet again in any way that has anything to do with him. But does that possibility exist any way? There seems to be an insoluble mystery in all this.

It might be suggested[4] that in ascetic death there results an absolute nothingness (for everyone and not just for the person concerned). This however is not apparently what Schopenhauer says. It may also be remembered that in expounding the notion of the Ideas (*WR* I 25, pp. 128-9; *WI* I, p. 167) Schopenhauer said that if a single being were annihilated the whole world would be annihilated with it. Does that confirm the suggestion that Schopenhauer means that if through the denial of the will one person ceases to exist the whole world will cease to exist as well. I do not think so, for he says of the suggestion that one being might be annihilated that it is an impossible suggestion. The denial of the will is not an abolition of the will in an absolute sense, only its abolition as far as that human-being is concerned. Hence the same must apply to the nothingness — it is so for that human-being.

Given all this it is also obscure why this kind of ending should be thought of as a form of salvation. In any obvious sense death is the end for an individual any way, and whether or not that is seen as a blessing (a question to which different thinkers have reacted differently) it is at any rate the end of suffering in this life. It is easy enough to see why some people should want more — a new life free from suffering — even if that is an illusion. But why want less, and what indeed could count as less for an individual than one's non-existence as the individual one is? It is of course much more obvious why the prelude to ascetic death, if Schopenhauer is right, should be seen as a form of salvation. For this is marked by 'true calm, and complete will-lessness'; it involves freedom from striving and in that way freedom from suffering. One might indeed think that the goal that Schopenhauer offers us of a tranquillity to be got through knowledge is enough in itself. What he offers in that respect is akin to the *ataraxia*, the freedom from fear and stress, that most of the post-Aristotelian schools in Greece, e.g. the Stoics and Sceptics, offered. For they thought that the philosopher who accepted whole-heartedly the truths that they thought were the real truths would attain such a state of *ataraxia*. While Schopenhauer offers that at least, he also offers more — nothingness — and it is the problem how that differs, as far as the individual is concerned, from ordinary death that seems insoluble. It is not really a salvation if it does not so differ.

There is a second way in which it is difficult to see all this as a form of salvation, but in this respect Schopenhauer faces up to the problem directly, whatever we think of his solution. This is that if all this is the result of the will's denial of itself, and is mediated through knowledge, it does not appear that there is anything that we as individuals can do about getting the salvation in question. In the first place, whether the will denies itself is not a function of our individual intentions; we cannot set out to produce that result, or at any rate not with any surety of success. In that respect it is like self-deception; we may perhaps set out to bring about the state of affairs of our being deceived on some matter, but if we do there is nothing that we can do that will guarantee success. One might indeed say that if we do succeed it will be because of factors that lie outside our control — by an act of grace, so to speak. So it is with the denial of the will.

This consideration is reinforced by the fact that for Schopenhauer the will's denial of itself is mediated by knowledge. What counts as having that knowledge? Did Schopenhauer himself have it, one might wonder? It is clearly not any old knowledge that is relevant here; it must be a form of knowledge that involves acceptance. The will is stilled by a form of knowledge that involves, to put it at its lowest, seeing the folly of individual striving and the suffering that it produces. It thus involves accepting everything simply as an aspect of oneself, and oneself as nothing separate from everything else. It is possible to see on occasion why this seeing of things in this way *sub specie aeternitatis* might result in a simple acceptance of it all and thus a comparative freedom from fear, striving and the pain that results from it. (It is perhaps less easy to see why the same outcome should be expected in relation to acute and unwished for physical pain, although even here it is not perhaps beyond the bounds of possibility.) This is perhaps something the attainment of which we might admire, even if it does nothing for the unwished for suffering of others. On Schopenhauerian terms, however, it is again something that we cannot *do* anything about achieving.

That is so because what we do is governed by motives; there is no real freedom at our disposal. We can, as we saw earlier, simply make use of the relative freedom involved in the possibility of further consideration of whether what immediately presents itself as a motive is what we should act on. In the end, however, what we will do will turn on what our real motive is in accordance with the principle of sufficient reason. Schopenhauer faces the difficulty that this presents for the denial of the will as a road to salvation. What we do, he reminds us (*WR* I 70, p. 404; *WI* I, p. 523), is subject to necessity, although the will itself is free. '*Necessity*', he adds, '*is the kingdom of nature; freedom is the kingdom of grace*'. Hence the will's denial of itself can be regarded as what the Church calls an *effect of grace*. Since the will's denial of itself 'comes from knowledge, but all knowledge and insight are as such independent of choice' so also 'that denial of willing, that entrance into freedom, is not to be forcibly gained by design, but comes from the innermost relation of knowing and willing in man; hence it comes suddenly, as if it had flown in from without' (*ibid*). It is because of this that if it comes it is like an effect of grace.

The result must be a change in the inner nature of the man, so that he no longer wills what he did (though how this is possible given Schopenhauer's views on the immutability of character is a puzzle). This too is like what the Church calls a *new birth or regeneration*. The theological parallels that Schopenhauer invokes are not really surprising. We can attain salvation only if that is the way in which the will works. But the will is not only quite free, not subject to motives or other causes; it is also blind. Hence if we regard the salvation when it comes as an act of grace, it is not an act of grace on the part of anything like a person. It is, one might say, just chance, without any suggestion of design. If we grasp the salvation when it comes with gratitude, there is really nothing that we have any reason to be grateful to. Moreover, if we admire the state of resignation and true calm, if and when it comes, we have no reason, if Schopenhauer is right, to admire the person who has attained it; it was not due to him.

As for the paradox of the will's denial *of itself*, Schopenhauer cannot here say that the will is deceived by the way in which it objectifies itself in knowledge, as he does in trying to explain the fact of suffering. In this context it is simply the transcendental freedom of the will itself that is responsible for the fact that one person may achieve a Schopenhauerian salvation, while another may not (and what is there in eternal justice that accounts for that?). That does not perhaps in the end alter the case, since even when knowledge is involved in a negative way rather than the supposedly positive way that is presupposed by salvation, the will is still in the end responsible for it, if it is the one underlying reality. We have noted a certain ambivalence in Schopenhauer's general attitude on that — the world is will *and* representation. In the end, however, representations exist only because the will objectifies itself in the form of individuals with brains that are responsible for those representations. Hence, in the end also, the will must be the only true reality.

If the will is free, however, in the sense that Schopenhauer says that it is, that reality must be irrational, because the will is blind and can have no principles in accordance with which to exercise its freedom. Such a freedom is an existentialist freedom — what some have called in connection with human-beings 'radical choice'. There is a strong streak of existentialism, as it came to be called, in Schopenhauer's thinking. Whatever we may think of the desirability and plausibility of that kind of freedom in a human-being, a world which is ultimately governed by it must be an intellectually unsatisfactory place for anyone of anything approaching a rationalist persuasion, no matter what order there seems to be in the world as a result. For even that order will be subject to the whim of fate, as it were. Whether or not a world of this kind is an intellectually satisfying place, that it is on Schopenhauer's view an uncomfortable one is abundantly clear.

Nevertheless, as far as he is concerned the only, but vastly superior, alternative for one who has experienced life in the world is nothingness — 'no will: no representation, no world' (WR I 71, p. 411; WI I, p. 531). Schopenhauer faces the objection that he is offering nothing in that nothingness, arguing that by comparison with the misery of our lot it is nothingness that provides the only clear contrast and the only real release. So, he says, 'we have to banish the dark impression of that nothingness, which as the final goal hovers behind all virtue and holiness, and which we fear as children fear darkness' (ibid). And he ends the first volume with the words that I quoted at the end of my introduction. Now, however, I quote also the preceding words, since they set Schopenhauer so clearly in relation to eastern thought, which he nevertheless admired so much: 'We must not instead evade that very thing, as the Indians do, by myths and meaningless words, such as the reabsorption in Brahman, or the Nirvana of the Buddhists. On the contrary we freely acknowledge it: what remains behind after the complete abolition of the will is, for all those who are still full of the will, indeed nothing. But also conversely, to those in whom the will has turned and denied itself, this so very real world of ours with all its suns and galaxies is — nothing.'[5]

8

Aspects of Human Life

There are a number of matters on which Schopenhauer says things that have achieved fame or in some cases notoriety that are not really part of the main fabric of his argument. I have touched on some of them in passing in earlier chapters. Some of them again can be thought of as consequences of the main argument, though others really lie outside it. Schopenhauer has, for example, acquired a certain notoriety for his views on women, views which could hardly please a feminist. There is an essay of this kind 'On Women' in the *Parerga and Paralipomena* (*PP* II, p. 614ff.). For the most part I do not think that the views expressed there follow in any way from the argument on which his main system is based; they no doubt reflect Schopenhauer's own temperament. For that reason I shall not say anything more about them, except in so far as they connect with any doctrine that *can* be regarded as a consequence of the main argument. Those that do mostly have regard to aspects of human life — birth, death, suicide and the metaphysics of sex. One might say that they have to do with 'birth, copulation and death'. I shall discuss them briefly.

Birth and death belong only to the phenomena of the will, and so to life, since the will is the will to live (*WR* I 54, p. 275; *WI* I, p. 355). They hold the balance, Schopenhauer says, as mutual conditions of each other. Birth comes as a gift, rising out of nothing, in that there is for the individual nothing before birth. Death comes as the loss of that gift, returning to nothing, since there is nothing for the individual after death. Hence we are in a sense born to die; death is our lot and becomes so when we are born. The life of our body is 'only a dying continually checked, an ever-deferred death' (*WR* I 57, p. 311; *WI* I, p. 401). The individual's real existence is in the present.

156

This antithesis between, yet mutual balancing of, birth and death — the life and the urge towards it on the one hand, and the death that must come, the tendency towards it despite the urge to postpone it on the other hand — suggests the kind of opposition that Freud stated when he invoked his two principles — the pleasure principle and the death instinct respectively. It cannot be denied, however, that Schopenhauer laid the greater weight on the urge towards life, since the will is simply the will to live, at any rate as it manifests itself in living creatures. If we ask why death occurs at all, the answer lies at one level in the properties of matter that constitutes bodies, and of course in their organization. The processes that bring about birth must in the end bring about death, and that is certainly one reason why birth and death are mutually supporting conditions. The result, given that human-beings are by their organization creatures with a brain and thus conscious, is that birth and death can be said to be 'the constant revival of the consciousness of what is in itself the endless and beginningless will' (WR II 41, p. 500; WI III, p. 297). After one life the will goes on in the life of another, and in one sense the overriding function of life is to make possible that continuance in the life of another member of the species.

At another level, however, Schopenhauer can regard death as 'the great reprimand that the will-to-live, and more particularly the egoism essential to it, receive through the course of nature; and it can be conceived as a punishment of our existence. . . . We are at bottom something that ought not to be; therefore we cease to be' (WR II 41, p. 507; WI III, p. 306). (Another example perhaps of eternal justice !) At death the ego lives on only in what formerly the person concerned had considered as non-ego. Yet at other times Schopenhauer can say (e.g. WR II, 41, p. 493; WI III, p. 287) that the complete answer to the question of the individual's existence after death is to be found in Kant's doctrine of the ideality of time. If that doctrine is taken seriously there is no question of existence after death, since there is no 'after'; with death time also ceases. Schopenhauer says that in this sense death is a mystery; for while it is in one way right to say that our true being continues, since it is not destroyed by death, in another way it is wrong, since given the ideality of time there is no scope for continuance. It remains true on Schopenhauer's view that in death one's true nature and being are not destroyed; they are indestructible.

There is nevertheless a certain tension in Schopenhauer's views on death. On the one hand he can quote with approval Epicurus' remark that death is nothing to us (WR II 41, p. 468; WI III, p.

255).[1] For this reason death is not to be feared, and it cannot be simply non-existence that we fear, or otherwise we should have the same attitude to the non-existence before birth as to the non-existence after death.[2] From the standpoint of consciousness and knowledge there is nothing there to be feared, any more than there is in the cessation of consciousness that occurs in sleep, which is in that sense a constant preparation for death. Death is terrible only to the will to live. That, however, is another case of the will being deceived by the intellect, since the will is led to think of the cessation of consciousness and of the organism that supports it as a threat to itself; but in fact death is merely the end of that individual consciousness and that particular organism, it does not affect the underlying will at all.

On the other hand, there is the fact implied by that last remark — that our true nature is not affected by death. Hence, whether or not it is right to say that that nature continues there must remain a sense in which it is true to say that we are indestructible. In the light of this Schopenhauer can speak (*WR* II 41, p. 487; *WI* III, p. 280) of the deep conviction that we all have of the impossibility of our extermination by death. That is a reasonable conviction only to the extent that a person thinks of himself as eternal. On the other hand, if he thinks of himself as having come out of nothing he must also think of himself as becoming nothing again. In that respect birth and death are on a par.

It seems, therefore, that there are two reasons for not being afraid of death, as far as Schopenhauer is concerned. One is that non-existence itself is not something that is a cause for fear; it is merely the cessation of consciousness, as occurs in sleep. It is nothing to us, it is not an event in life. On the other hand, there is the reason that we are after all eternal and indestructible. It all depends on whether we think of ourselves as bound by time or as eternal. I doubt if in fact either of these reasons would provide any consolation for one who does fear death. For the sense in which we are eternal is one in which we are not individuals, while the sense in which we are individuals is one in which non-existence for ever must come. It is indeed not non-existence as such that is terrible (*if* it is, for it cannot be denied, and Schopenhauer emphasizes the point, that death may sometimes be welcome); it is the cessation for ever of life as we are aware of it. To stress the similarity between death and sleep may be a sound move on the intellectual level; the cessation of consciousness is the same in each case. It remains true that death is for ever as far as the individual is concerned. Hence it is the *anticipation of nothingness without return* that makes the difference both from sleep and from the nothingness before birth.

Schopenhauer may well be right to emphasize the force of the will to live in all this, even if the meaning of that phrase 'the will to live' be interpreted in the mundane and non-metaphysical sense. For most people perhaps life, once tasted, is difficult to give up. That is not by any means universally so, however, for a variety of reasons, and it is perhaps impossible not to think that cultural factors affect that fact. There are cultures in which individuality is not given so much importance as in our western, perhaps Christian influenced, culture. It *is* possible for cessation of individual existence to be given quite genuinely a much lesser importance than some other things, such as the continuance of the society, nation, or species. Yet fear of death is pervasive, and understandably so, even if there is much irrationality in that fear also. To say 'Death is nothing to us' may well be a consolation for those who think that death brings some terrible or potentially terrible form of further existence (and it was no doubt those whom Epicurus had in mind when he said it); it may do nothing for those who fear the cessation for ever of existence or life itself, whether that fear is rational or irrational. To say that our real being is eternal, in the sense that Schopenhauer has in mind, may well do even less. It is difficult to take a *rational* view of death, however one regards it.

Schopenhauer also has well known, perhaps even notorious, views on suicide. Once again, however, there is a certain tension in his views on it. On the one hand, he sees no reason for a moral condemnation of suicide as such, and sees no reason for legal prohibition of it. On the other hand, he says that it provides no escape; we remain what we really are (cf. WR I 65, p. 366; WI I, p. 473). Suicide remains therefore a 'useless and foolish act' (WR I 69, p. 399; WI I, p. 515), since the will as thing-in-itself remains unaffected by it. Suicide is no escape from the will as the will's denial of itself in asceticism may be; it is indeed a form of affirmation of the will.

That may seem paradoxical. Schopenhauer expresses the contrast between the denial of the will and suicide by saying that in the former it is merely the pleasures of life, not its sorrows, that are shunned, while the suicide 'wills life, and is dissatisfied merely with the conditions under which it has come about for him' (WR I 69, p. 398; WI I, p. 515). Those conditions — suffering and the like — make impossible the development of the will to live in these phenomena. The will therefore decides on the cessation of these phenomena, but does not of course thereby remove itself. 'Just because the suicide cannot cease to will, he ceases to live; and the will affirms itself here even through the abolition of one of its own phenomena, because it can no more affirm itself otherwise' (*WR* I 69, p. 399; *WI* I, p. 516). The only valid procedure in the face of suffering is the denial of the will; but the suicide rejects this, like a man rejecting a painful operation that would cure him. In consequence he destroys the 'will's phenomenon, the body, so that the will may remain unbroken' (*ibid*.). Why however is that useless? It should be so only if the suicide thinks that he thereby destroys his real nature and being; for it is clear that on Schopenhauer's terms he cannot do that. But the suicide does remove his sufferings, and if death is not to be feared in general it is not to be feared in this case either. Suicide is useless only if in those circumstances there is something better to be achieved. Schopenhauer of course thinks that there *is*, in the denial of the will, but it is the very obscurity that attaches to the question what that state brings for the person concerned that is different from ordinary death that casts doubt on the claim that suicide is by comparison useless.

In the *Parerga and Paralipomena* there is a short and somewhat fragmentary essay on suicide, which ends with two brief and epigrammatic remarks. The first (*PP* II, § 159, p. 311) says 'if in heavy, terrible dreams anxiety reaches its highest degree, that itself causes us to wake up, as a result of which all the monsters of the night vanish. The same happens in the dream of life when the highest degree of anxiety forces us to break it off.' But the analogy surely breaks down; when we break off the dream of life it is surely not *us* who wake to a reality free from anxiety, or not in a sense that preserves our individual identity. In any case, one would have thought that, given the nature of life, the continuance of it, to the extent that it involves consciousness, is likely to be as much subject to misery and anxiety as it was before, even if not for the suicide in his strict individuality. Misery remains, that is, for the phenomena of the will. It is indeed somewhat strange that Schopenhauer makes this remark, although it is in a context in which he has been discussing condemnations of suicide and the overcoming of reluctance to take the step.

The second remark (*ibid*., § 160) reads 'Suicide can also be regarded as an experiment, a question which one puts to nature and wants to force her to answer, namely what change the existence and knowledge of man experiences through death. But it is an awkward experiment, for it abolishes the identity of the consciousness that would have to listen to the answer.' If that was truly what suicide was, there would indeed be a futility about it; for the description describes a procedure which is self-frustrating — in carrying it out we prevent its success. In any case, however, it has seemed to many that the same question is put by death it-self, and it is the impossibility of an answer that many have thought the terrifying thing about death. If the suicide actively raises the question, it is a question which is there for all of us all the same.

Birth and death are then for Schopenhauer necessary bound-aries to what the will to live produces, but it is only when it produces an organism that is conscious that difficulties arise. For there comes with it the fear of death and a possible self-frustrating attempt to end the sufferings that are the condition of conscious life. Whichever way it is, however, death must eventually come, and the individual ceases to exist even if the species continues. The continuation of the species depends, however, on its propagation, and that in turn depends on sex. Hence we should expect that on this subject too the paramount emphasis in Schopenhauer's thought should be on the will to live. So it turns out to be. There is a chapter in the second volume of the main work (WR II 44, pp. 531ff.; WI III, pp. 336ff.) entitled 'The metaphysics of sexual love' in which Schopenhauer expatiates on the real nature of love in what many would think an extremely cynical way. It is, as one might expect, nothing but the will to live. That is the driving force that governs all the phenomena of love, having as its aim the preservation of the species. That is so even if it is the last thing that lovers think that they have in their mind. It is all dominant. Much of what Schopenhauer says about it can be regarded as having been written in sorrow that such an impulse is as dominant as it is and so much a source of self-deception.

Schopenhauer describes in glowing colours, but often in terms of horror, what this dominant impulse can lead to, to the extent that all the things that we think important, honourable and worthy may be sacrificed to it. It is, he thinks, a gross delusion implanted in the individual by nature − that is to say, instinct − as a result of which he thinks that anything that is good for the species is good for himself. Men see beauty in the beloved, think that union with her is an end in itself, when all the time the true end is the preservation of the species. Moreover, the whole character of love is determined by that. A man's love diminishes from the moment of satisfaction, and he always looks round for other women. The woman, by contrast, is such that her love is increased from the moment of satisfaction, and she clings to the one man. The whole thing is dictated by what is likely to produce and support off-spring and has no other end. The same applies to the kind of features that a lover sees as attractive in the beloved. Marriages of love are contracted in the interest of the species and are likely to prove unhappy, while arranged marriages are likely to prove the opposite just because there are other governing considerations, such as money. And so on and on.

In general, Schopenhauer says (*WR* II 44, p. 559; *WI* III, p. 373), when a man in love hangs with abandon on the eyes of the beloved it is 'his *immortal part* which longs for her; it is always the mortal part alone that longs for everything else.' It is the immortal part that is, of course, his real nature, and that is the will to live. Hence in fact his species is nearer to him than the individual, and all the paraphernalia of love and matters of the heart have really no end other than that — the persistence of the species. (There is even an appendix to the chapter in which homosexuality — what he calls pederasty — is explained, perhaps rather surprisingly, on the same principles.)

It is clear enough that the main principles which underlie Schopenhauer's treatment of these matters fit in with the metaphysics. Hence it ought to be no surprise that the subject receives the kind of treatment that it does. The details and the vehemence with which it is written, however, suggest that the subject provoked in Schopenhauer a whole range of feelings the precise nature and origins of which is something about which one can only speculate. I mentioned earlier that some of the subjects on which he writes, e.g. women, do not seem to have much to do with his central metaphysical argument. That there are important differences between men and women is something that does fit in with his views on the metaphysics of sexual love. There is, however much there too that can only reflect his personal and sometimes idiosyncratic feelings.

It is also once again evident how little a part a reference to cultural differences and cultural factors plays in his theory on these matters. It is the real nature of human-beings, as he sees it, that is his real concern, and he sees everything in that light. According to him, therefore, we are born into a life in which egoism is the dominant personal motivation — a life which can only end in death after considerable suffering and misery, combined with merely temporary gratifications and pleasures. When each of us dies the species continues, because it reflects the underlying, indestructible will. Despite philosophy, science and the arts, despite occasional evidence of saintliness, Schopenhauer seems to think that much of what goes on between birth and death is simply the expression of the will, blindly promoting life in one form or another, but in the interests of the species. The individual is in the end not very important.

It is not a picture of things that many, perhaps, will find attractive. Schopenhauer has been described as the philosopher of pessimism, and we saw earlier that he went so far as to describe optimism as an immoral way of thinking. It is, however, a pessimism that he thought the only appropriate attitude in the face of the world as he saw it. In his eyes it is a world that is in every way the likely result of the blind force that the will consists in; and that the underlying nature of the world and everything in it is indeed the will he thought he had shown beyond question. We have seen that the argument for that conclusion is in fact invalid. That fact does not diminish the grandeur of his general argument and scheme of thought. Nor does it mean that we have no reason to listen to what he has to say about human-beings and their place in the scheme of things — although pessimistic indeed is what he has to say on that topic. Schopenhauer's was a great but uncompromising mind. There is much to admire in such a mind, however unpalatable its thoughts may be.

9

Conclusion

When reading Schopenhauer's writings one cannot help feeling that one is in the presence of a great and forceful mind, as I said at the end of the previous chapter. It is also a mind with a splendid talent for expressing its thoughts. It is no doubt a flawed mind. There is often an element of the peevish and spiteful in Schopenhauer's attitude to things, particularly of course in relation to his contemporaries. (The same thing can be observed in his personal life, but that is true of many great minds.) There can be no doubt, however, that considering the range and depth of his interests, and his truly synoptic view of the world from a philosophical point of view, his was a very great mind indeed.

I shall not say anything here about his influence on other philosophers. The influence on Nietzsche is perhaps obvious for anyone who knows anything of the two philosophers; the influence on Wittgenstein has been sufficiently remarked upon by others.[1] In any case, for present purposes what is important is not that but the status of his own philosophy as an argued system. An assessment of that is not easy. From one point of view it has to be said that the argument is in a strict sense invalid at many points. For one interested only in valid argument that must be that. It would, however, be unfortunate if the matter were left there. It is possible to have an admiration for a system of thought, even to see truth in it, while accepting that in a strict sense its supporting argument is entirely invalid. There may still be much to learn from the incidental, and perhaps more than incidental, insights; and there may be much to admire in the sweeping grandeur of the argument as a whole. That is how it must be with Schopenhauer.

There is no doubt that Schopenhauer derived an immense amount from Kant, and there may be some who will say that all that is good in him is to be found in Kant. That would be a mistake. It is not just that Schopenhauer thought that he could take things beyond the place at which Kant left them. Others thought that they could do that, including Hegel whom Schopenhauer so much despised. Schopenhauer thought that he could provide a simplification of Kant's architectonic in two important ways in particular, and it was from these two, ultimately simple, points that everything else flowed (or nearly everything else, since it is difficult to see the paradox of the ways in which the will denies itself as *flowing* from the central insights). These two great simplifications of Kant's architectonic, if that is what they are, are to be found in *The Fourfold Root* and in the argument for the identification of the thing-in-itself with the will. They are at all events the crucial points in the argument.

It is arguable that one outcome of *The Fourfold Root* — the thesis of the conditioned nature of all necessity and the consequent rejection of all absolutes — is one that Kant himself ought to have seen and accepted. Synthetic *a priori* truths are for Kant all relative to possible experience; only analytic truths provide anything that might be called absolute necessity. Even here, however, it is arguable that such truths are, in being necessary, necessary only to other things — the concepts in terms of which such judgments are made and the laws of thought that lie at the back of them, the acceptability of which is itself a condition of the possibility of intelligible thought. Schopenhauer's *The Fourfold Root* is an attempt to give such suggestions a relatively simple expression in a systematic way.

It presupposes a scheme of faculties which differs from Kant's at certain points — particularly in his conception of the relative roles of understanding and reason — and it is not altogether the better for that. It nevertheless depends on the conception of *a* scheme of faculties, and by including in it the forms of consciousness by which we are aware of our motives for action it provides a link with the second cardinal point of doctrine, that which invokes the will. It cannot be said that in his simplification of Kant's scheme of categories into the one notion of causality Schopenhauer provides any better support than Kant did for the thesis of the *a priori* character of principles governing experience and understanding (even if the critique of Kant's ideas in that respect involves some subtle and interesting points). The outcome of it all — the conditioned nature of all representations of whatever kind — is nevertheless supposedly an *a priori* truth both in general and in its details. The truth of that supposed insight is very difficult to assess, just because it does depend on the scheme of faculties, and even more important because it presupposes the transcendental idealism that Schopenhauer inherited from Kant.

It is perhaps a curious fact that Schopenhauer never saw any substantial need for a justification for that transcendental idealism until he came to write the supplementary essays in the second volume of the main work, and the arguments there leave much to be desired. Such was the influence that Kant exerted upon him. In a sense, the transcendental idealism is the ultimate premise on which everything else depends. Without it there would be no room for the 'fourfold root', let alone anything else. The trouble with transcendental idealism is that it presupposes the epistemological apparatus which Kant inherited from his empiricist forebears and from the tradition of epistemological individualism that Descartes initiated – the suggestion that reality is a matter either for construction or for discovery on the part of each individual by himself (a position that is implicit in Descartes' 'cogito'). The anthropocentrism that has today largely replaced transcendental idealism in European philosophical thinking[2] might be thought of as a socially based transcendental idealism, and has been taken in that way by many proponents of the sociology of knowledge. It is arguable, however, that it is quite consistent with, and even indeed presupposes, a form of realism, in that the only conditions under which anthropocentrism can gain application are those which presuppose a world independent of human judgment, a world to which human-beings can react in regular ways, given their own nature and make-up. That is sometimes put by saying that epistemology should start, not from an 'I', but from a 'we', and that that *presupposes* in its application much of what an 'I'-centred epistemology thought that it had to justify. That is to say that the sort of scepticism that Descartes initiated presupposes for its intelligibility the very objectivity and publicity that it seeks to doubt. While, therefore, transcendental idealism is, in its compatability with empirical realism, much the most acceptable form of idealism, its terms of reference may be seen as misguided.

One has, therefore, to waive misgivings about the starting-point of Schopenhauer's inquiry if one is to have any sympathy towards his project in *The Fourfold Root*. If one can do that and accept in turn the scheme of faculties that is presupposed, the argument of *The Fourfold Root* is likely to seem impressive, if not convincing in all its details. The general outcome – the conditioned nature of all representations – is vital for what is to follow. For it is in the, by contrast, unconditioned awareness of willing that there is to be found, according to Schopenhauer, the key to the door that opens to a world beyond that of representation alone.

That is the second simple point on which Schopenhauer's argument depends. Or at any rate it would be simple if that were all that was to it. To the extent that Schopenhauer's argument at this point is valid at all it takes us to just that — to an aspect of reality which is different from that given in representations alone. That, however, is just to say that there is a respect in which human-beings differ from the rest of nature — they *act* in a true sense and have a direct and unconditional awareness of that fact. Indeed, unless they had that awareness they could not be said to act in the true sense. A difference between human-beings and the rest of nature in this respect is not enough, however, to justify a claim for the identification of things-in-themselves, or *a* thing-in-itself, as will and thus different from all representation. If we can learn a lesson from Schopenhauer concerning the nature of action and the will, and thereby concerning the place of human-beings in the scheme of things, it is another matter to accept that in the will we can see the true reality.

If we do accept that, if only for the sake of argument, it is necessary also to be given an account of the relation that exists between the will and representations generally, between the will and phenomena. Schopenhauer thinks that a crucial factor in providing such an account is to be found in the relation that we are aware of between our will and the phenomena of the will, i.e. what we are aware of in ourselves in action. For he takes it that just as the will that we are aware of in ourselves is the same will as that which is the thing-in-itself for all phenomena, so in being aware of the phenomena of the will as subject to motives in accordance with the principle of sufficient reason we are aware of the very same principle that governs all expressions or objectifications of the will. Motives, in other words, constitute causality seen from within in a very literal sense. Perhaps the only argument for this conclusion in the end is that inasmuch as the will as thing-in-itself is not subject to those aspects of the principle of sufficient reason that make plurality possible there can be only one will, and its objectifications must be governed in their relation to each other by the same principle — causality — even if this takes various forms in different kinds of objectification of the will — human-beings, animals and organic life, and inorganic matter.

In other words, there is no argument for the claim that we can find within ourselves the clue to the underlying nature of reality apart from the argument that *if* what we find within ourselves as will is the thing-in-itself, and *if* this, lying outside representations and their conditions, can only be one, then this too must be what underlies all other phenomena. Moreover, such phenomena must be related to each other in consequence just as the phenomena of our will are related to each other. Hence, everything turns on the argument for the thesis that the will is thing-in-itself. In arguing for that Schopenhauer *ipso facto* argues for the thesis of the one will of which all phenomena are objectifications. He also argues *ipso facto* for the thesis that the relation between the will and its phenomena cannot be anything like that which obtains between phenomena themselves; in particular that relation cannot be that of causality. Everything, therefore, turns on the argument for the will as thing-in-itself, and although that argument cannot be said to be valid it raises issues of great interest.

Once given this, the rest follows with greater or less cogency. The will, being distinct from the intellect which is merely its objectification through the brain, must be blind, irrational, and concerned only with its own being. The all-important question why it objectifies itself in phenomena at all, let alone why it should ever get into the position of denying itself, receives, and can receive, no answer. Nor is it clear how Schopenhauer can speak, as he sometimes does, of the will being deceived by the intellect, its phenomenon, so as to turn, so to speak, against itself. In Kant, the thing-in-itself merely lies outside the scope of any of the principles that the human understanding brings to bear on phenomena. If there is something inexplicable in it in consequence, something perhaps irrational even, that does not really matter since the thing-in-itself is not given any distinctive work to do. The concept of a thing-in-itself is for Kant a merely negative or limiting concept. For Schopenhauer it is much more than that, and the thing-in-itself has a definite, positive role to play. In consequence there is on Schopenhauer's way of thinking a fundamental inexplicability and irrationality in the order of things, however much phenomena as such are subject to the principle of sufficient reason. The relations between phenomena may be ordered, but there is no explanation why they exist at all in the form that they do. There is thus a definite existentialist element in Schopenhauer's thought, which is accentuated when the will is said to deny itself.

That paradox finds expression first in the quieting of the will that is said to take place via contemplation of works of art, these themselves involving the exemplification of Ideas or grades of objectification of the will. The second, more profound, expression of the paradox is to be found in the final mystery of the permanent quieting of the will through a penetration of the *principium individuationis* combined with asceticism. By this stage of Schopenhauer's argument the will has been explicitly identified as the will to live, this being the form of its persistence in being which is found in human and animal life (though, strictly speaking, the will can have no aim, since aims˚are a matter of the intellect). The will's actuality, one might put it in Aristotelian terms, is simply *being* (or, to invoke the converse of the Thomist doctrine, its *actus* is *esse*). In the two ways in question — art and asceticism — the intellect, although the will's objectification, manages to quieten, temporarily or permanently, the very thing of which it is an objectification. That is a paradox indeed, and it is not dissolved merely by appeal to the will's blindness.

In between, there comes Schopenhauer's ethics and his account of other human phenomena. Here things are much more straight-forward. It reduces to the idea that the governing principle of human existence is simply the will to live, i.e. egoism. If human-beings do manage to get beyond that it is simply because the intellect provides them with a realization that their differences from others are merely phenomenal and have no basis in reality. Hence, once again it is the intellect that plays a part in opposition to what is, at any rate immediately, the workings of the will. This may do something to substantiate the claims of philosophy to have a practical importance, since the intellect's realization of the basis for true sympathy with others is the realization of a meta-physical truth on Schopenhauer's account. It does not, however, lessen the puzzle why on Schopenhauer's account it happens at all. Why indeed are there phenomena at all, let alone the phenomena that actually obtain? Schopenhauer's tendency to moralize about human phenomena, in terms of the moral worthlessness of men and in terms of eternal justice for the sin of existence, does not help to answer these questions, whatever one may think of it in itself.

It might be argued that in this part of his work he is caught up in his general attitudes to mankind, his pessimism and misan-thropy, such as are evident in some of the essays. There would be some justification for that view of the matter, although Schop-enhauer is never far from his metaphysical basis for his views. What is perhaps even more evident is the relative detachment from the initial idealism that colours this part of his work. It is almost as if that part of his theory had been forgotten. I do not mean to suggest by that that what is said in the last book of the main work is inconsistent with the initial idealism. It is simply that references to the idealism and what that entails seem to have faded into the background. What looms large in the book is the all-dominant force of the will. Intellect plays a part, on the whole, merely as something that may mislead the will. That is true at any rate until the intellect makes possible an insight into the real nature of things and thereby a move beyond the veil of Mâyâ. But that is not an intellect of the kind responsible for ordinary phenomena. It is an intellect in the service of philosophy.

In one way that is one of the more important messages that Schopenhauer wishes to convey. Philosophy is not just an academic discipline which at best increases our understanding of things, even if that understanding is of a world where misery and suffering are inevitable. It can bring with it a form of salvation too. For the asceticism that brings about the quieting of the will must, in Schopenhauer's view, be mediated by an understanding and acceptance of the philosophical truth that there is in the end nothing but that will — or just nothing. The world is will and representation. But it could be, or could have been, just will, and an acceptance of that fact brings not only, Schopenhauer thinks, the realization that phenomena are in fact nothing in reality, but also the possible, but only, release from the will — in nothingness.

It is in many ways a mysterious doctrine. It is, perhaps, on any account an austere message, and one that Schopenhauer was conscious would attract few. But as he saw it, it was the only truth. One can respect that, perhaps even admire it, while recognizing that at crucial points the argument that leads to that conclusion goes sadly astray. It is difficult to think of anyone these days wanting to say either 'Yes' or 'No' to Schopenhauer's philosophy as a whole; perhaps not even to large parts of it. It remains a magnificent intellectual construction, and one from which there is still much to learn. A great mind indeed.

Notes

CHAPTER 1   INTRODUCTION

1 For further details on this see chapter 3.
2 That Schopenhauer occasionally says (e.g. *WR* I 7. p. 34; *WI* I, p. 44) that he starts from representation, as the first fact of consciousness does not really gainsay that point in relation to Kant.

CHAPTER 2   *THE FOURFOLD ROOT*

1 For the notion of *immediate presence* see my later discussion on p. 37.
2 Or perhaps 'intuition'. The word is 'Anschauung'. Translators tend to translate this either as 'perception' or as 'intuition' according to context. I think, however, that it ought to be recognized that behind Schopenhauer's use of the word lies the Kantian contrast between intuitions and concepts. Perception, like knowledge or consciousness, is treated by Schopenhauer as an awareness of something and hence intuitive. It is one of the oddities of translations that the conventions for translating key words in Schopenhauer tend to be different from those that hold good over Kant, despite the Kantian context in which Schopenhauer so often speaks. The oddities become positively misleading when the *a priori* intuitions of space and time, for example, are referred to as 'intuition or perception [sic!] prior to all experience' (*WR* I 10, p. 50).
3 I shall return to further considerations about sensation and perception in chapter 4.
4 I have discussed these issues elsewhere and I shall not repeat the arguments here. See my *Theory of Knowledge*, ch. 3 and *Experience and the Growth of Understanding*, ch. 2. I shall return to what Schopenhauer has to say about concepts in chapter 4.
5 See Michael Dummett, 'Truth' and other papers in his *Truth and Other Enigmas*.
6 Cf. what I said earlier about Aristotle's treatment of the principle of

contradiction. For the general theme see my article 'Contingent and necessary statements' in *The Encyclopaedia of Philosophy*, ed. P. Edwards.

7 In the 'Fragments for the history of philosophy' (*PP* I, pp. 104-5), however, he disagrees with Kant, claiming that, while time is *a priori* infinite, the limitedness or unlimitedness of space is an empirical matter.

8 It has indeed been argued. It is implicit in Wittgenstein's so-called 'private language argument'. For a discussion of this in relation to Schopenhauer see my 'Schopenhauer on the principle of sufficient reason', p. 155.

CHAPTER 3   SCHOPENHAUER AND KANT

1 Some may think that I have laboured the obvious in so spelling out the nature of transcendental idealism, especially when I have taken it for granted earlier. It is, however, important to be clear about it if we are to assess Schopenhauer's relation to the doctrine and to Kant.

2 Cf. on this in particular Kant's 'Refutation of Idealism'.

3 See on this my *Theory of Knowledge*, ch. 1.

CHAPTER 4   THE WORLD AS REPRESENTATION

1 D.M. Armstrong, *Bodily Sensations* (1962).

2 I suspect that the difficulty concerning the content of the consciousness applies to Armstrong's account also, but he is not committed to the second point.

3 Cf. Bernard Williams's treatment in his paper 'Imagination and the self' in his *Problems of the Self* of a similar point in Berkeley.

4 Particularly of course the view of Karl Popper.

CHAPTER 5   THE WORLD AS WILL

1 See G. E. M. Anscombe *Intention*, pp. 13ff. and S.N. Hampshire *Thought and Action*, pp. 103ff.

2 P.L. Gardiner, *Schopenhauer*, pp. 169ff.

3 See also on this my 'Schopenhauer on action and the will' in *Idealism: Past and Present*.

4 This is what is called the 'accordion effect' by Joel Feinberg in 'Action and responsibility', in A.R. White (ed.), *The Philosophy of Action*, pp. 95-119, esp. p. 106; but see also the discussion in Eric D'Arcy, *Human Acts*, pp. 15ff.

5 See my 'Thinking' in *Contemporary British Philosophy*, 4th Series, ed. H.D. Lewis, pp. 100-12.

6 For these notions see W.V. Quine, e.g. 'Reference and modality' in *From a Logical Point of View*, pp. 139-59, and *Word and Object*, ch. 4.

7 See again my 'Schopenhauer on action and the will'.

CHAPTER 6   THE IDEAS

1 See my earlier discussion of this in chapter 2, pp. 32-3.

2 Another possible model would be the Kantian notion of space, which is the notion of something that is necessarily one, but such that every phenomenon manifests it wholly by occupying part of it. But that parallel, if it is valid, brings as many problems with it as it solves. The notion of a Platonic Idea, properly speaking, involves an incoherence as is revealed in the 'third man argument' in Plato's *Parmenides*.

3 Cf. what I said towards the end of chapter 5 about the problem why the brain exists. But the paradox of the intellect overcoming the will involves an even more extreme difficulty.

4 See R.V. Scruton, *The Aesthetics of Architecture*, p. 127.

5 Cf. R.V. Scruton, 'Representation in music', *Philosophy* 1976, pp. 273-87.

6 See note 2 to this chapter.

7 Cf. the role of the created gods in Plato's *Timaeus*. See also my earlier reference to Plotinus.

CHAPTER 7   ETHICS

1 Cf. P.L. Gardiner, *Schopenhauer*, p. 251.

2 It is not clear of course how this is to be applied to other forms of punishment, e.g. that of children by parents.

3 See my 'The phenomena of love and hate', *Philosophy* 1978, pp. 5-20.

4 It has indeed been suggested to me by Professor A.P. Griffiths.

5 But then he spoils it by adding a footnote, as I do, indicating that this is after all Buddhist doctrine.

CHAPTER 8   ASPECTS OF HUMAN LIFE

1 Cf. Wittgenstein's remark at *Tractatus* 6.4311 about death not being an event in life.

2 This is not a very good argument, given the asymmetry between past and future. See Thomas Nagel, 'Death' in his *Mortal Questions*, pp. 1-10.

CHAPTER 9   CONCLUSION

1 By e.g. G.E.M. Anscombe, *An Introduction to Wittgenstein's Tractatus*, ch. 13; P.L. Gardiner, *Schopenhauer*, pp. 278ff. See also E. Stenius, *Wittgenstein's Tractatus*.

2 Cf. Wittgenstein's emphasis on agreement in judgments as a condition of the intelligibility of language as a means of communication and thereby of much else, but also the kind of thinking implied in the writings of M. Merleau-Ponty. Much of modern American philosophical thinking, on the other hand, perhaps because of its pragmatist leanings and origins, seems to ignore the whole issue. The materialism that Schopenhauer thought of as a gross illusion now seems to be taken largely for granted.

Bibliography

1 WORKS OF SCHOPENHAUER

(a) German Editions

Schopenhauers sämtliche Werke, ed. Arthur Hübscher, 7 vols (Wiesbaden: Brockhaus, 1946-50); also available in paperback, 3rd edn, 1972 as *Zürcher Ausgabe*, 10 vols (Zurich; Diogenes, 1977).

Schopenhauers sämtliche Werke, ed. W. Frhr, von Löhneysen, 5 vols (Stuttgart and Frankfurt: Cotta/Insel, 1960-5).

(b) Translations in English

On the Basis of Morality, trans. E.F.J. Payne (Indianapolis/New York: Bobbs-Merrill, Library of Liberal Arts, 1965).

On The Freedom of the Will, trans. Konstantin Kolenda (Indianapolis/New York: Bobbs-Merrill, Library of Liberal Arts, 1960).

Parerga and Paralipomena, 2 vols, trans. E.F.J. Payne (Oxford: Clarendon Press, 1974).

The Fourfold Root of the Principle of Sufficient Reason and *On the Will in Nature*, trans. Mme Karl Hillebrand (London: Bell, 1915).

The Fourfold Root of the Principle of Sufficient Reason, trans. E.F.J. Payne (La Salle, Illinois: Open Court, 1974) (also includes a translation of chapter 1 of *On Seeing and Colours*).

The World as Will and Idea, 3 vols, trans. R.B. Haldane and J. Kemp (London: Routledge, 1883).

The World as Will and Representation, 2 vols, trans. E. F. J. Payne (Indian Hills, Colorado: Falcon's Wing Press, 1958; paperback, New York: Dover, 1969).

(Bibliographies in many of the above works contain references to other collections of essays, selected from the *Parerga and Paralipomena*.)

174

BIBLIOGRAPHY

2 WORKS ON SCHOPENHAUER

(Bibliographies included with most of the above translations of Schopenhauer give references to a number of works on Schopenhauer. Not many of these works are recent or philosophically illuminating. I give references only to such works as meet both those criteria. They are very few indeed.)

F.C. Copleston, *Arthur Schopenhauer: Philosopher of Pessimism* (London: Burns, Oates & Washbourne, 1947).

M. Fox (ed.), *Schopenhauer: His Philosophical Achievement* (Brighton: Harvester, 1980).

P.L. Gardiner, *Schopenhauer* (Harmondsworth: Penguin, 1967).

A.P. Griffiths, 'Wittgenstein, Schopenhauer and Ethics' in *Understanding Wittgenstein*, R.I.P. Lectures, vol. 7, 1972-3, ed. G.N.A. Vesey (London: Macmillan, 1974), pp. 96-116.

A.P. Griffiths, 'Wittgenstein on the Fourfold Root of the Principle of Sufficient Reason', *Proc. Arist. Soc.* Supp. vol. 1976, pp. 1-20.

D.W. Hamlyn, 'Schopenhauer on the Principle of Sufficient Reason' in *Reason and Reality*, R.I.P. Lectures, vol. 5, 1970-1, ed. G.N.A. Vesey (London: Macmillan 1972), pp. 145-62.

D.W. Hamlyn, 'Schopenhauer on Action and the Will' in *Idealism: Past and Present*, R.I.P. Lectures, vol. 13, 1978-9, ed. G.N.A. Vesey (Brighton: Harvester, 1980).

R. Taylor, 'Schopenhauer' in *A Critical History of Western Philosophy*, ed. D.J. O'Connor (London: Collier-Macmillan 1964), pp. 365-83.

Perhaps also worthy of mention is:

R.A. Tsanoff, *Schopenhauer's Criticism of Kant's Theory of Experience* (New York; Longmans, Green, 1911).

3 OTHER WORKS REFERRED TO

G.E.M. Anscombe, *An Introduction to Wittgenstein's Tractatus* (London: Hutchinson, 1959).

G.E.M. Anscombe, *Intention* (Oxford: Blackwell, 1957).

D.M. Armstrong, *Bodily Sensations* (London: Routledge & Kegan Paul, 1962).

E.D'Arcy, *Human Acts* (Oxford: Clarendon Press, 1963).

M. Dummett, *Truth and Other Enigmas* (London: Duckworth, 1978).

P. Edwards (ed.) *The Encyclopaedia of Philosophy* (London: Collier-Macmillan; New York: Macmillan and Free Press, 1967).

J. Feinberg, 'Action and Responsibility' in *The Philosophy of Action*, ed. A.R. White (London: Oxford University Press, 1968) (originally in *Philosophy in America*, ed. M. Black (London: Allen & Unwin, 1965)),

D.W. Hamlyn, *Experience and the Growth of Understanding* (London: Routledge & Kegan Paul, 1978).

D.W. Hamlyn, 'The Phenomena of Love and Hate', *Philosophy*, vol. 53 no. 203 (1978), pp. 5-20.

D.W. Hamlyn, *The Theory of Knowledge* (London: Macmillan, 1971).

D.W. Hamlyn, 'Thinking' in *Contemporary British Philosophy, Fourth Series*, ed. H.D. Lewis (London: Allen & Unwin, 1976), pp. 100-12.

S.N. Hampshire, *Thought and Action* (London: Chatto & Windus, 1959).

I. Kant, *Critique of Pure Reason*, trans. N. Kemp Smith (London: Macmillan, 1929).

M. Merleau-Ponty, *The Phenomenology of Perception*, trans. C. Smith (London: Routledge & Kegan Paul, 1962).

T. Nagel, *Mortal Questions* (Cambridge University Press, 1979).

Plato, *Meno*; *Republic*; *Timaeus*.

W.V. Quine, *From a Logical Point of View* (Cambridge, Mass., Harvard University Press, 1953).

W.V. Quine, *Word and Object* (New York: Technology Press of MIT and Wiley, 1960).

R.V. Scruton, 'Representation in Music', *Philosophy*, vol. 51, no. 197 (1976), pp. 273-87.

R.V. Scruton, *The Aesthetics of Architecture* (London: Methuen, 1979).

E. Stenius, *Wittgenstein's Tractatus* (Oxford: Blackwell, 1960).

P.F. Strawson, *Individuals* (London: Methuen, 1959).

B.A.O. Williams, *Problems of the Self* (Cambridge University Press, 1973).

L. Wittgenstein, *Notebooks*, *1914-16*, trans. G.E.M. Anscombe (Oxford: Blackwell, 1961).

L. Wittgenstein, *Tractatus Logico-Philosophicus*, trans. D.F. Pears and B.F. McGuinness (London: Routledge & Kegan Paul, 1961).

Index